Entrepreneur. MAGAZINE'S

ULTIMATE
GUIDE TO
Linked in
FOR BUSINESS

How to Get Connected with 150 Million+
Customers in 10 Minutes

TED PRODROMOU

EP
Entrepreneur
PRESS®

Entrepreneur Press, Publisher
Cover Design: Beth Hansen-Winter
Production and Composition: Eliot House Productions

This publication is designed to provide accurate and authoritative information in regard to the
subject matter covered. It is sold with the understanding that the publisher is not engaged in
rendering legal, accounting or other professional services. If legal advice or other expert assistance is
required, the services of a competent professional person should be sought.

Library of Congress Cataloging-in-Publication Data
Prodromou, Ted.
        Ultimate guide to LinkedIn for business: how to get connected with 150 million+ customers
in 10 minutes/ by Ted Prodromou.
        p.   cm.
        ISBN-13: 978-1-59918-451-7 (alk. paper)
        ISBN-10: 1-59918-451-6 (alk. paper)
        1. LinkedIn (Electronic resource) 2. Business networks. 3. Online social networks.
4. Internet marketing. I. Title.
HD69.S8P75 2012
658.8'72—dc23   2012018777

Printed in the United States of America

16 15 14 13 12   10 9 8 7 6 5 4 3 2 1

This book is dedicated to the most supportive, encouraging, and loving person in my life—my mother, Sophia. I wouldn't be where I am today without her continuous love and support—in good times and especially during the trying times. I love you, Mom.

Contents

Acknowledgments xi

Foreword by Perry Marshall xiii

Preface xv

CHAPTER 1
Why LinkedIn? 1
    The Info Gold Mine 1
    Souped-Up Search Engine 2
    Conclusion 2

CHAPTER 2
Getting Started on LinkedIn 3
    Determine Your LinkedIn Objective 5
    What About Other Networking Websites? 7
    Conclusion 8

CHAPTER 3
Creating Your LinkedIn Account. 9
    Conclusion 13

CHAPTER 4
Supercharging Your LinkedIn Profile 15
    Profile Headline 16
    Profile Picture. 18

Status Update. 20
Experience. 20
Education 23
Additional Information. 24
Adding Your Social Media Accounts 26
Conclusion 28

CHAPTER 5

LinkedIn Privacy Settings. 29
Public Profile 30
Conclusion 31

CHAPTER 6

A Tour of Your LinkedIn Homepage 33
Conclusion 36

CHAPTER 7

LinkedIn for Companies 39
Components of a Company Profile. 40
Company Status Updates. 44
Creating Your Company Page 44
Conclusion 46

CHAPTER 8

LinkedIn Search 47
Keywords Are King. 48
Taking Advantage of the Sort Option 50
Advanced LinkedIn Search 53
Sales Rep Selling Customer Relationship Management Software. 54
A More Direct Route to Hot Prospects. 57
LinkedIn Reference Search 60
Saved Searches 60
Advanced Job Search 60
Advanced Answers Search 61
The Dark Side of LinkedIn Search 61
Conclusion 64

CHAPTER 9

Getting Found on LinkedIn. 65
Keyword Selection 66
Competitive Analysis 67
The Google Keyword Tool 70

Conclusion 72

CHAPTER 10
Giving and Receiving LinkedIn Recommendations 75
How Can Social Proof Get You Hired in Today's Economy?. 77
What Are LinkedIn Recommendations?. 78
Why Do I Need LinkedIn Recommendations? 80
How Many LinkedIn Recommendations Should I Have?. 81
What Makes a LinkedIn Recommendation Great?. 81
What to Say in Your Recommendations 82
Who Should I Recommend? 83
How to Ask for Recommendations .87
Conclusion 89

CHAPTER 11
Connecting with Others 91
Strategic Networking 92
Open Networking 93
Pop Quiz. 94
Connection Request Etiquette. 96
Removing a Connection 97
Conclusion 97

CHAPTER 12
Using LinkedIn InMail to Reach Out 99
LinkedIn InMail Vs. Introductions .99
What Is InMail? 100
Tips for Writing InMails to Increase Your Response Rates. 105
Conclusion 108

CHAPTER 13
LinkedIn Groups. 109
What Are LinkedIn Groups?. 109
What Is the Best Way to Use Groups? 115
Conclusion 116

CHAPTER 14
Mastering LinkedIn Answers. 117
LinkedIn's version of the BBS 118
Asking a Question 119
Answering Questions 122
Let's Practice 123

Make a Plan 124
Let's Answer Some Questions!. 125
Your Options When Answering Questions 126
Writing Great Answers 128
Earning Expertise 130
Conclusion 130

CHAPTER 15
Monitoring Your Network **131**
Using Tags. 134
Conclusion 134

CHAPTER 16
LinkedIn Apps. **135**
Tweets 135
SlideShare Presentations 137
Google Presentation. 138
Creative Portfolio Display 139
E-Bookshelf 139
WordPress 139
Blog Link 141
Projects and Teamspaces 141
Events 142
Reading List by Amazon 142
MyTravel. 143
GitHub. 143
Polls 143
Real Estate Pro 144
Lawyer Ratings 145
Box.net. 146
Conclusion 146

CHAPTER 17
LinkedIn Tools **147**
LinkedIn Mobile 147
CardMunch 148
LinkedIn Labs. 149
Conclusion 151

CHAPTER 18
Creating and Managing LinkedIn Groups **153**
How to Start a Group. 153

Group Settings 154

Permissions 155

Restrictions 155

Membership 155

Managing the Group 160

Conclusion 162

CHAPTER 19

Recruiting New Employees 163

Tips to Help Your Recruiting Effort 167

LinkedIn Recruiting Solutions 169

LinkedIn Recruiter Corporate Edition 169

Recruiter Professional Services 170

Referral Engine 172

Talent Direct 172

The Jobs Network 173

LinkedIn Career Pages 176

Work With Us 178

Recruitment Ads 179

Recruitment Insights 180

Conclusion 181

CHAPTER 20

LinkedIn for Sales and Marketing Professionals 183

Building Your LinkedIn Network 184

Should You Go Anonymous? 188

Leveraging Your Company Page 189

Leveraging Your Company Group 190

Prospecting on LinkedIn 190

LinkedIn Company Groups 193

Conclusion 199

CHAPTER 21

LinkedIn Advertising 201

Advertising Options 202

Lead Collection in LinkedIn Ads 202

Self-Service Advertising 203

Enhanced Marketing Solutions 204

Answers Sponsorships 205

Content Ads 207

InMail Partner Messages 208

Polls Sponsorship 209

Social or Recommendation Ads 210
Conclusion 212

CHAPTER 22
Creating LinkedIn Ads That Convert Like Crazy 213
Selling on LinkedIn 214
Create Laser-Focused Campaigns 215
Writing Effective Ads 216
LinkedIn Self-Service Ads 217
Creating Attention-Grabbing Headlines 217
Factors That Generate Clicks 218
Brainstorming Headlines 220
The Old Magazine Rack Trick 220
Create a Swipe File 223
Writing Your Ad Copy 224
The Power of Images 224
Follow Editorial Guidelines 225
A/B Split Testing 226
Targeting Your Ads 227
Bidding 228
How to Measure Success and Improve Your Performance 228
Conclusion 229

CHAPTER 23
Finding a Job on LinkedIn 231
Let's Find a Job! 242
Job Seeker Premium 252
Conclusion 254

CHAPTER 24
Commencement 255

LinkedIn Glossary 259

Index 263

Acknowledgments

I have to start by thanking my friends, Dieter Schien and Paige Gaines, who accompanied me to a "free" lunch one day in 2004 where we were introduced to the world of internet marketing. The lunch workshop introduced me to search engine optimization, e-commerce, online marketing, and pay-per-click marketing. Of course, I was intrigued by the idea of owning my own online business so I could work from home and not have to worry about where my next consulting client would come from. That free lunch was the beginning of my online journey, which led me into the world of social media and, eventually, LinkedIn.

Over the years, I've learned from some of the best online marketers and social media experts, including Chris Brogan, Ed Dale, Mike Filsaime, Tom Beal, Dan Kennedy, Bill Glazer, Russell Brunson, Dan Theis, Leslie Rohde, Rand Fiskin, and many more. They've all had a major influence on my career and helped me get to where I am today.

I have to thank my wife, Ellen, and my children, Alicia and Mike, for their support after my career became a roller coaster subsequent to the dotcom crash of 2000. They've been supportive and loving through thick and thin, while encouraging me to keep moving forward and not give up.

I especially have to thank my mentor, Perry Marshall, who saw something in me and encouraged me to write a book way back in 2008. I didn't think I knew enough to be a recognized expert in my field, but Perry believed in me. He reached out to me when the opportunity arose and encouraged me to write this book about LinkedIn. Perry has been a tremendous mentor and role model for the past nine years. I will forever be grateful to him for everything he taught me about building a sustainable business and for the opportunity to share my expertise with the world. Thank you, Perry!

Foreword
by Perry Marshall

If you could truly see through the social media smoke and mirrors, you would almost certainly discover that for most businesses it is a massive time suck and productivity drain. Reality has little to do with the oft-repeated fantasies.

But for those who know how to use social media as a *power tool*—as a search engine for business expertise, for talent and intelligence, for those who understand how to deliver real value to their network—LinkedIn is a way to ensure you never go hungry again.

As author of *Ultimate Guide to Google AdWords* and *Ultimate Guide to Facebook Advertising*, my publisher, Entrepreneur Press, asked me who should write their book on LinkedIn. I told them, "Get Ted Prodromou." Ted is an expert practitioner of direct marketing whom I've enlisted to teach my own students on several occasions. He's a highly respected social media specialist in the Bay area.

In writing this book, Ted Prodromou has defied conventional wisdom. Much of the recommendations you'll find in these pages fly in the face of run-of-the-mill social media fluff. This book thankfully goes far deeper than urging you to "join the party" or "enter the conversation." It's a detailed manual, not a pep talk.

The other day the wife of a nationally prominent surgeon told me, "They don't teach you *anything* about business in medical school."

Likewise, in all the other majors in school, they teach you the skills you need to do the job, but they don't teach you how to find one.

It's not good enough to know how to *do* something anymore. You have to be able to communicate what you know in a way that earns you *respect*. This book is the 21st-century knowledge worker's handbook to becoming well known, easily found, and in demand in whatever corner of the world you occupy.

One last thing: The lines between employee and entrepreneur have been forever blurred. Once at a music clinic, a gigging drummer told the audience, "As a musician, you *are* your business." Amen. No matter what you do, even if you've been employed at the same firm for 20 years, there is always a sense in which you are self-employed. That's why you need to take Ted's sections about targeted LinkedIn advertising seriously, too.

LinkedIn is the world's largest business network, so if networking for business matters to you, mastering this book is not optional. It's mandatory.

—Perry Marshall, Author, *Ultimate Guide to Google AdWords*
and *Ultimate Guide to Facebook Advertising*
Chicago, Illinois

Preface

What comes to mind when someone mentions LinkedIn? Most people think LinkedIn is a place to post your resume and someone will contact you for a job interview. Others think it's a business networking website where you can network with like-minded people and generate leads for your business. Most people don't understand LinkedIn, but they signed up because they received an invitation from a friend or colleague.

I'm sure you created a profile on LinkedIn and wondered what to do next. Millions of business professionals have joined LinkedIn over the past few years but most rarely take advantage of the vast opportunities on the site. They don't take the time to learn what LinkedIn can do for their career or business, so they're missing a huge opportunity.

When the economy turned in late 2008, millions of people lost their jobs. They may have heard on the news or from friends that LinkedIn was a good place to find a job, so they created an account. They partially filled out their profile and waited. And waited. And waited, but nobody contacted them for a job interview. They assumed LinkedIn was a waste of time and never returned.

In 2008, the bottom fell out for most businesses, too. Many large and small businesses filed for bankruptcy soon after the economy collapsed.

Most of these businesses were running on very small margins and couldn't withstand the sudden downturn in the economy. While many businesses struggled, others thrived during the worst downturn in the economy since the great depression in the 1930s. My friend Perry Marshall expanded his business significantly in 2009–2010, releasing many new high-priced products. The worse the economy got, the faster his business grew.

Why did some companies thrive while others went out of business? Those that thrived during this downturn had already built a strong network of followers before the collapse. These businesses had loyal followers on social media sites such as LinkedIn, Facebook, and Twitter. These businesses built large email databases of loyal followers and continued to communicate with them on a regular basis when times were tough. They created products and services that could help businesses survive the economic downturn. By building a loyal network of followers during the good times, these businesses had a huge safety net for outreach when times got tough. Surprisingly, these loyal followers were more than willing to open their wallets and invest in new products and training while others hoarded their money trying to ride out the storm.

What the companies that failed didn't know is that it takes more than filling out your company profile to succeed on LinkedIn (or in the business world for that matter). Filling out your company profile on LinkedIn is like creating a flier to advertise your business. If you create an ad for your business but never send it to anyone, how do you expect anyone to know you are in business?

Most people don't understand how to use LinkedIn to its full advantage to promote their business or consulting practice. For example, I see a lot of great individual and company profiles but I don't see those people participating in Group discussions or answering questions in the Answers section. These are the people with a powerful, well-written resume and cover letter. They took the time to clearly define the services that their business or practice provides skillfully, summarize their work history, and spell out their skills in an easy-to-read format. They know how to post their resume on the online job sites and get a response. Their weakness is they haven't taken the time to learn how to network. Business networking is a skill that takes time to hone and you only learn by practicing. It takes years to become an expert business networker but it's well worth the effort. Networking on LinkedIn is relatively easy if you take the time to learn how to use the tools.

I see others doing a fantastic job demonstrating their expertise in the Groups and Answers section but their profile suggests they are a "Jack of All Trades and Master of None." They have a diverse skill set and work history, so they end up creating a fragmented company profile because they're trying to cover all bases in their profile summary. To me, it's a sign of desperation when I see a mixed-bag profile. There is no focus or clarity, which makes it difficult to tell what products or services they are providing and they don't exude confidence in any of their skills. These people are good at networking because they're participating in the Groups and Answers sections. They know how to connect with others and help others without self-promoting, which will eventually turn into paid projects. If they would pick one expertise and focus their company profile on that expertise, they would have unlimited opportunities coming their way.

It's pretty easy to succeed on LinkedIn if you know how to network in person. We've all been to networking events or cocktail parties where you meet the guy that can't stop telling you how wonderful he is or how great his product is. It's all about him and you can't get a word in edgewise. You try to break away from the conversation and he's like gum on the bottom of your shoe and won't let you escape.

I see those people on LinkedIn, too. Their profiles are full of self-promotion. They participate in Group discussions by promoting their own products or services instead of answering the questions. The focus is on them instead of focusing on building relationships with other Group members. It's a one-way monologue and nobody's listening.

In addition to the information and instruction in this book, I recommend spending one hour in the LinkedIn Learning Center. It shows how to create a compelling, searchable profile and how to use the vast array of networking tools LinkedIn provides. The combination of a clear, complete profile and the ability to network will help you succeed on LinkedIn. But learning how to build a strong LinkedIn profile and how to network isn't enough. The key to success on LinkedIn is to take what you learn from this book and take action. Commit time in your schedule to build that complete personal profile and company profile. Schedule time every day to connect with others on LinkedIn and participate in discussions. Take action on a regular basis and you will succeed on LinkedIn and in business.

By the time you read this book, LinkedIn will have added new tools and features. To keep up with the latest LinkedIn updates, I invite you to visit http://tedprodromou. com/LinkedIn frequently where I will be posting articles and videos demonstrating the latest LinkedIn features.

How much more powerful would LinkedIn be if everyone had a complete profile and used the networking tools effectively? LinkedIn would be exponentially more useful than it is today—which is hard to imagine.

MY PERSONAL LINKEDIN STORY

When I first moved to San Francisco in 1979, it was easy to find a job. Silicon Valley was growing like crazy and the high-tech industry was desperately looking for skilled workers. Companies were growing so fast they posted job openings on billboards outside their sprawling tech campuses. I could drive around Silicon Valley, drop off my resume at the security desk, and have multiple job offers by the end of the day. For more than 20 years, I had the most secure career ever, knowing I could change jobs and get a significant raise whenever I wanted.

The high-tech boom of the 1980s and '90s was a very wild ride. I built a strong network of contacts in the high-tech industry over 20 years and felt on top of the world in my career as a network manager working for companies like IBM, Cellular One, and Digital Equipment Corporation. Life was great and I was a recognized leader in my field. I was featured in trade magazines and even an annual report of a networking company.

The internet boom of the late 1990s was like pouring gasoline on a fire, accelerating the growth of the high-tech industry exponentially.

Then came Y2K and the turn of the century. The dotcom boom imploded, collapsing the entire tech industry. It was the end of an era. High-tech companies began laying off employees for the first time ever.

Soon many companies closed their doors. Others sold themselves off for pennies on the dollar as the entire industry collapsed. Within one year, more than 500,000 high-tech workers lost their jobs in Silicon Valley alone. Most of the remaining jobs were outsourced overseas. Salaries collapsed for those lucky enough to keep a job, but most of us were unable to find work for the first time in our careers.

When my consulting practice went under in late 2001, I began reaching out to my network of colleagues for work. I didn't care if it was a consulting gig or full-time job. I was looking to my network because I knew someone would have a lead for me.

A funny thing happened when I reached out. I couldn't get in contact with most of my network. Emails bounced back. Telephones were disconnected. I only had business cards with company email addresses and telephone numbers in my Rolodex (yes, that old-fashioned contraption). I didn't have a private email address for my network because email was still fairly new at that time and we didn't have private email addresses. Cell phones were also fairly new and not everyone carried one because it was still pretty expensive. Many of my colleagues moved out of the area because of the high cost of living and the lack of career opportunities.

I felt lost. I had no way to reach my network that took 20 years to build. I couldn't find them in the phone book (that's how we used to find people in the old days) and lost touch with most of them. My safety net was gone and I was starting my career over from the beginning. This was devastating for someone in his early 40s in the high-tech arena where 20-somethings ruled the roost.

There were no online networking websites like LinkedIn in 2001, so I joined a local business networking group. We met once a week for breakfast and traded leads. Most of the leads were worthless, but occasionally a lead would pan out. It also gave everyone in the network an excuse to get out of the house, since we were all struggling, work-at-home consultants.

My business treaded water for the next few years as the economy recovered from the dotcom crash and 9/11. The only way to get new projects was from referrals, in-person networking, and cold calling because I couldn't afford to advertise.

In 2004, I received an email invitation from a friend who wanted to connect with me on LinkedIn. I didn't know what LinkedIn was, but I registered to check it out. I am LinkedIn member number 2,239,835. You can determine your member number by going to Profile, View Profile on the LinkedIn main menu. Your member number is the number in your profile URL.

I signed in to LinkedIn and looked around a bit but there wasn't much to see. I joined a couple of alumni groups, searched for some old co-workers, and then pretty much ignored LinkedIn for the next year.

I slowly filled out parts of my profile after people would invite me to connect with them, but never spent much time on the site. When LinkedIn first launched, there really wasn't much you could do other than fill out your profile and connect with colleagues and former co-workers. I considered LinkedIn nothing more than an online resume website.

Eventually I reconnected with some of my original network. It was great to see most of them had landed on their feet and some were doing extremely well. I was excited to see some of the people I hired right out of college were now directors and vice presidents at large tech companies. I guess my mentoring paid off for them and we're still close today.

Over time, LinkedIn has added more features, which made the site more useful. Answers and Groups were added, so there was more interaction between members. Adding the ability to interact with others was the turning point for LinkedIn, and membership began to increase.

I quickly discovered if I answered questions in the Answers sections, people started reaching out to me with contract opportunities. I also posted provocative questions, which attracted a lot of attention and created some interesting conversations.

LinkedIn became a useful tool for me when I owned my own consulting practice. My network expanded significantly as I connected with more people and joined groups. After being a passive observer of LinkedIn for years, I realized the more I participated, the more consulting work came my way.

Today I work full time as an online marketing/SEO analyst for a large software company so I use LinkedIn in a very different way. I'm not trying to generate leads for my consulting practice. I manage our LinkedIn group, update our company status with news items, schedule events, and manage our company page. My job now is to get exposure for our company on LinkedIn, which in turn gives us more exposure on Google. I used to generate leads for my own business by answering questions in Groups and the Answers section. Today I generate leads by posting provocative statements in our status, with links to landing pages where people can download valuable white papers. I also manage our paid ads on LinkedIn, which are extremely targeted and very effective. I'll share more details about LinkedIn advertising later in the book.

WHAT YOU'LL FIND IN THIS BOOK

Throughout this book I'll share my perspective of LinkedIn from the keyword and search engine ranking perspective. I'll also share tips to help you get maximum exposure for your personal profile and your company.

Most LinkedIn books teach you the fundamentals of LinkedIn and don't go into much detail. You learn how to create a basic profile and how to use the LinkedIn tools from the 10,000-foot level, but you don't get into the nitty-gritty details that make you a LinkedIn Expert.

We're going to go deep in this LinkedIn book, very deep. We'll start with the basics of LinkedIn, and then I'll show you the advanced tips and tricks that will separate you from your competitors. I'll start out teaching you the fundamentals of LinkedIn to help first-timers or users with minimal experience using LinkedIn. Once you master the fundamentals, we'll move on to the advanced features of LinkedIn to help you get the most out of your LinkedIn experience. Throughout the entire book, you will learn lots of great tips to help you get maximum exposure and find what you are looking for to grow your business or advance your career.

First, I'll show you the ins and outs of LinkedIn by introducing you to the vast array of features and tools available to you. I'll explain each feature and tool in detail and show you some best practices for each. Some of the LinkedIn features you will learn about include:

- Your Homepage
- Profiles
- Jobs
- Groups
- LinkedIn Today and Signal
- Twitter
- Company Pages
- Answers
- Applications
- Tools

- Mobile ✓
- Settings/Personalization ✓
- Advertising ✓
- LinkedIn Premium ✓
- Job Seeker Premium ✓

I'm going to show you how to leverage the power of LinkedIn so you and your company can appear in the LinkedIn and Google search results. I'll show you exactly how to create a searchable LinkedIn profile that will rise to the top of the search results in both LinkedIn and Google.

After you master the basics of LinkedIn, I'll show you how experts get the most out of LinkedIn. We'll review step-by-step case studies demonstrating how to use LinkedIn for various outcomes. If you are looking to grow your business, I'll show you how to use LinkedIn to find your perfect clients or customers. If you're looking to hire a new employee, I'll show you how to find your dream employee.

Here's a list of the case studies so you can see exactly how to use LinkedIn to its full extent.

- Sales professionals/business development/lead generation
- Finding your ideal employees
- Recruiters

I'm sure you have a compelling business story to tell if you've survived the dotcom crash in 2000 to 2001, or the collapse of the economy in 2008. Maybe your business wasn't lucky enough to survive two major downturns in less than ten years. My business didn't and from that experience I learned the importance of building and nurturing a strong business network.

Today, the business world is changing constantly. You need to be well connected so your business continues to thrive through the peaks and valleys of the economic swings. You need to build a strong, stable professional network that can provide guidance and support during the trying times. During your boom times, you can provide guidance and support to those in your network who are struggling. In the next chapter, I'll show you the benefits of joining LinkedIn and show you how it can help you build your ideal professional network and grow your business.

Why LinkedIn?

You know when you're thinking about buying a new car and all of a sudden you see that car everywhere? You never noticed many on the road but now that you're thinking about buying one, it seems like everyone is driving your new car.

I have the same problem when I see online ads and keywords. Sometimes I feel like Don Draper from the TV show *Mad Men*, analyzing every ad and keyword I see. Since I'm a search engine optimization and online marketing expert by trade, I see the internet from a different perspective than most. Whether I like it or not, I see the internet from the perspective of online ads, keywords, and search rankings. I'm always trying to figure out how a company gets top rankings or maximum exposure from their marketing campaigns. I look for the same patterns on LinkedIn. Which companies appear consistently in LinkedIn? Which people get the most exposure on LinkedIn? Which keywords get the most traction in LinkedIn?

THE INFO GOLD MINE

With more than 150 million members and growing, LinkedIn has become a gold mine of demographic information and business intelligence. Unfortunately, most LinkedIn members don't see LinkedIn as a powerful business tool. They see LinkedIn as a place to post their profile and expect others to hunt them down without providing any value to the site.

Today, LinkedIn has become a very powerful business-oriented search engine. With the advanced search features, you can find great employees to hire, find the perfect company to work for, find highly targeted leads to sell to, and network with the thought leaders of your industry.

You can mine deeply into the LinkedIn database and find a treasure trove of information that will change the way you do business. You'll know so much about a prospect, their company, their competitors, their industry, and their products before you ever meet the person. LinkedIn is changing the sales process and making it easier than ever to find targeted prospects for your business.

SOUPED-UP SEARCH ENGINE

Not many people consider LinkedIn a search engine, but I invite you to consider the possibility. What if your profile or company appeared when someone did a people search on LinkedIn? What if your LinkedIn profile or company profile appeared when a prospect searched Google for keywords related to your product or service? What would that do for your career or company? What would your bottom line look like if you could identify highly targeted prospects just by searching on LinkedIn or Google?

If you still don't believe LinkedIn is a powerful search engine, then why do LinkedIn search results appear in Google search results? If Google understands the power of LinkedIn, you should, too.

Throughout this book I'll be sharing my perspective of LinkedIn from the keyword and search engine ranking perspective. I'll also share tips to help you get maximum exposure for your personal profile and your company.

CONCLUSION

You now know that LinkedIn is the fastest growing and most successful business networking site in the world. You see the benefits of joining and participating in the networking groups and demonstrating your expertise by helping others. In the next chapter, I'll show you how to get started on LinkedIn, so you can begin growing your professional network and become a recognized thought leader in your industry.

Getting Started on LinkedIn

Why did you sign up for LinkedIn? Did your friend invite you when she signed up for LinkedIn and clicked on the automated invitation? You may have read about LinkedIn in *The Wall Street Journal* or your local newspaper. Maybe you read about LinkedIn in a magazine or on someone's blog. Or maybe your colleagues at work signed up and told you to sign up, too.

For whatever reason you joined LinkedIn, you are now a member of the largest professional business networking community in the world. At the time of this writing, LinkedIn just surpassed 150 million members. LinkedIn is often called a networking community, but it's becoming much more than just a networking website. It's become the largest job-related website with thousands of job postings. Recruiters and job seekers are finding LinkedIn the perfect place to connect.

Many people ask me if LinkedIn is better than Facebook for connecting with people. To me, I prefer to use LinkedIn to build my professional network and use Facebook to connect with my personal network. Facebook is trying hard to become both a personal and professional network; this may work for some people, but I prefer to keep my networks separate. Of course, I'm friends with some people on Facebook who are also connected with me on LinkedIn, which is fine with me. My differentiation is focused on what I put on both networks.

I post personal comments and pictures on Facebook, whereas I post business-oriented information on LinkedIn. Personally I don't like to see people's business-oriented status updates or Tweets on Facebook. When I'm on Facebook, I want to turn off my business-oriented brain and have fun. When I'm on LinkedIn, my business-oriented brain is turned on and I prefer to see only business-related information. That's just my opinion, but I think most people prefer to keep their business and personal networks separate. Do you have a preference? I'd love to hear what you think. Send me an email at ted@tedprodromou.com and let me know whether you keep your business and personal networks separate.

LinkedIn is also becoming the largest B2B lead-generation website where businesses can connect with their ideal customers and potential business partners. LinkedIn is where you can reconnect with past co-workers and classmates. LinkedIn has become so much more than a job hunting website, which most people mistakenly think is its only function; it is invaluable for so much more. Here is just a small sampling:

- Keeping up with news and trends in your industry
- Demonstrating your particular expertise
- Finding great professional referrals
- Promoting your events
- Recommending people to others

LinkedIn has become the one-stop portal for you to connect with like-minded people. There is hardly anyone who doesn't benefit in some way from its network and tools. It's perfect for:

- An employee for a company
- Marketing and sales professionals
- Job seekers, HR personnel, and recruiters
- Entrepreneurs and small-business owners

Through LinkedIn Groups, you can demonstrate your expertise to attract new clients and connect with other industry experts. You can share your knowledge or keep up with the latest industry news on LinkedIn Today. LinkedIn is expanding its tools and services to attract the best business professionals, so the quality of the community continues to improve and exceed all other business networking communities.

Unfortunately, many people become LinkedIn members and don't take advantage of the unlimited opportunities in the community. They create their account, partially fill out their profile, connect with a few close friends and never come back. They complain there is nothing for them on LinkedIn because they think it is only a job opportunity website and they are already employed.

The real reason they are frustrated with LinkedIn is because they don't have a reason for being a LinkedIn member. Like any community you join, you have to have a reason to join it if you want to take full advantage of all the opportunities it has to offer.

When people join Facebook, they expect to connect with past and current friends in a casual environment. Facebook is all about taking a break from our busy lives by viewing vacation pictures posted by our friends, engaging in chats, and playing games. Your expectations are very clear when you join Facebook, and the level of engagement is incredibly high.

When people join LinkedIn, they used to expect to find a new job but today they can expect to connect with a lot of like-minded business professionals. As LinkedIn provides more networking tools and ways to engage others in conversation, the level of engagement increases proportionally. I spend most of my day logged into LinkedIn checking status updates from my connections and learning about industry news. When I leave work, I spend my personal time engaging with friends on Facebook. My expectations of both websites are very clear, so I have no problem engaging with people on both networks.

Do I think Facebook will ever replace LinkedIn or vice versa as an all-in-one networking site? My personal opinion is no, because people like to keep their personal life separate from their work life. More and more businesses are building a presence on Facebook—which could change my opinion in the future—but I'm not ready to merge my personal life with my business life yet.

DETERMINE YOUR LINKEDIN OBJECTIVE

What is your LinkedIn objective? Most people don't have one when they join LinkedIn, which explains why many profiles are incomplete and their profiles show little or no activity. They signed up because they were invited to connect with a co-worker or colleague, but they aren't looking for a job or looking to network with others so they rarely return. They assumed LinkedIn was only for job-hunting, so they never took the time to explore the incredible networking opportunities and professional communities.

Even if you're gainfully employed and not looking for a job, it's important for you to be on LinkedIn and complete your profile. Your LinkedIn profile is a dynamic electronic billboard displaying your skills and expertise to millions of potential readers. By keeping your profile up-to-date, participating in Answers, connecting with others, engaging in groups, and demonstrating your expertise, you are showing the business world you are in touch with the latest trends and technologies. The more you participate on LinkedIn, the more your name will pop up in the LinkedIn sidebar and on Google, creating unexpected opportunities to help potential customers, partners, and employers find you.

With the uncertain job market and corporate instability, you never know when your company will be acquired or go out of business. It's also impossible to predict when you'll be restructured or downsized out of a job. There is no security in today's marketplace, and no one is safe when corporations downsize or get acquired. If your company is acquired or merges with another business, the chances of job loss increase.

My parents grew up in the generation where they got a job after they finished school, worked for the same company for 40 years, and retired. There was complete job security and they never worried about being laid off or their company being acquired. If a company was acquired, they usually kept all employees whether they were needed or not. Layoffs were rare back then.

Unfortunately, those days are long gone and today we have to be prepared to change jobs, or even careers, in an instant. If your LinkedIn profile is active and current, there's a good chance you will land on your feet in a short period of time if the worst happens. If you wait until you're unemployed to update your LinkedIn profile and build your connections, it will take longer for you to find your next job. So take a few minutes every day and complete your LinkedIn profile, get the minimum three recommendations, connect with some colleagues, and participate in some Groups. Take it one step at a time and in no time you will be logging into LinkedIn every day to participate in the vibrant community discussions.

Once you are on LinkedIn and you have finished your profile, you should determine how LinkedIn can best serve you. There are four basic functions of LinkedIn:

1. Establishing your professional profile
2. Staying in touch with colleagues and friends
3. Exploring opportunities
4. Finding experts and answers to your business-related questions

Your objective could be one of these functions, all of these functions, or any combination. You should have the objective of establishing your professional profile, even if you aren't actively looking for work. Remember, LinkedIn is your electronic business card that could be seen by more than 150 million professionals, so you want a complete, up-to-date profile. You never know when a once-in-a-lifetime opportunity will arise because the right person came across your profile in a LinkedIn search or read some of your comments in a Group discussion.

It's also good practice to keep in touch with colleagues and friends, even if it's just commenting on one of their status updates. By "pinging" your network on a regular basis, you keep your name in front of them and they're more likely to consider you for an opportunity when it arises. Many great career opportunities present themselves when you least expect it. I have to say, since I completed my profile and optimized it to appear when people search for popular search terms, I have received numerous opportunities even though I am not looking for them. This proves to me that LinkedIn is a powerful tool, and I will never have to worry about finding a new job if something unforeseen suddenly happens to my current role.

As I mentioned earlier, you should always keep your eyes open for new opportunities given the unstable business environment. Companies are in a constant state of flux and won't hesitate to lay off thousands of workers if they see a downturn in business on the horizon. I'm not telling you to always be actively looking for new opportunities, but I am telling you to keep one eye open for better, more stable opportunities as they appear on your radar.

LinkedIn is a fantastic business resource if you're doing research or looking for expertise in an unfamiliar area. You will receive great advice from many experts in a matter of minutes by posting a question in the Answers section of LinkedIn. In the past you would have to hire a consultant to help you navigate unfamiliar areas of expertise. Today you have access to thousands of subject matter experts at your fingertips who will gladly answer your question for free in the Answers section. Many times you will end up hiring the consultant who provides quality recommendations or advice—I know this for a fact because I was hired many times after I answered questions—so it's a win-win for you and the subject matter expert.

WHAT ABOUT OTHER NETWORKING WEBSITES?

There are other professional business communities online, but none is as vibrant and dynamic as LinkedIn. Friendster was the original online social network, but it wasn't focused on business networking. It was the most popular personal social networking site for years until MySpace and Facebook came along.

Ryze was launched a few years ago with a lot of fanfare, and they claim to have more than 500,000 members in 200 countries. Since then they've lost momentum. Like the early days of LinkedIn, it seems people don't know what to do once they log in. The idea behind Ryze is that you "rise up" through quality networking. I see some current postings on the site, but they have disabled the ability to create new accounts so it looks like Ryze's days are numbered.

Xing is the most popular business networking website in Germany and has a strong following in Europe. Xing is free to join and they offer premium accounts for about $10 per month. The premium accounts let you see who searched your profile; filter your searches for better targeting; and allow you to send messages to people you are not connected to. Xing has a lot of the same features and tools as LinkedIn, including groups, jobs, events, apps, and company pages. It's very user-friendly and a great business networking community for Europeans.

Some people prefer to network on these other sites for various reasons, but I think they're missing out by not focusing on LinkedIn. Maybe they have a nice niche network on one of these other sites that's working for them, but there is so much opportunity on LinkedIn that they're crazy not to build a network on LinkedIn, too. LinkedIn is exponentially larger than Xing (LinkedIn has more than 150 million users, while Xing has more than 5 million users primarily in the DACH region [Deutschland, Austria, and Switzerland]), so why not belong to both networks and expand your reach significantly? Why be the salmon swimming upstream against the current, when you can easily ride the wave to success by using LinkedIn?

CONCLUSION

There are other business networking websites, but none is near the quality of LinkedIn for growing your professional network. You've established your reason for joining LinkedIn and your networking strategy is beginning to take shape. In the next chapter, we'll create your LinkedIn account, start creating your optimized profile, and begin expanding your professional network.

Creating Your LinkedIn Account

When you create your LinkedIn account, you will be prompted to answer some questions as you populate your profile. Filling out your profile completely will help you connect with others faster than if you leave out important details.

You will be asked if you are Employed, a Job Seeker, or a Student. You will be led through a custom wizard, as you see in Figure 3–1 on page 10, which is tailored to your selection so you can easily build a profile optimized for your objective.

After you enter your country, ZIP code, job title, and company and click Create my Profile, your profile will be created.

Next you will be asked if you want to import your contacts into LinkedIn. If you choose this option, LinkedIn will automatically import all of your contacts from your Outlook, Gmail, or any other email program you use. LinkedIn will tell you which of your contacts are already on LinkedIn, so you can send them invitations to connect automatically. If your contacts are not on LinkedIn, you can send them an email from LinkedIn inviting them to connect with you on LinkedIn. This is an easy way to quickly connect with your existing network on LinkedIn.

Personally, I do not like using automated connection tools. I feel it's impersonal and almost like spamming your current network.

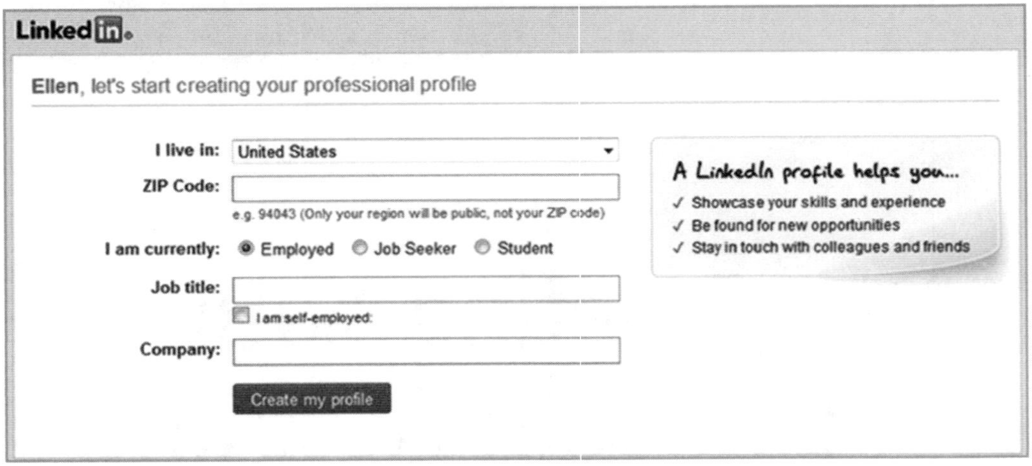

FIGURE 3–1. Using the LinkedIn Profile Wizard

LinkedIn sends a canned invitation message to your existing contacts and you can't customize the message for each person. I prefer to reach out to my existing network manually and choose whom I want to connect with on LinkedIn. I prefer to build my LinkedIn network with a small number of quality contacts instead of everyone who is in my address book. I may have met a person at a networking event and corresponded with him a few years ago, but he may not be appropriate for my LinkedIn network today.

I'll leave it up to you if you want to use the automation tools to build your network quickly, but most professionals prefer the "quality over quantity" method of building their network.

Next you will be prompted to share on Facebook and Twitter that you just joined LinkedIn. When people click on the link you will be connected to them on LinkedIn. Again, I don't like this method of connecting with people because you are sending a blind invitation to all of your friends on Facebook and your followers on Twitter. I connect with people on Facebook on a personal level, not as a business networking venue. I like to keep my Facebook life separate from my business life, which I share on LinkedIn. With Twitter, I have no control of who follows me and I may not want them to be part of my professional network on LinkedIn. Again I'll leave it up to you if you want to automatically share an open invitation on Facebook and Twitter, but I don't recommend it.

The next step in the registration wizard will ask you if you want to sign up for the premium paid version or use the free basic version of LinkedIn. I'll go into greater detail about the premium version throughout this book, but I highly recommend staying with the free version for now, unless you have an immediate need for the advanced LinkedIn features.

The wizard will now prompt you to enter your current job information including your hire date and details about the position. The wizard will continue to prompt you to complete your past job titles, responsibilities, and the dates you worked at that position. You can enter up to five past positions in LinkedIn.

As you enter your job information, the wizard will ask you: "What did you do as *your job title will appear here*?" Enter the details of your job responsibilities and remember to add your skills when possible. Some people write a brief description of their responsibilities in the first person, while others create a bulleted list of responsibilities. An example of a first-person job description would be, "I was responsible for search engine optimization and online advertising for our regions around the world. I was also responsible for email marketing campaign development, brand development, and website traffic growth."

Some people write their summaries in the third person. An example of a third-person summary would be: "Ted was responsible for search engine optimization and online advertising for the company's regions around the world. Ted was also responsible for email marketing campaign development, brand development, and website traffic growth."

Personally, I prefer to use the first-person voice when I write my profile summary because it sounds like it's coming from me personally. To me, third-person narrative sounds like it was written by someone else so it's less personal and not as friendly as a first-person profile summary. I know there is an ongoing debate about which style works better, so I suggest trying first person for a few months and switch to third person to see which gets the best result for you.

Another way to phrase your summary would be like this:

A dynamic online marketing manager with over ten years of experience, including search engine optimization (SEO), pay-per-click (PPC) advertising, and search engine marketing (SEM).

- Thrives in chaotic environments, cool-headed in stressful situations; ability to manage multiple projects concurrently and get things done
- Excellent communicator; often serves as the liaison between other departments, customers and offshore teams
- Flexible and resourceful, applying exceptional organizational, time-management, and planning skills to deliver projects on time and on budget
- Drives adoption of new technologies and innovative solutions.

Here's another example of a bulleted-list job description:
Responsibilities included:

- Search engine optimization (SEO)
- Online banner advertising for regions around the world
- Creating and managing pay-per-click (PPC) ad campaigns internationally
- Email marketing campaign development and management
- Brand development
- Website traffic growth

Notice how the list contains keyword phrases and three-letter acronyms where appropriate. I added SEO after search engine optimization, so the LinkedIn search algorithm can find these keywords and related acronyms in my profile. Now I'm easily found when someone searches for SEO or search engine optimization.

There is no right or wrong way to create your profile summary. The main objective is to use your keyword phrases so you're easily found and people can get a quick overview of your skill sets as they scan your professional profile.

Once you've entered your current and past jobs, the LinkedIn wizard will prompt you to enter your education. Here you enter the school you attended, the degree(s) you earned, if any, and the dates you attended the school. If you are a current student you can enter your expected graduation date. If you didn't graduate from that school, you can just note the dates you attended the school and the courses you studied. The wizard will continue to prompt you to enter more schools until you've entered all of those you attended.

A lot of people ask me if they should include their high school in the education profile if they have college or advanced degrees. If you enter your high school, LinkedIn will show you people who also attended your high school so you can easily add them to your network. If you think it would be valuable to have people from your high school in your professional network, then you should add your high school in your education profile.

After you complete the education portion of your profile, the wizard will move to your skills. It's important to use your keyword phrases in the skills section of your profile so your profile is search friendly. You can add up to 50 skills to your profile, which will dramatically increase the chances of someone finding you when they search for that skill set. As you start typing, the system will suggest skills that are already being used on LinkedIn. Select as many variations of your keywords as possible to optimize your profile.

At this point you have a basic LinkedIn profile and you will start seeing new items appear in your sidebar. LinkedIn is reading your profile and building a list of recommendations based on the keywords you post in your jobs, education, summary, and skills. The People You May Know section will begin recommending new, targeted connections you may want to add to your network. As you add connections, Your

LinkedIn network will update automatically. It will tell you how many connections and how many new people are in your network. You will also see recommended jobs and groups you may want to join based on your profile and network data. You will also see a list of companies you may want to start following so you can keep up with your industry trends or watch them to see if you may want to work there some day.

Keep adding appropriate connections to your network and this sidebar data continues to update automatically. LinkedIn is constantly learning and suggesting appropriate recommendations as your extended network grows. You receive targeted information automatically, which saves you a ton of time when you're looking for people to connect with or looking for companies to learn more about.

Your personal profile should complement your company profile using the same terminology and keywords. People like to see congruency when they view your company profile and then visit your employee profiles. This helps present a more professional image for you and your company, which gives potential clients a positive and lasting impression.

CONCLUSION

Your basic LinkedIn profile is now live and you will start receiving invitations to connect with others. You will also have the opportunity to reach out to others, but I recommend waiting a bit before connecting with others until you are more familiar with LinkedIn.

In the next chapter, I'll show you how to optimize your LinkedIn profile so you will appear near the top of LinkedIn and Google search results for your skills and target keyword phrases.

Supercharging Your LinkedIn Profile

Your LinkedIn profile represents your professional image on the internet and can be found through searches on LinkedIn or search engines like Google, Bing, and Yahoo. When people search the internet for your name, your LinkedIn profile will most likely be one of the top search results so you want to make a great first impression.

Think of LinkedIn as your online resume and your profile as the introductory paragraph of your resume. As people scan your profile, they should be able to understand exactly what you do as they read your headline.

Your LinkedIn profile provides people with a comprehensive summary of you, your education, work experience, and your achievements. Your LinkedIn profile also links people to other social media properties and websites where you can showcase your expertise.

Your LinkedIn profile consists of:

- Your headline
- Your photo
- Status updates
- Vanity URL
- Summary
- Applications

- Experience
- Education
- Recommendations
- Additional information
- Personal information
- Contact information

PROFILE HEADLINE

Your profile headline is the single most important part of your profile. Your profile headline will appear next to your name in the search results. As your name appears in the search results, your headline must

> ### LINKEDIN PROFILE TIP
>
> In this age of text messaging and auto-correct, our society has become very careless about spelling and grammar. Your LinkedIn profile is a reflection of your professional image, so be 100 percent sure your profile is correctly formatted and free of spelling and grammatical errors.

be compelling enough to make people want to click on your profile to learn more about you. You should never put just your name and company name in your headline.

Some people like to add symbols to their profile headline to attract attention. Some of the symbols I've seen include ♥ ♦ # * ◊ and many other unprofessional symbols. I searched Google to see how people added the symbols to their profile and they just copy and paste them from other people's profiles. You can also add the symbols from a Word document by using Insert, Symbols or Insert, Shapes.

Personally, I don't think it's professional to add symbols to your profile, and it diminishes your credibility. If you are really good at what you do you shouldn't have to trick people into reading your profile. When I see symbols in someone's profile, I think of those cheap restaurants with the flashing signs out front advertising their specials and cheap prices. You know the restaurant is a dive and the food is horrible, but they catch your attention with the flashing lights and cheap prices. You always regret eating there because you always leave with a stomachache, but you were seduced by the bright, flashing lights.

I usually feel the same way after wasting my time reading a LinkedIn profile that contains flashy symbols. If the symbols do catch my attention, I take a moment to read the profile and it's usually very unprofessional. The person typically overuses keywords, overstates his experience, and uses tricks to rank well in the LinkedIn and Google searches. Eventually, LinkedIn and Google catch up with profiles like this and lower their rankings, although they do get their 15 minutes of fame and maybe even a few clients.

You will also select your location and industry in this section of your profile setup. You can also create multilingual profiles in the Basic Information section of your profile as shown in Figure 4–1.

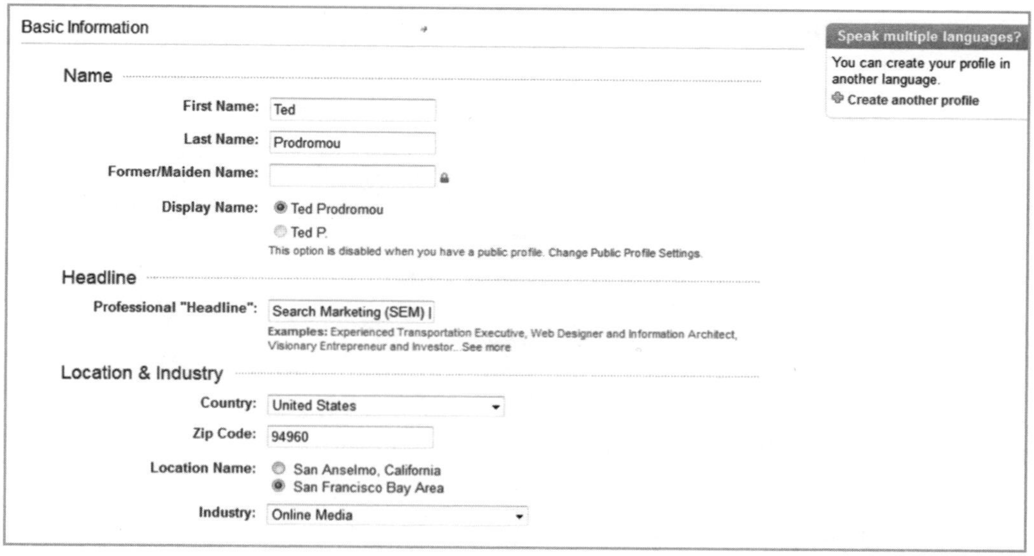

Basic Information

Name

First Name: Ted

Last Name: Prodromou

Former/Maiden Name:

Display Name: ● Ted Prodromou
○ Ted P.
This option is disabled when you have a public profile. Change Public Profile Settings.

Headline

Professional "Headline": Search Marketing (SEM) |
Examples: Experienced Transportation Executive, Web Designer and Information Architect,
Visionary Entrepreneur and Investor...See more

Location & Industry

Country: United States

Zip Code: 94960

Location Name: ○ San Anselmo, California
● San Francisco Bay Area

Industry: Online Media

Speak multiple languages?
You can create your profile in another language.
⊕ Create another profile

FIGURE 4–1. Basic Information Section

Here's my profile headline in Figure 4–2 with my name and profile headline, using my target keyword phrases, location, and industry.

Ted Prodromou

Search Marketing (SEM) | Search Engine Optimization (SEO) Expert
San Francisco Bay Area | Online Media

FIGURE 4–2. Location and Industry Headline

Figure 4–3 on page 18 shows us the profile headline for Viveka von Rosen, a well-known LinkedIn expert. You know exactly what she does for a living within seconds of reading her profile headline.

And here's why it's important to use your target keyword phrases in your LinkedIn profile headline. Viveka is the top search result in Google for "LinkedIn expert" out of 159 million search results. Also notice her public profile link, www.linkedin.com/in/linkedinexpert, which makes it very easy for prospective customers to find her, as shown in Figure 4–4 on page 18.

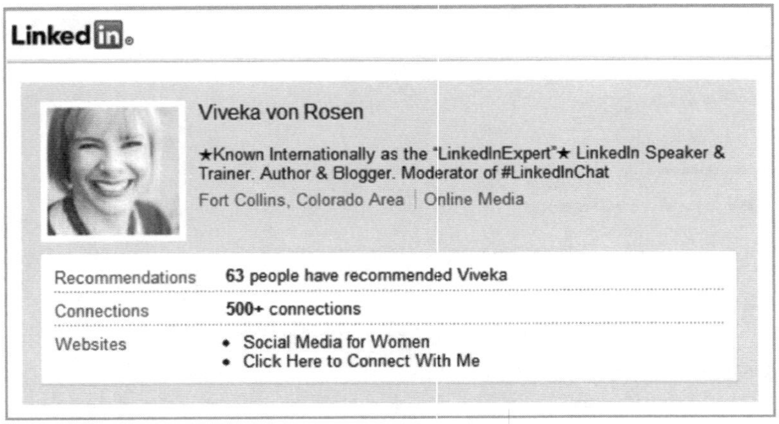

FIGURE 4–3. Profile Headline for Viveka von Rosen

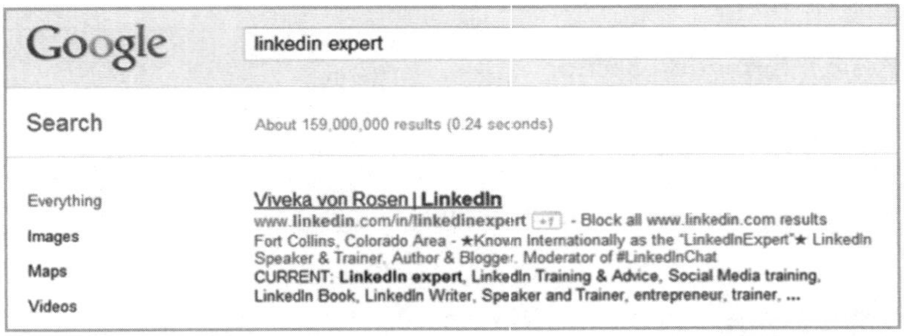

FIGURE 4–4. LinkedIn Expert Google Search

Take the time now to create your compelling profile headline using your target keyword phrases.

PROFILE PICTURE

It's very important to use a professional picture in your LinkedIn profile. You are trying to project a professional image on LinkedIn and a professional profile picture will make a lasting impression when people view your LinkedIn profile. First impressions are very important and people will judge you within a few seconds when they see your LinkedIn profile. Save your casual pictures for Facebook and Twitter. The best LinkedIn profile pictures are engaging and inviting. I recommend a headshot focusing on your smiling face. You are establishing your professional brand on LinkedIn and your profile photo is your personal logo. Your profile will be associated with your company so you want to present a consistent, professional image. This is why I recommend using a professional headshot of yourself instead of avatars, caricatures, or other images that aren't congruent with the image you are establishing for you and your business.

Never use your company logo as your personal profile picture. First, it's not engaging and doesn't give people a chance to get to know you. Second, it's a violation of the LinkedIn End User License Agreement (EULA; www.linkedin.com/static?key=user_agreement).

Your profile photo must meet the following format:

- You can upload JPG, GIF, or PNG files
- Maximum file size is 4MB
- Pixel size: 80 x 80 minimum and 500 x 500 maximum

As you upload your profile picture, you can choose who will be allowed to view your profile picture. I recommend choosing "Everyone," so people may see your picture when they are viewing your profile even if you are not connected with them.

In addition to users I message, my profile photo is visible to:

○ My Connections
○ My Network
○ Everyone

I like to see a person's picture when I'm deciding whether that person is a good fit for my network. I've never rejected linking with a person because I didn't like a profile picture, but I have turned down invitations to connect with people if they don't have a picture in their profile or have chosen not to make it available. To me there is nothing worse than a LinkedIn profile with a missing picture.

I feel strongly that you should have a complete profile on LinkedIn, including a professional picture. When I see a partial LinkedIn profile or a profile without a professional picture, I feel this is a negative reflection on that person. If those individuals don't take the time to complete their LinkedIn profiles, chances are they don't take the time to complete other work tasks as thoroughly as they should. I judge this based on the fact that some people I know don't have a complete LinkedIn profile and they are not very detail-oriented. They finish 80 to 90 percent of a project, but don't complete it. These are not people I want working for me, and I would not want to recommend these people to others because it could reflect negatively on me. This is just my personal opinion and, while it may not hold true in all cases, I feel very strongly about finishing what we begin.

STATUS UPDATE

Below your Basic Information is your Status Update section. Your updates for "Share" will appear right under your Basic Information as well as under All Updates on the LinkedIn home page. You can configure your LinkedIn account so your Tweets will automatically appear as your status, as you see in Figure 4–5.

FIGURE 4–5. My Status Update

You can Share your status using this box, which is located on the LinkedIn home page. By checking the box you see in Figure 4-6, your Share will also be Tweeted.

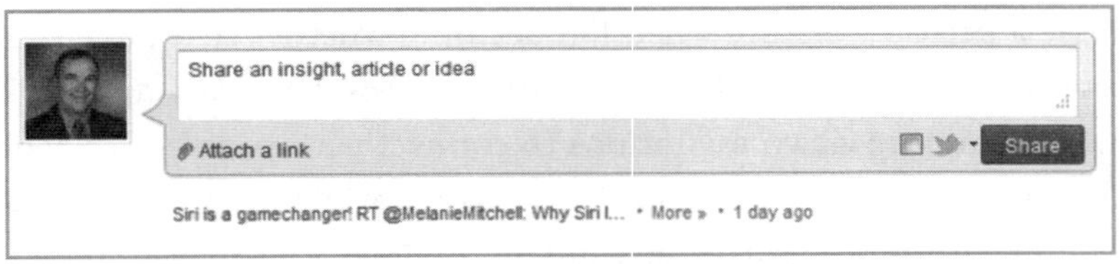

FIGURE 4–6. Tweet Status

EXPERIENCE

Now we'll move into your Experience or Employment section. To add your current and previous positions, click + Add a Position, as seen in Figure 4–7 on page 21. Your current position and your past three positions will be displayed in your profile. Up to three additional positions will be displayed if the viewer clicks on View All.

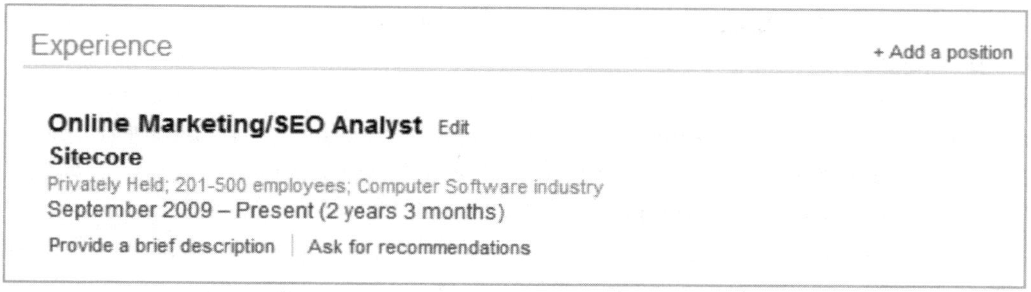

Experience + Add a position

Online Marketing/SEO Analyst Edit
Sitecore
Privately Held; 201-500 employees; Computer Software industry
September 2009 – Present (2 years 3 months)
Provide a brief description | Ask for recommendations

FIGURE 4–7. My Current Experience Summary

Simply fill out the form and click Save Changes. Figure 4–8 shows you the Add Position form. Make sure you add a brief but clear description for each position. Use your target keywords in your description, so you will be found when people search for your skill sets. You can also "Ask for Recommendations" from previous co-workers or clients in this form.

Add Position

Company Name:
Title:
Location:
Time Period: ☐ I currently work here
Choose... ▾ Year to Choose... ▾ Year
Description:

See examples

Save Changes or Cancel

FIGURE 4–8. Add Position Form

If you are going to Request Recommendations, I recommend sending personal invitations to one person at a time. Often I receive mass requests from people using the standard LinkedIn message:

I'm sending this to ask you for a brief recommendation of my work that I can include in my LinkedIn profile. If you have any questions, let me know.

Thanks in advance for helping me out.

I am going to cover giving and receiving recommendations in greater detail in Chapter 10. For now, I'll provide you with some important pointers as you get started. First, it is critical you know that I rarely recommend someone who sends me a mass request and doesn't take the time to write a personal invitation. This is a huge pet peeve of mine, and I will reiterate it numerous times throughout this book. *Don't use the tools in LinkedIn to send mass invitations!* LinkedIn is about building strong personal connections, and using automated tools is not the way to build a strong connection with me or with others. If you want a good recommendation from someone, take the time to write a personal invitation and you will receive a much better recommendation than you would from a mass invitation.

You can Ask for a Recommendation in this section by clicking on the link. Fill out the form shown in Figure 4–9 and a recommendation request will be sent to the contacts you choose.

Make sure you include personal details about how you met, projects you've worked together on, and other details about your working relationship. Specify exactly what

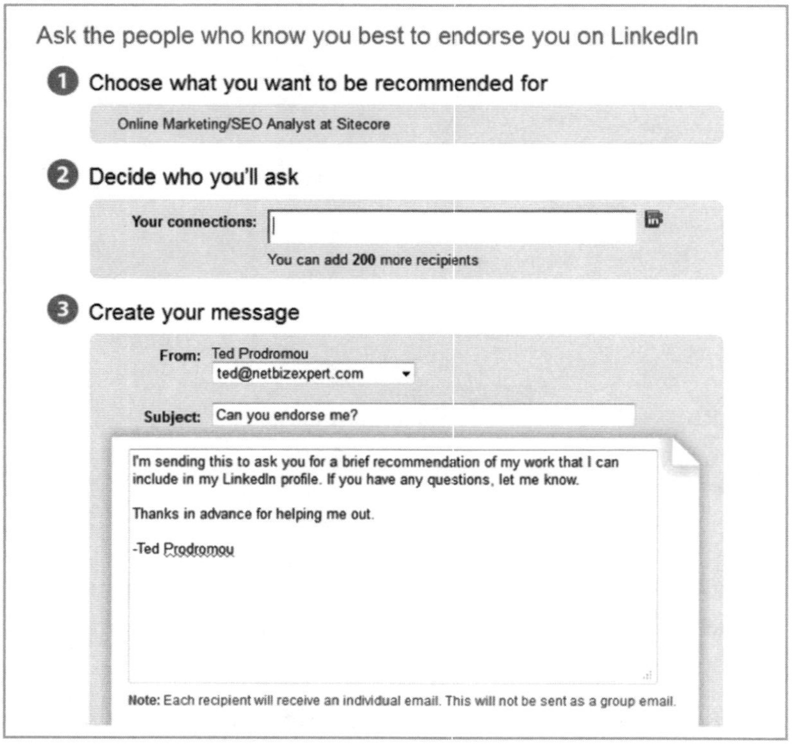

FIGURE 4–9. Recommendation Form

you want in the endorsement, such as a specific project you worked on together or to highlight a certain skill set of yours. Some people even prefer that you send them a brief endorsement you've written about yourself they can edit or modify to save them time.

Your Recommendations are displayed next as shown in Figure 4–10.

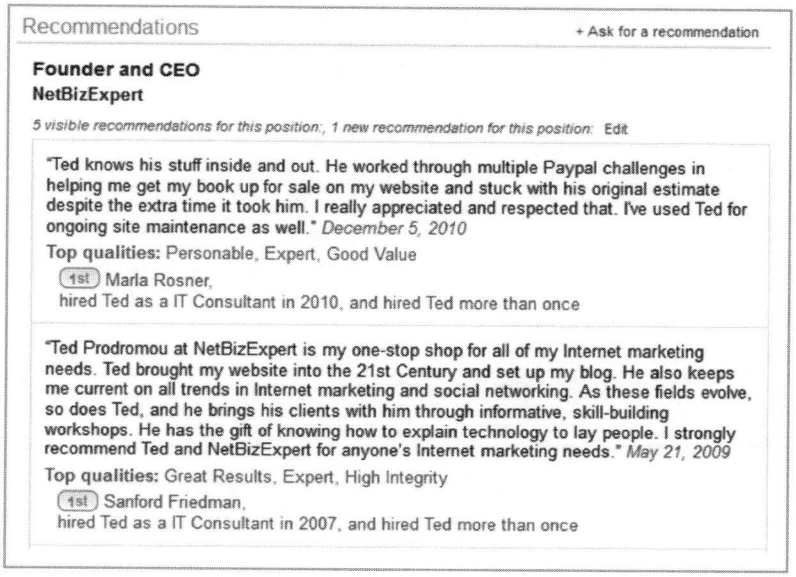

Recommendations   + Ask for a recommendation

Founder and CEO
NetBizExpert

5 visible recommendations for this position:, 1 new recommendation for this position: Edit

"Ted knows his stuff inside and out. He worked through multiple Paypal challenges in helping me get my book up for sale on my website and stuck with his original estimate despite the extra time it took him. I really appreciated and respected that. I've used Ted for ongoing site maintenance as well." *December 5, 2010*
Top qualities: Personable, Expert, Good Value
(1st) Marla Rosner,
hired Ted as a IT Consultant in 2010, and hired Ted more than once

"Ted Prodromou at NetBizExpert is my one-stop shop for all of my Internet marketing needs. Ted brought my website into the 21st Century and set up my blog. He also keeps me current on all trends in Internet marketing and social networking. As these fields evolve, so does Ted, and he brings his clients with him through informative, skill-building workshops. He has the gift of knowing how to explain technology to lay people. I strongly recommend Ted and NetBizExpert for anyone's Internet marketing needs." *May 21, 2009*
Top qualities: Great Results, Expert, High Integrity
(1st) Sanford Friedman,
hired Ted as a IT Consultant in 2007, and hired Ted more than once

FIGURE 4–10. Some of My Recommendations

EDUCATION

Once you've added your current and previous positions, you'll move to your education. Simply click Add a School to enter your schools, years attended, and your major. Figure 4–11 on page 24 shows the Add Education form.

You can also Request Recommendations from classmates and educators as shown in Figure 4–12 on page 24.

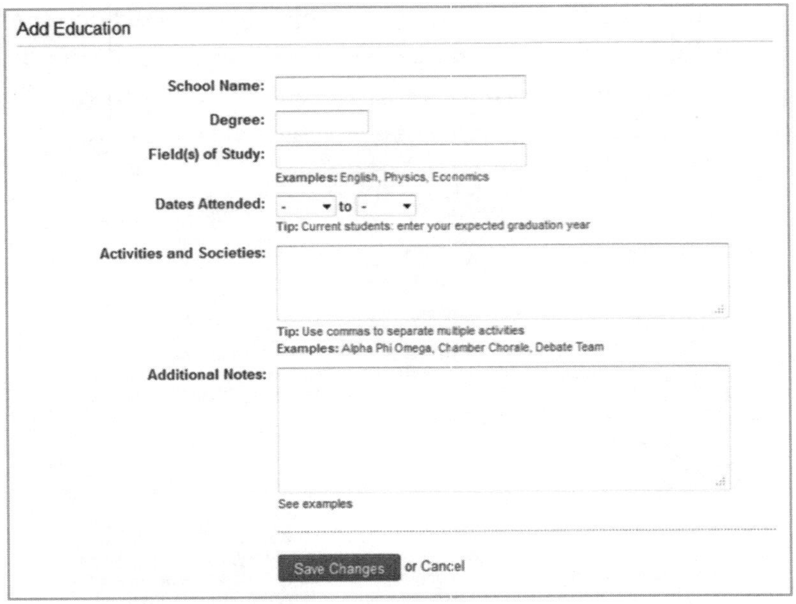

FIGURE 4–11. Add Education Form

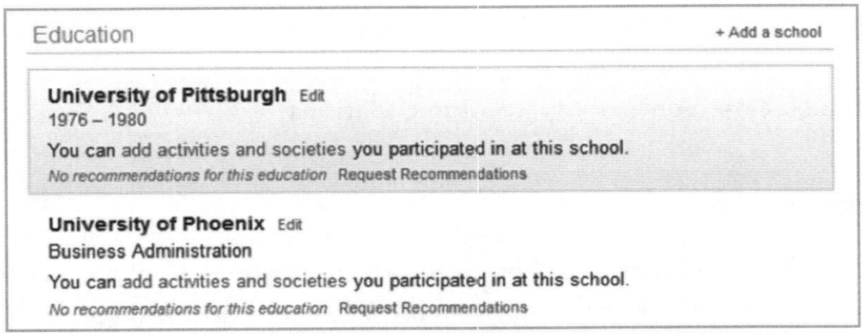

FIGURE 4–12. Education List with Request Recommendations Link

ADDITIONAL INFORMATION

This is the section where you can add links to your website and blog, which will generate lots of web traffic and help your search rankings. Links from popular sites like LinkedIn are very valuable, so you want to use this trick when you enter your website or blog URL.

One of the most common mistakes people make when adding their website or blog URLs to their LinkedIn profile is to choose one of the default options like Personal Website or Blog.

If you choose Company Website or one of the other options in the dropdown list as shown in Figure 4–13 on page 25, your listing will look something like Figure 4–1.

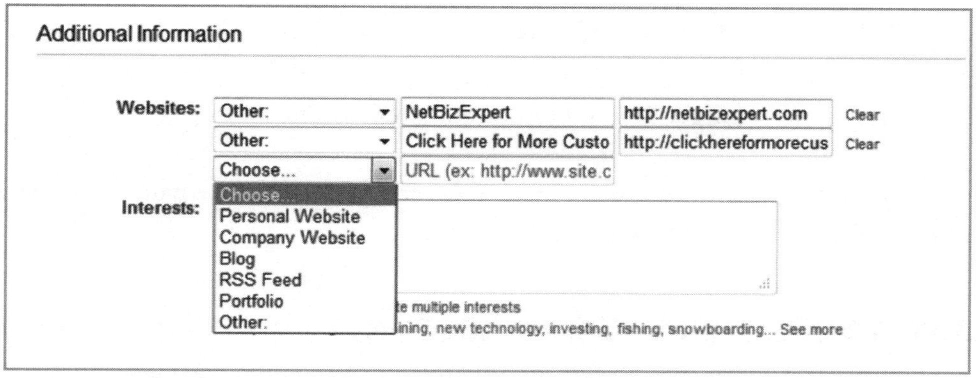

FIGURE 4–13. Additional Profile Information

I chose Company Website so you can see how it displays Company Website instead of my actual company name or target keyword phrase. This helps add valuable links and keyword phrases in your LinkedIn profile that will help your Google search rankings.

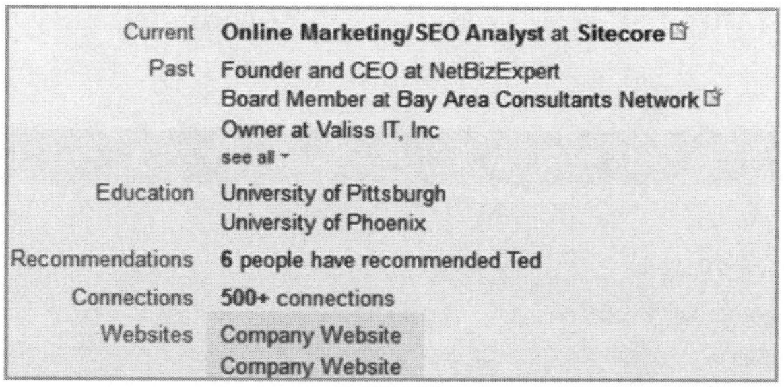

FIGURE 4–14. The Default Option—Company Website

LINKEDIN SEO TIP

Choose Other and enter your company name or keyword phrases in the middle box shown below.

FIGURE 4–15. Displaying Your Keywords Instead of the Words "Company Name"

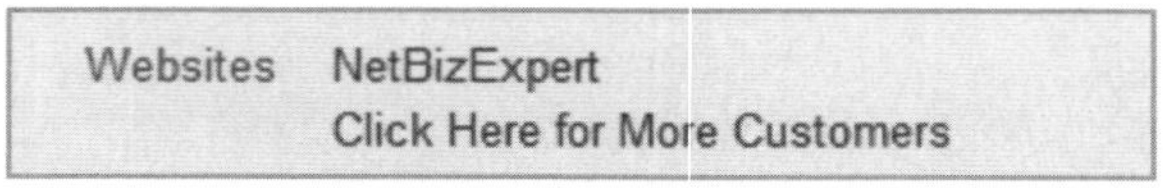

| Websites | NetBizExpert |
| | Click Here for More Customers |

FIGURE 4–16. Search Optimized Links to Your Website

Now your listing will look like Figure 4–16 and your company name or keyword phrases are clickable links to your blog or website.

ADDING YOUR SOCIAL MEDIA ACCOUNTS

LinkedIn lets you add social media feeds to your LinkedIn profile. This lets your profile visitors see what you're up to on the social media front.

Adding Your Twitter Account

Open your LinkedIn profile, click on Add Twitter Account and enter your Twitter user name. I prefer to display my Twitter account on my LinkedIn profile by checking the box. This allows me to Tweet from Twitter and shows my Tweets in my LinkedIn profile, as well as my Share status. Figure 4–17 shows you how to manage your Twitter settings.

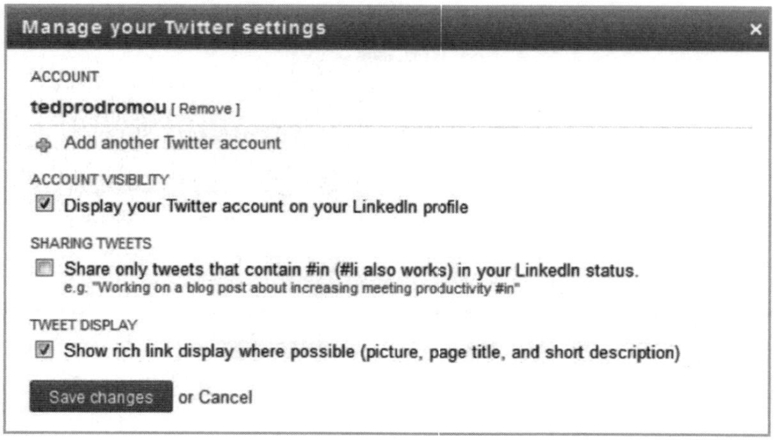

FIGURE 4–17. Adding Twitter to Your LinkedIn Profile

Now my Twitter account is connected to my LinkedIn profile, so my Tweets appear in my Status box as you see in Figure 4–18 on page 27.

FIGURE 4–18. Profile with Twitter

People can easily see your full status activity by clicking on See All Activity, where they will see a full listing of your LinkedIn activity as shown in Figure 4–19.

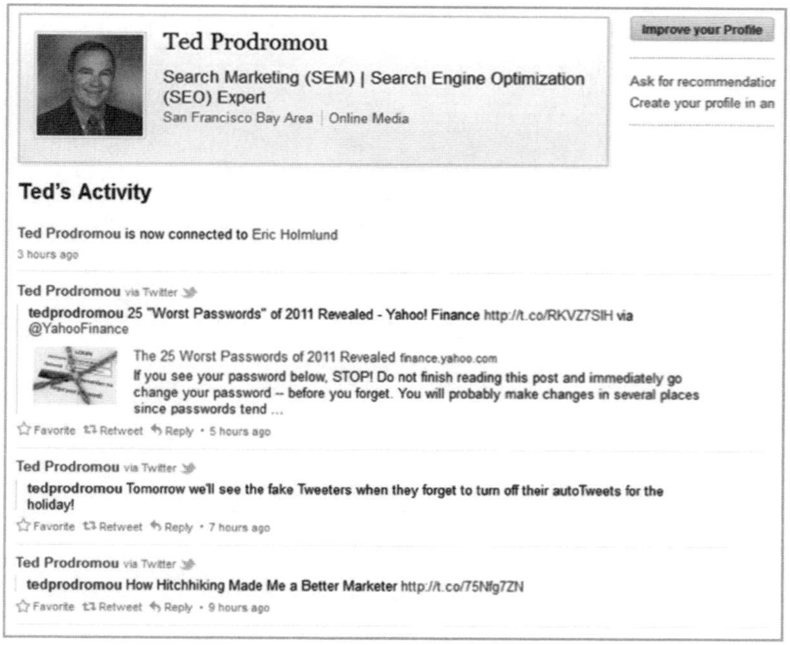

FIGURE 4–19. See All Activity

CONCLUSION

Your LinkedIn profile is now optimized for the search engines and ready to promote. Edit your public profile and choose Create a Profile Badge to promote your LinkedIn profile or use your Public Profile link. Add links to your LinkedIn profile from your website, blog, and email signature to generate traffic and improve your search rankings.

In the next chapter, I'll introduce you to the LinkedIn Privacy settings, where you can control when and where LinkedIn and its partner websites may use your profile information. I'll show you why it's important for you to configure your privacy settings properly to prevent your profile from appearing in inappropriate places like an ad near your competitor's company profile.

LinkedIn
Privacy Settings

Now that your LinkedIn profile is complete, we can configure your privacy settings. LinkedIn lets you control how your data is displayed and who is allowed to see your activity on LinkedIn. Internet privacy is a very controversial topic these days because people are becoming concerned about how much personal and private information is being collected by websites and how they are using it. Your LinkedIn profile does not contain any personal information like your address or telephone numbers, unless you voluntarily add them to your profile. I do not recommend adding any such personal information on your account. It is appropriate to include your work telephone number so prospects and customers can easily reach you and I'll leave it up to you if you want to include your cell phone number. Remember, more than 150 million people potentially have access to this information, which could be a blessing or a curse depending on who gets access to your cell phone number. People will also be able to get your company telephone number from your LinkedIn company page, so you want to add a link to your company page in your profile. Make it easy for prospects and customers to connect with you.

You have two profiles on LinkedIn. Your primary profile is the profile people see when they are logged into LinkedIn. They will see the details of your current and past jobs, the details of your education, your recommendations, your websites, Twitter account information, and which LinkedIn Groups you have joined. In the right column of your profile, people will see all of your LinkedIn activity, including your Tweets and Share updates.

People can also see all of your connections and get a sense of who you are and whom you're associated with. This helps people connect with like-minded people, so they can grow their network. Many believe this is a great way to grow your professional network because you're being totally transparent with other LinkedIn members.

If you don't want to let people see your connections, you can change your privacy settings so you are the only one who can view your connections. Some people do believe that not sharing their connections with others gives them a competitive advantage. A common practice of LinkedIn members is to find out whom their competitors are connected to and reach out to these connections to see if they are interesting in bringing their business to your company. If the person doesn't share their contacts with other LinkedIn members, you wouldn't have the opportunity to connect with their customers and steal them away from your competitor.

When you participate in the Q&A, your answers will be displayed in your sidebar. When you answer 25 questions or more in one area of expertise, you receive a star in that category. This is a fantastic way for you to demonstrate your expertise. Spend some time in the Q&A section answering questions and your expertise will be on display in your profile sidebar.

When you recommend others on LinkedIn, your recommendation will appear in your profile sidebar. This lets people see whom you do business with and helps them find great resources when they need assistance. People always prefer working with service providers who have been recommended instead of working with unknowns.

The last section of your profile sidebar displays Viewers of This Profile Also Viewed . . . . After people view your profile, they often view your connections' profiles. This section shows you the other profiles viewed after yours. This lets you see people LinkedIn has associated with your profile because you work for the same company, work in the same industry, have similar job skills, or have other similarities. This often shows you people you should be connected with on LinkedIn because of these similarities.

PUBLIC PROFILE

One profile is called your Public Profile, which can be viewed by people who are not logged into LinkedIn. This profile appears in Google searches if you choose to make it visible to the search engines. You can edit Public Profile settings and control which parts of your profile are displayed publicly. You can open up your profile completely so all information is accessible to the search engines and people not logged into LinkedIn.

You can also make your Public Profile completely private if you don't want to be found in the search engines. The third option is to customize the display of different elements of your profile. For example, you can display your basic information, headline, and summary and block the rest of your profile from the search engines. Most people use the custom configuration and display some of their profile and block sensitive information if it's included in their profile.

CONCLUSION

If you are a consultant or small-business owner and want to get your name out there, I see no reason to block any of your content from the search engines. You are on LinkedIn so people can find you and blocking your listing from search engines is self-defeating. It would be similar to owning a small business and having an unlisted telephone number. Opening up your profile completely will get your target keywords into the search engines, giving you maximum exposure.

In the next chapter, we'll take a tour of your LinkedIn homepage. I'll show you how to customize your homepage layout so you can easily see a snapshot of your important LinkedIn data.

A Tour of Your LinkedIn Homepage

L et's take a tour of your LinkedIn homepage. Every LinkedIn member has his or her own customizable homepage, which is like your start page on Yahoo, Google, or MSN. You select what you want to appear on your homepage so you can easily see what's important to you in a single glance. Figure 6–1 on page 34 is a view of a typical LinkedIn homepage.

1. This is your LinkedIn toolbar or menu. The menu options include:

   - Home: Obviously, this takes you back to your LinkedIn homepage.
   - Profile: This is where you can view and edit your LinkedIn profile.
   - Contacts: This is where you can add and manage your LinkedIn connections. You can also view your network statistics from this menu item.
   - Groups: This is where you create new groups, find new groups to join, see which groups you belong to, and see a complete directory of LinkedIn groups.
   - Jobs: You can post job openings for your company. This is where you can look for a job, post and manage jobs, and access premium services like Job Seeker Premium and Recruiting Solutions. I'll explain the premium solutions in Chapter 19, "Recruiting New Employees," and Chapter 23, "Finding a Job on LinkedIn."

FIGURE 6–1. A Typical LinkedIn Homepage

- Inbox: This is your LinkedIn email system.
- Companies: This is where you can search for companies and access companies you are following.
- News: This is where you can access LinkedIn Today, Signal, and articles you have saved. This is the section you can customize to view current news events in one screen.
- More: This is where you access Answers, the Learning Center, Skills, and your LinkedIn Apps

2. *LinkedIn Search.* This is where you search for people, companies, and groups on LinkedIn. I'll show you how to do advanced searches on LinkedIn in Chapter 8, "LinkedIn Search."

3. *Self-Service Text Ads.* Near the top of Figure 6-1 you will see where your LinkedIn self-service text ads will be displayed.

4. *Share Box.* This is where you post your status updates.

5. *People You May Know.* This is where the LinkedIn search algorithm will recommend people you may want to connect with based on who you are connected with, companies you have in your profile or follow, or former co-workers.

6. *LinkedIn Today.* This is a customizable news widget where you can display current news items from various industries and websites.

7. *Content Ads.* This is where LinkedIn Premium Content ads are displayed.

8. *Updates.* Your updates and updates from your connections are displayed here.

9. *Who's Viewed Your Profile.* This widget lets you know how many people viewed your profile in the past week. Clicking on the link will give you some details about who clicked, and LinkedIn Premium members will get full contact information about who viewed your profile.

10. *Your LinkedIn Network.* This is where you see how many first-level connections you have and how many new people joined your network in the past day.

Your LinkedIn homepage contains many sidebar widgets, which are customizable. Figure 6–2 on page 36 shows the widgets that come from configurable options in your LinkedIn account. You can choose whether you want to display these widgets under your Settings, Profile section.

11. *Jobs You May be Interested In.* Based on the job titles and keywords in your profile, LinkedIn will recommend jobs you may be interested in.

12. *Groups You May Like.* Based on the groups you belong to, job titles, and keywords in your profile, LinkedIn will recommend groups you may want to join.

13. *Companies You May Want to Follow.* Based on the companies you have listed in your profile, your industry, keywords in your profile, and other companies you follow, LinkedIn recommends other companies you may want to follow.

You can also display the LinkedIn apps you are using in your sidebar. Figure 6–3 on page 37 shows how you can display your blog posts from the WordPress App and your PowerPoint presentations that you've uploaded to your SlideShare account.

14. *WordPress.* This is the WordPress application that shows your latest blog posts in the sidebar of your LinkedIn profile page and your LinkedIn homepage. Blogging on a regular basis shows your LinkedIn connections that you are a subject-matter expert in your field.

15. *SlideShare Presentations.* This LinkedIn app displays PowerPoint presentations and articles you have written and posted to SlideShare.

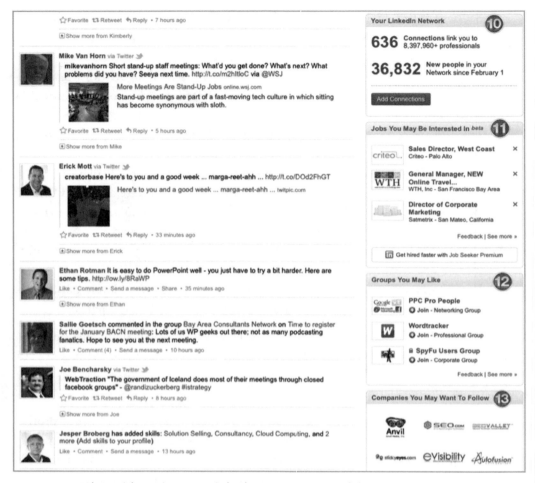

FIGURE 6–2. The Widgets in Your LinkedIn Homepage Sidebar

Other LinkedIn apps that you have installed will appear down the right column. You have to be careful to make sure you don't display too many apps because it will make your sidebar scroll too far down the page. If this occurs, people may not see an excellent article or presentation that you posted at the very bottom of your page.

CONCLUSION

You are now familiar with your LinkedIn homepage and how you can configure it to display the content that is most appropriate for you. You can change many of the content modules so your homepage gives you an efficient snapshot of the data you want to see.

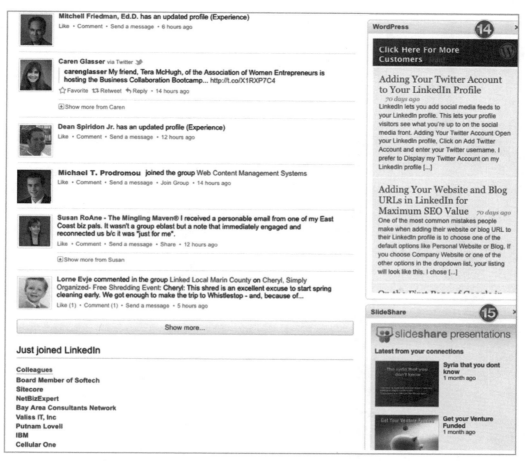

FIGURE 6–3. Displaying LinkedIn Apps on your LinkedIn Homepage

In the next chapter, I'm going to show you how to set up your LinkedIn company page and customize it to give your company maximum exposure.

LinkedIn
for Companies

LinkedIn company pages are like a LinkedIn personal profile for your company. Your company page is a mini-website for your company, but it's located on LinkedIn so it's easy for LinkedIn members to find. You'll want to use the same search optimization techniques that you used when you set up your personal profile when you're setting up your company page. I'll show you exactly how to search-optimize your company profile later in this chapter.

Your company page will always appear when a member types your company's name in LinkedIn's search box on their home page or on the Companies link on the top toolbar. Your LinkedIn company page will also appear in Google search results. Because LinkedIn is a very popular and trusted website, LinkedIn company pages rank well in Google. This is very significant because your LinkedIn company page will rank highly in Google search results and people can view your LinkedIn company page without logging into LinkedIn, giving your company significant exposure. For this reason, you want to make sure your LinkedIn company page is complete and updated frequently with your latest company news and product offerings.

Other ways your company page will appear include:

- When you view the LinkedIn profile of one of your employees
- Receive a notification when your products or services are recommended by one of your employees' connections
- See an open position from your company via a job search under Jobs You May Be Interested In

> **LINKEDIN COMPANY PAGE TIP**
>
> Your LinkedIn company page URL will be www.linkedin.com/company/*Your-CompanyName*

- See your company under Companies You May Be Interested in Following, which appears in the right sidebar on your homepage.
- Follow your company and receive status updates.

For LinkedIn members, company pages are a great way to research companies. There is a treasure trove of detailed information about almost any company—even if the company does not have a company page. When you do a search from the LinkedIn top toolbar and switch the search type to companies, you will see search results from the company page (if there is one) and all companies who work closely or partner with that company.

For example, when you do a company search for Microsoft, you will see the Microsoft company page followed by a list of Microsoft Certified Partners. Click on the Microsoft company page and you'll find a list of people in your network who are affiliated with Microsoft. You'll also be provided with a list of Microsoft employees who are in LinkedIn and are your first-, second-, or third-degree connections.

You can follow companies on their company page so you can stay up-to-date with their new products or services, review their products or services, and see who they are hiring. You can also follow competitors and know what they're up to!

Company pages let your customers and prospects get to know the people in your company. You can feature the employees behind your brand and show how customers use your products. Your company page is a great way to solidify your reputation and build trust with your clients and prospects.

COMPONENTS OF A COMPANY PROFILE

Figure 7–1 on page 41 shows you a typical company profile and the options you have to customize it for your needs.

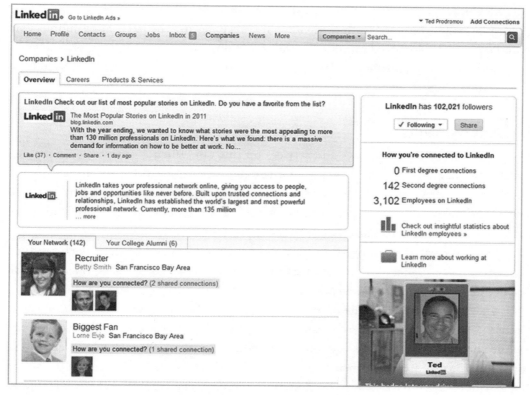

FIGURE 7–1. A Typical Company Profile

Overview of Your Company Homepage

The Overview tab shows the viewer a snapshot of your company, including your latest Share post, a brief description of your company, and all employees in the network, including first-, second-, and third-degree connections. You can also display your company's blog posts and Twitter feeds on the Overview tab. It's a great way to give people a quick overview of your company and an opportunity for you to make a direct connection with them if they follow your company.

Careers

This is where any job openings you've posted on LinkedIn will appear. If you purchase a Silver or Gold Career Page, you can also add a brief description of your company culture and people can get a good idea of how fantastic it is to work there. The Silver and Gold Career Page also lets you feature top employees and create targeted messaging to help fill your open positions quickly with the best talent. If you have a Gold Careers Page, your jobs will be targeted to the individual member viewing the page. For example, you can target members based on industry, job function, seniority, and geography, so your message to a programmer in Silicon Valley is different from your message to a sales professional in Sydney.

Products and Services

You can feature your products and services on this tab. When a prospect or customer visits this page, he sees how many of their network connections recommend your product and they can add their own recommendations. You can also add the contact details of the product manager or sales representative responsible for each product in case the reader wants to learn more about the product.

You can create a directory-style listing of your products and services. Each product or service can also include descriptions, features, images, display banners, videos, special offers, and the ability to add recommendations.

The most powerful feature of the products page is the ability to display personalized content to your audience. You can show technical product details to a developer while showing cost benefit details to an executive decision maker. You can create up to 30 distinct audience segments for different versions of this tab, based on a variety of attributes such as industry, job function, seniority, geography, and company size, providing targeted content to each member.

Analytics

This tab is visible only to an administrator of your company page. The Analytics tab shows you who your visitors are, what they do, and which other companies they follow. You gain valuable insight into what content they are most interested in, their job function, industry, company, and which products they are researching.

Key Statistics

This data is located in a widget on the right sidebar of the company page. LinkedIn uses data from employees' profiles to compile summaries of job functions, years of experience, education degree, and university attended. You can see where your company compares with other companies in your industry with respect to these categories. Your customers and prospects can also compare your company with your competitors to see which company has the most experienced workers, as well as the best educated; you can even find out which schools your employees attended.

Company Description

This is where you add a brief description of your company using your target keyword phrases and help influence the rank of your company's page in the search results. Make your company description clear and concise, so readers know exactly what your company does and how you can help them.

Company Employees

This is a list of LinkedIn users in your network (up to two degrees of separation from you) who currently work at this company. Viewers can see who works at your company and how they are connected to your employees, which makes it easy for them to reach out for an introduction if they want to connect. This is a powerful feature if you are looking for a job and want to get hired at a certain company; it can also be valuable if you are in sales and are looking for an introduction to a key decision maker.

New Hires

When someone hires on at a company and updates their LinkedIn profile, they will show up as a new hire at that company. Their profile will be displayed in the New Hires section so you can see what level of talent the company is hiring. This is great information for recruiters looking to place people at specific companies and for job seekers looking to get hired. Knowing the background of new hires helps a job seeker update their resume and/or skill set to match the talent being hired at that company.

Recent Promotions and Changes

When a LinkedIn user updates her profile with a new position at this company, the new profile will appear here. This is valuable information for recruiters looking to place people at this company and for job seekers looking for a position in this company. When a person is promoted, the company is often looking for a replacement to fill the old position.

Popular Profiles

These are company employees who are featured because they are in the company news, referenced in blogs, participating in industry groups, and/or frequently the result of searches and other activities within the LinkedIn network. Users appear on this list when they have the most profile views at their company. Most of the time, the most popular profiles in a company are the C-level executives who are featured in press releases, company news, and in the media. It's important for C-level executives to have a complete, search-optimized profile, because people will often review their profiles before doing business with their company.

COMPANY STATUS UPDATES

Company status updates are posts made by the company to share company news, product releases, promotions, or relevant industry news. Company status updates are a powerful communication tool, allowing you to send messages and links directly to your followers.

Company posts can be seen on the company's Overview tab by any LinkedIn member and in a member's network update stream. If you follow the company, you will see the company status updates directly on your homepage so it's easy to know what's happening with that company, your competitors, or in your industry. All LinkedIn members have the ability to view company status updates, click on embedded links, or view posted videos. They can also comment on, like, or share a company status update, allowing your updates to spread virally to grow your following and engage your members.

CREATING YOUR COMPANY PAGE

When you are ready to create your company page, go to Companies on the top toolbar. On the right side of the page near the top, click on Add a Company. Enter your company name and company email address and check the box next to the verification message: "I verify that I am the official representative of this company and have the right to act on behalf of my company in the creation of this page." You must use an email address from your company, not a Gmail or other free email address.

Next you will enter a wizard shown in Figure 7–2 on page 45 that will guide you through the setup of your new company page.

You can select any language for your company page. When you select any language other than English, the wizard changes; this eliminates all configuration options on the Overview tab, except Company Description. You can still add items to the Careers and Products & Services tabs if you select a language other than English.

If you choose English for your company page, you need to choose who will be authorized to be the company page administrators (admins). The default choice is "All employees with a valid email registered to the company domain," which I don't recommend. It's best to manually designate your admins, so you have consistency of and control over what is posted on your company page. Allowing every employee to have

Companies > NetBizExpert (edit mode)

Overview   Careers   Products & Services   Analytics

14/2011 by Ted Prodromou

Publish   Cancel

* Indicates required field

ert

e description for other languages: English

id email registered to the company domain

dates

our Company's Followers, via your Company Page Overview tab. To turn on
ignate an admin or admins responsible for managing your company page.

* Company Type
Public Company

* Company Size
myself only

* Company Website URL

* Main Company Industry
Accounting

* Company Operating Status
Operating

Year Founded

pany Page Setup Wizard

admin access to your company page can result in inappropriate content being posted and inconsistent management of your company page.

Designate at least two administrators for your company page. You may want to add more if you work for a large company and will have a lot of activity on your page. For example, if you will be posting a lot of job openings on your company page, you can designate a member of your human resources department as administrator and allow her to post and remove job openings. It would be smart to have an administrator from human resources, sales, public relations, and marketing, so they can each efficiently manage their respective areas of your company page. The marketing person could manage the Products & Services section; public relations could post your Share updates with current company news and product announcements; and sales could monitor the discussions, in case any pre-sales questions are posted on your company page.

It's imperative that someone is assigned to constantly monitor your company page, in case inappropriate content is posted. Any offending content should be removed immediately.

Negative remarks don't necessarily have to be removed, if you address them in an appropriate way. Every company has at least a small number of dissatisfied customers who may post negative comments about their products. Instead of just removing the negative comment, you can respond in a positive way by addressing the issue publicly. Sometimes the issue is a simple misunderstanding of how to use the product, which you can explain. On other occasions, there could be a legitimate problem with your product or service. If this is the case then proper communication with the customer not only leads to resolution, it may even build your company's reputation. Admitting mistakes, speedy solutions, and strong communication demonstrate that you care about your customers and provide excellent customer service.

CONCLUSION

Your LinkedIn company page is a mini-website where you can share company news, updates, and current job openings. Your LinkedIn company page is easily found in LinkedIn searches giving your company great exposure to millions of LinkedIn members and in Google search results.

In the next chapter, we'll explore LinkedIn Search, which is your most powerful tool on LinkedIn. Mastering LinkedIn Search will give you access to the invaluable data available in the rapidly growing LinkedIn database.

LinkedIn Search

L inkedIn is essentially a business-oriented search engine and works the same way as other search engines like Google and Yahoo. LinkedIn has its own proprietary search algorithm that isn't as sophisticated as the Google search algorithm (no search engine is as sophisticated as Google's), but it's evolving rapidly.

LinkedIn Search has two functions. First, it can be used to find other people, companies, and groups on LinkedIn so you can build your professional network, follow companies, and join industry-related groups. The second function of LinkedIn Search is for people to find you. Most people don't think of LinkedIn Search from that perspective, but I think you need to stop and consider the possibilities. What would it do for your business or career if you appeared when people searched for specific skills or industry terms? With more than 150 million of the best top business professionals looking for industry experts by searching LinkedIn, you career would skyrocket if you appeared on the first page of the search results. If you want to optimize your LinkedIn profile so you appear in search results, I invite you to visit Chapter 4, "Supercharging Your LinkedIn Profile."

Let's start with using LinkedIn Search to find people, companies, and groups. As you can see in Figure 8–1 on page 48, the LinkedIn search box is located on the right side of the LinkedIn menu or toolbar.

FIGURE 8–1. The LinkedIn Menu or Toolbar

The search box gives you seven search options in a dropdown box. This lets you narrow your search results to People, Updates, Jobs, Companies, Answers, Inbox, and Groups. If you leave the search box on the default People search and just click the magnifying glass, LinkedIn will display a list of all of your connections. You can also see a full list of your connections if you go to the Contacts, Connections tab on the LinkedIn menu. If you want to find people outside your network, you need to enter specific keywords like a job title, company name, industry, school, or skill.

LinkedIn People Search is a very powerful tool that can help you find new customers, recruit new employees, and build your professional network. You can also use LinkedIn People Search to:

- Find an industry expert to speak at an event your company is hosting.
- Find an industry expert to hire as a consultant for a project.
- Find people you want to meet with when you are traveling to another city.
- Find speaking engagements.
- Find consulting engagements.
- Connect with other industry experts to join you in a project or business venture.
- Find people who want to join you for charity events.
- Find people who want to start a local networking group.

When you have the ability to search a database of more than 150 million business professionals, the benefits of LinkedIn People Search are endless.

KEYWORDS ARE KING

Keywords, keywords, keywords! You are going to get tired of hearing me talk about keywords, but they are the foundation of LinkedIn Search so it's important that you understand how to use them effectively. In the next chapter, "Getting Found on LinkedIn," I'm going to teach you everything you ever wanted to know about keywords (and probably a little more!), but for now let's focus on the fundamentals of using the LinkedIn Search function.

LinkedIn Search works a little differently from a Google search. If I search Google for "web marketing expert," without the quote marks, I will see results that contain the word web or marketing or expert. This is called a broad match search because Google will return all results that contain any of the keywords I used in my search.

I can also do a phrase search to narrow my results. If I search Google for "web marketing expert" with the quote marks, I will only see results that contain the entire phrase "web marketing expert." This gives me a more focused search result, saving me time.

When I search for "web marketing expert" on LinkedIn, however, I have the ability to sort my search results by Relevance, Relationship, Relationship, + Recommendations, Connections, and Keywords. If I change my sort criteria to Keywords, the search result will display the phrase match search results just like Google would. If I use any of the other sort criteria, the search results will consider these factors when displaying the results.

Competitive Analysis

Let's get into more detail about doing a competitive analysis search, and I'll show you how to use the Search sort option to expand your search results and find exactly who or what you are looking for. A great example of a competitive search is one to see what keywords your competitors are targeting.

Figure 8–2 shows your sorting options that are available after you've completed your initial search.

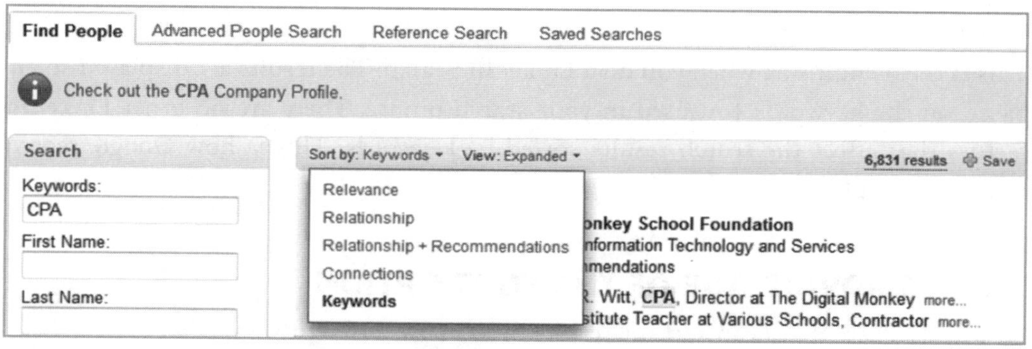

FIGURE 8–2. Keyword Search and Sorting Options

Relevance

Relevance is determined by the proprietary LinkedIn algorithm, which the site is constantly improving to help you receive optimal search results. Relevance results are based on the searcher's activity on LinkedIn, the profiles returned by the query, and other members who have made similar searches in determining the search result order.

Relationship

When you sort by Relationship, LinkedIn displays the results by degree (first through third), and then groups—in that order. This means your first-degree connections will be displayed first followed by your second-degree connections. Your third-degree connections are displayed next, and then the people who are in the groups you joined.

Relationship + Recommendations

The Relationship + Recommendations sort is displayed by the degree of your connection and the number of Recommendations. A second-degree connection with 20 Recommendations will appear before a first-degree connection with no Recommendations.

Connections

When you choose to sort by Connections, the search results are displayed in order based on the number of LinkedIn Connections the member has.

Keywords

This is the default sort when you do a LinkedIn Search. The results are displayed solely based on the keywords you used in your search phrase. There are no other LinkedIn factors that affect the search results sorted by keywords. This is how Google search results are displayed.

TAKING ADVANTAGE OF THE SORT OPTION

So why do I care that I can sort my results in so many different ways?

Let me show you how and why you would want to use these different sorting options. I'll start with the default sort result, Keywords.

Suppose you are a divorce attorney and you're just getting started on LinkedIn. You know very little about LinkedIn and you know you have a lot of competition. You want to check out your potential competition so you enter "divorce attorney" in the LinkedIn Search box and you get a long list of attorneys in the search results.

How do you get to the top of the search results for "divorce attorney"? The first thing you want to do is look at the Sort by Keywords option to see what keyword phrases your competitors are using. Since your law practice is only in the Chicago area, we want to back up one step and narrow your search to "divorce attorney" in the Chicago area.

Next to the magnifying glass in the Search box, you see a link called Advanced. Click on that link and you will enter the Advanced People Search screen as seen in Figure 8–3. Don't worry about the numerous Advanced Search options right now. Just enter "divorce attorney" in the keywords box and enter your postal code. Leave all the other options the way they are and click Search.

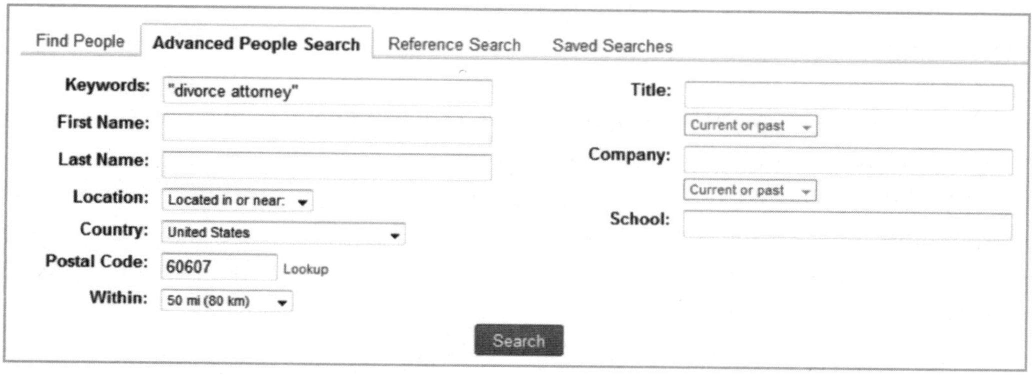

| Find People | **Advanced People Search** | Reference Search | Saved Searches |

Keywords:	"divorce attorney"		Title:	
First Name:				Current or past
Last Name:			Company:	
Location:	Located in or near:			Current or past
Country:	United States		School:	
Postal Code:	60607	Lookup		
Within:	50 mi (80 km)			

Search

FIGURE 8–3. The LinkedIn Advanced People Search

You will see a list of all divorce attorneys within 50 miles of your postal code. Make sure your sort is by keyword and start browsing your competition. Notice how many times the top search results use "divorce attorney" in their profile. Notice where they place their target keywords, such as in their job titles, job descriptions, recommendation titles, and recommendation content. Make a list and compare the top ten search results, so you can see how they tailored their profile to reach the top ten in a keyword sorted search result. Remember, the sort by keyword search result provides search results solely based on the keywords used in your LinkedIn profile.

Let's try the sort by Connections search result next. Using the same example of the Chicago divorce attorney, change your sort result to Connections. Notice the list has completely changed order. Start clicking on the profiles from top to bottom and you will see the person with the most Connections is number one and the person with the least amount of Connections is at the bottom of the search result. How does this help you? If the person at the top of the list only has 200 Connections, you can surpass him or her if you get 201 Connections. Now don't run out and connect with 201 people just to become number one in the search result. Connect with the right people and eventually you will move to the top position.

Why does the number of Connections matter? People like to see that you are connected to a fair amount of other professionals in your field. This shows that you are not a lone ranger and you work in a vacuum. Just to clarify: You don't necessarily need a *lot of* Connections, just a good number of *quality* Connections.

Let's move on to the next sorting option, Relationship + Recommendations. Notice the list changed again, maybe not as significantly as when you changed from Keywords to Connections. You see some familiar faces in the list that are the same as the Connections sort. The Relationship + Recommendations list is important to you because as you connect with more people you will have to receive more Recommendations than them to surpass them in the search rankings.

If you have 201 Connections and 20 Recommendations and the number-one person on the search result has 201 Connections and 22 Recommendations, you can surpass them if you receive three more Recommendations.

Why does the Relationship + Recommendations sort result matter? This measurement shows someone searching for a divorce attorney that you are well connected and you have a lot of Recommendations. This is better than just having a lot of Connections or a lot of Recommendations.

The sort by Relationship is next. Why is this measurement important to someone looking for a divorce attorney? This shows the person searching for a divorce attorney their potential connection to you. If I search for a divorce attorney near my home and I see that I already have a first-degree connection with a divorce attorney, I would probably contact that person. If I didn't want to use that individual as my divorce attorney because we were good friends and it may impact our friendship, I would ask for a referral. If I didn't have a first-degree connection with a divorce attorney but I had a second-degree connection, I would contact my first-degree connection who is connected with that divorce attorney and ask for an introduction. See how important it is to have a healthy number of connections in LinkedIn? The more connections you have, the bigger your second- and third-degree networks become.

Relevance is the last sorting option, but it is not the least important option. Remember, Relevance is determined by the LinkedIn algorithm where it factors in the keywords you entered with similar searches done by others in your LinkedIn network. As more people in your network search for certain keywords, LinkedIn remembers those keyword searches and the actions they took when they saw the search results. LinkedIn will display the most relevant search results to you based on the history of similar keyword searches and the actions taken after the search. This is a form of artificial intelligence that learns over time so you receive the best search result for your personal situation.

ADVANCED LINKEDIN SEARCH

Okay, you've had a couple of tastes of the basic LinkedIn Search and now it's time to dig into the main course: Advanced LinkedIn Search. This is the skill you need to master to become a top-tier LinkedIn user. Whether you are in sales hunting for prospects, a recruiter looking for top talent, or just a regular LinkedIn member, becoming an expert at searching on LinkedIn will take your career to the next level.

At your fingertips, you have access to more than 150 million business professionals from around the world. Obviously you don't need to connect with all of them, but you can build a strong professional network of 150 colleagues that you can carry with you for the rest of your career. No longer will you have to worry about recessions and high unemployment. When you surround yourself with a strong international professional network, recessions will have little or no impact on your career.

Think about this. When we entered the new millennium, everyone was worried that the Y2K date problem in older computers would bring businesses to their knees. We survived Y2K without a hitch, but the dotcom collapse crushed our economy and changed the high-tech world forever. Thousands lost their jobs, but eventually most people found new jobs or careers. In 2008, the banking crisis collapsed the world economy, with millions of people around the world losing their jobs. Not only did they lose their jobs, many lost their homes and their life savings. The past 10 years have been a wild roller-coaster ride for many middle-class citizens around the world.

While the economy and unemployment were bouncing up and down over the past 10 years, the number of millionaires and billionaires around the world increased significantly. According to a finding in *The Wall Street Journal* in the year 2000, there were 306 billionaires in the world. In 2011 there were *1210 billionaires*—a fourfold increase.

How did so many people become billionaires during the worst economic conditions in our lifetime? They built a strong personal network around themselves, so they could withstand the recession and actually make a significant amount of money during the past few years.

I know it seems like I'm drifting a bit off track and you're probably wondering how this relates to LinkedIn Search. It's *directly* related to LinkedIn Search because you have the opportunity to build a powerful personal network from the LinkedIn database. Everyone you need to know is on LinkedIn. If for some reason you need to connect with someone who is not on LinkedIn, a LinkedIn connection can lead you to that person. Remember, success in business is about *who* you know not *what* you know.

The better you get at LinkedIn Search, the closer you come to putting your personal dream network together. Mining through the LinkedIn database, looking for the nuggets of gold, will put you in a position where you will never have to worry about not earning money again. When you need a new project, one of your connections will know someone who needs your expertise. Looking for some new sales prospects? A few of your second- and third-degree connections are sure to need your product. It's all about leveraging the power of the rapidly growing LinkedIn network. Since I started writing this book two months ago, LinkedIn grew from 130 million members to 150 million members. By the time this book hits the bookshelves, LinkedIn will likely be well over 200 million members, since statistically they are adding two members every second.

The following sections offer just a few examples how you can use Advanced LinkedIn Search.

SALES REP SELLING CUSTOMER RELATIONSHIP MANAGEMENT SOFTWARE

You are a sales rep who sells customer relationship management (CRM) software to enterprise-level clients. Your key decision maker is usually at the CXO level and your target companies are in the Fortune 500. Your software has a 6- to 12-month buying cycle and there are many departments involved in the decision-making process, including sales, information technology, and sometimes marketing. There are also project managers from these departments involved in the purchase decision.

Your initial contact is usually with a manager in the IT or sales department who does the initial evaluation of your product. After she does the initial evaluation, an IT or sales director gets involved. You want to use LinkedIn Advanced Search to find managers who are doing the initial evaluation or directors who are involved in the second phase of the project.

One way to find managers or directors who are shopping for CRM systems is to search LinkedIn Answers for phrases like:

- What is the best CRM software?
- I am looking for insight . . .
- Looking for advice . . .
- I want a GREAT CRM system. What is the best?
- What is your current CRM?

You can also look for Questions posted by people looking for help with their current CRM. They may be frustrated with their CRM, having problems, or outgrowing it. Many companies start with a free or low-cost CRM and upgrade once they outgrow the capacity or need additional functionality.

You get it. Search through the Questions and read all relevant Answers to see who is asking the questions. Chances are they are shopping for a CRM and they want to gather some social proof before they start reaching out to CRM vendors.

When you are searching through the Answers, make sure you select All Answers and sort by Date, so you can see the most recent Questions and Answers. It won't do you any good to reach out to someone who was shopping for a CRM two years ago. You can also select the Open Questions tab, so you will only see recent Questions and Answers. Remember that Questions only remain open for seven days by default, which means that Open Questions are very recent conversations. The person asking the Question may be in the very beginning of his or her evaluation process, so you may want to monitor the conversation and not be too aggressive while the Question is still Open.

Figure 8–4 is a great example of how to become a LinkedIn detective to track down hot prospects!

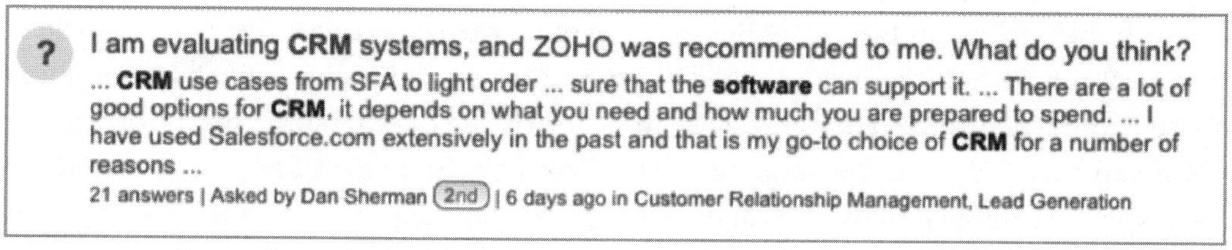

> **?** I am evaluating **CRM** systems, and ZOHO was recommended to me. What do you think?
> ... **CRM** use cases from SFA to light order ... sure that the **software** can support it. ... There are a lot of good options for **CRM**, it depends on what you need and how much you are prepared to spend. ... I have used Salesforce.com extensively in the past and that is my go-to choice of **CRM** for a number of reasons ...
> 21 answers | Asked by Dan Sherman (2nd) | 6 days ago in Customer Relationship Management, Lead Generation

FIGURE 8–4. Open Question with 21 Answers

You can learn a lot from this simple screenshot in which Dan Sherman asks an Open Question. Dan is a second-level connection of mine, because one of my first-level connections knows him. I'm only one step away from getting a direct introduction to Dan by one of his friends. Let's not get carried away and try to contact Dan until we do some more detective work.

You also see the question was asked in the Customer Relationship Management, Lead Generation category in Answers. We can monitor that category to find more prospects and see if Dan has been asking other questions related to CRMs. While monitoring the Customer Relationship Management, Lead Generation category, you can start answering some questions to build some credibility in the forum. You can also join some CRM-related Groups and participate in some conversations to build up your reputation. Remember, you are not selling when you answer questions. Just provide unbiased information that will answer the question and build a level of trust around you.

If someone asks for specific product recommendations, you can respond with a list of features they would benefit from without mentioning your product. Of course, it would be nice if only your product had those features so you would then have an opportunity to make an indirect recommendation of your product.

FIGURE 8–5. Learn More About the Person Who Asked the Question

Back to our detective work. Click on Dan's name at the bottom of his question to get some more background information about him. Figure 8–5 shows us Dan's profile headline and our relationship to him.

We see Dan's profile headline in the summary on the left and a link to see every question he's asked on LinkedIn. Before we explore the other questions Dan has asked, let's look at his headline. He's a LinkedIn Expert Author and Trainer who has more than 11,000 contacts. From first glance Dan may not fit the demographic of our enterprise CRM software. Click on his name to see his profile in more detail as you see in Figure 8–6. Now we can see if he works for a Fortune 500 company.

FIGURE 8–6. Dan Sherman's Full Profile

It looks like Dan is the owner of Linked Success, which has 1 to 10 employees, so he's not in our target audience. We would then move on to another question in the Answers section.

Let's pretend Dan did work for a Fortune 500 company and he did fit our demographic for an enterprise CRM system. Let's see if any of Dan's connections match mine in my LinkedIn network.

On the sidebar of Dan's profile you see this widget with a list of people in my network who are directly connected to Dan. Figure 8–7 tells me I have more than a couple connections that could introduce me to Dan. See how easy it is to get connected to hot prospects?

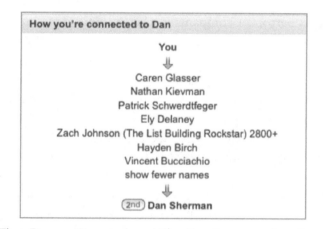

FIGURE 8–7. My First-Degree Connections Who Are Connected to Dan Sherman

As you see, it's relatively easy to search through the Questions and Answers to find potential prospects who are researching products. That entire process of finding Dan took me less than two minutes. You can spend less than 30 minutes a day scanning Questions and Answers and Groups to see who's in research mode for CRM software. You will find similar conversations in the Groups and you use the same approach of being an active participant in the Group helping others in an unbiased way. When they trust you and see you are an expert, they will reach out to you when they realize you sell the solution to their problem.

A MORE DIRECT ROUTE TO HOT PROSPECTS

While it was very easy to look for prospects in the Answers section, you saw the obvious drawback. There is no easy way to prequalify the potential leads you find in Answers. You have to take that extra step of reviewing the profile of the person asking the questions to find out if she works for a company that meets your demographic target. Unfortunately, there isn't an Advanced Search capability for LinkedIn Answers that lets you filter by anything other than the Answers category. It would be nice to be able to filter Questions and Answers by the same ones as the People Search provides—but LinkedIn can't do that yet.

From my experience, it's rare to see high-level executives asking Questions in the Answers section, since they enter the buying process towards the end after much due diligence by the managers and directors. You can target managers and directors in the Answers section, but you have to use a different approach to connect with the C-level executives who are the final decision makers.

I prefer to use the Advanced Search under People when I'm looking for very specific information about a person or company. In this example, you could do an Advanced Search to find C-level execs or managers and directors in Fortune 500 companies located in your territory.

To do an Advanced Search for specific people, make sure the Search is set to People and click the Advanced link next to the magnifying glass. The Advanced People Search tab will appear with a slew of options.

Let's keep it simple and search for C-level executives who work for Fortune 500 companies within a 100-mile radius of your office. Leave all of the fields empty except for your postal code and change the "Within:" to 100 mi. On the Seniority Level check the CXO box. This will search for all C-level executives. Check the appropriate boxes under Fortune 1000 to select only the Fortune 500. Figures 8–8 below and 8–9 on page 59 show you what your search criteria should look like.

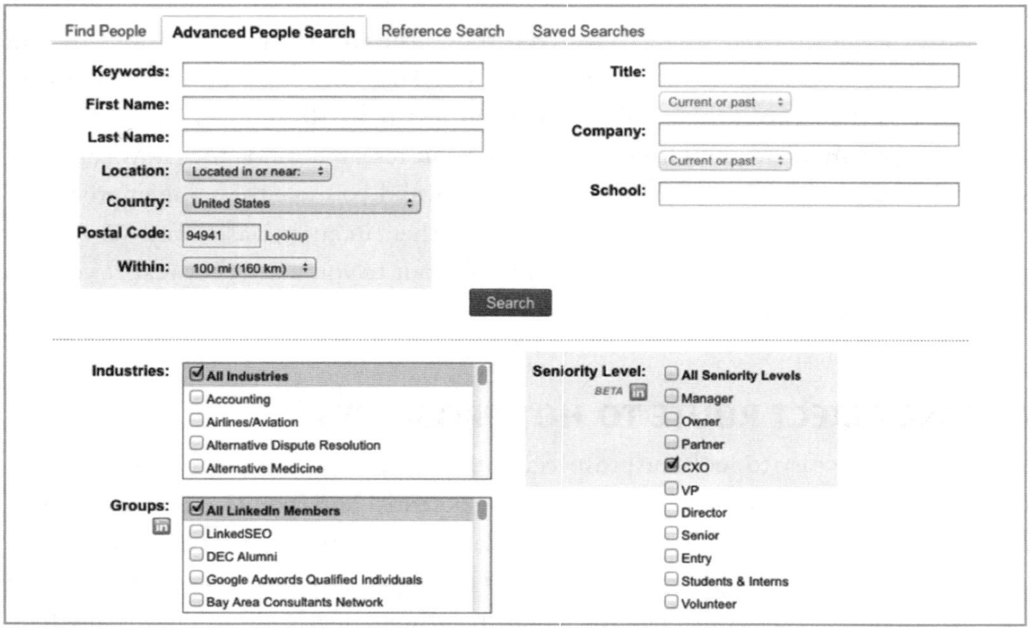

FIGURE 8–8. Selecting CXO Level People Within 100 Miles of You

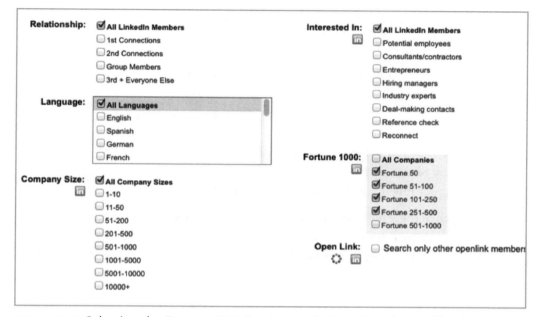

FIGURE 8–9. Selecting the Fortune 500 Companies in Your Search Specifications

Click Search and you will see a list of all C-level executives who work for Fortune 500 companies within 100 miles of your office. You can sort your results using the same options I described earlier to organize your search results. Sort your results by Relevance, Relationship, Relationship + Recommendations, Connections, or Keywords.

If you notice a manager or director from a certain company researching CRM options in the Answers section or in Groups, you can use the Advanced Search to find other managers, directors, and C-level execs so you will know who will probably be involved in the decision-making process.

You can see your relationship to them and ask for introductions from your first-level connections when the time is right. You can also modify your search to specific companies once you know which companies are researching new CRM systems.

There are hundreds of ways you can slice and dice your searches using the Advanced People Search. I can't get into every combination of searches you can do, but here are the high-level categories offered in the Advanced People Search:

- Keywords
- Name
- Title
- Company
- School

- Location
- Industries
- Seniority Level (only if you are a LinkedIn Premium Member)
- Groups (only if you are a LinkedIn Premium Member)
- Relationship
- Interested In (only if you are a LinkedIn Premium Member)
- Language
- Fortune 1000 (only if you are a LinkedIn Premium Member)
- Company Size (only if you are a LinkedIn Premium Member)
- Open Link (only if you are a LinkedIn Premium Member)

Within each of these high-level categories, you can select many subcategories, making your filtering options almost limitless. With more than 150 million LinkedIn members, you have access to the world's largest—and highest quality—business intelligence data anywhere.

LINKEDIN REFERENCE SEARCH

If the Advanced People Search didn't provide what you were looking for (though if this is the case it may mean you haven't tried hard enough!) then you can click on the tab to the right of the Advanced People Search tab and you will have access to the Reference Search. The Reference Search is for LinkedIn Premium Members only.

The LinkedIn Reference Search lets you find references who can give you feedback on candidates before you hire them. You can reach out to past employers and colleagues via Introductions or InMail to get honest feedback on job applicants. You can also keep track of your references in your Profile Organizer, which comes with your LinkedIn Premium subscription.

SAVED SEARCHES

Over time you will create custom Advanced People Searches that return great results. With your LinkedIn Premium subscription, you can retain your search criteria in the Saved Searches tab. This is very handy and timesaving because it can take a lot of time to refine your Advanced People Search and get your desired results.

ADVANCED JOB SEARCH

You can search for jobs using Job Title, Keywords, or Company Name in the basic Jobs Search box. LinkedIn also provides advanced search capabilities in Jobs. The filters work the same way as the Advanced People Search filters, but they are tailored to help you narrow down your search results when looking for a new job. A great trick is to use the Advanced Job Search when you are looking to hire new employees. Search for jobs similar to the job you want to fill and see how other companies describe the job, what skills and keywords they are using, and how they position the job. You can learn a lot by "spying" on your competitors.

You can filter your job search by the following categories:

1. Keywords
2. Job Title
3. Location
4. Company
5. Functions
6. Experience
7. Industries
8. Date Posted
9. Salary (this is accessible if you upgrade to the Job Seeker or Job Seeker Plus sub-scription levels)

Each of these categories has numerous subcategories to help you zero in on jobs compatible for you that will pay the salary you're targeting. The Advanced Job Search is a great tool, considering LinkedIn is becoming the top place for companies to post jobs and for people to find new jobs.

LinkedIn Jobs also lets you save your favorite searches in the Saved Searches tab. When you find jobs you are interested in, you can save them in the Saved Jobs tab.

ADVANCED ANSWERS SEARCH

This is the last search option that provides advanced search capabilities. The Advanced Answers Search lets you filter LinkedIn Answers by category and subcategory to make it easier to do research and find answers to your questions. You can also view the Questions and Answers or just the Questions, if you want.

When you want to answer questions to demonstrate your expertise and to build up some social proof, you can select Show Only Unanswered Questions in the Options tab. This is a great feature because this guarantees you will be the first person to answer the question, giving you lots of exposure and credibility.

THE DARK SIDE OF LINKEDIN SEARCH

The LinkedIn search algorithm gives relevant results when you search for People, Companies, and Groups, but it's still relatively easy to trick the algorithm so you can rank highly for your target skills or keywords. It's like the old days when you could add some HTML metatags to your web page and rank highly in Google for many search terms by overstuffing the meta keyword tag.

I don't recommend abusing the system to gain a high rank because eventually the LinkedIn algorithm will mature and you will lose your high ranking. Also, it's pretty easy to see who's tricking the system when you look at certain LinkedIn profiles.

Let me show you how you can easily trick the LinkedIn search algorithm to gain a high ranking. Before I demonstrate it, I want you to know that I do not recommend these "black hat" search engine optimization techniques—whether it's on LinkedIn or any other search engine—as they are considered unethical. Eventually you will get caught and your website can be banned from Google and you can be removed from LinkedIn for violating their terms of service. Being ranked at the top of the search results for a short period of time is not worth the risk of being banned from the largest professional networking website. Also, you will see that modifying your profile to rank highly will not bring you more business because of the overuse of certain keywords.

Okay, here we go. Again, don't try this at home without adult supervision!

Go to the LinkedIn Search box and do a People search for "SEO," which is the acronym for search engine optimization. You would think this is one of the most difficult phrases to rank highly for because you are competing against the best search engine optimization specialists in the world. The competition on Google is fierce for the top ranking of SEO and SEO-related keywords because SEO experts take pride in beating their competitors for their industry keywords. If you rank on the first page of Google for SEO-related keywords, you are considered among the "best of the best" SEO experts in the world.

So what happens when you search on LinkedIn for "SEO"? Take a look at Figure 8–10.

FIGURE 8–10. Search Results for SEO

I blurred the names of the top two search results because they do not deserve any recognition in this book. They used black-hat SEO techniques, which may have included one or more of the following:

■ Violated search engine terms of service

■ Created a poor user experience by overusing keywords or creating low quality content that is optimized for search engine ranking instead of creating high quality content that is beneficial to the web visitor

■ Unethically presented content to search engine bots and search engine users. This includes creating invisible text, which is only seen by the search engine bots. This is not a problem on LinkedIn because we don't have the ability to modify the website code.

Again, I strongly recommend against using black-hat SEO techniques. You would be deceiving the search engines for the benefit of you or your business. When you practice black-hat SEO techniques, it is no different than practicing unethical business practices in any profession—except you won't go to jail when you get caught. However, if Google catches you practicing black-hat SEO or violating their terms of service, they can ban your company URL from their search rankings. How would you explain that to your boss if you were the in-house SEO at your company? Whether you are practicing black-hat SEO or any other unethical business practice, your reputation will be permanently damaged when you get caught—so don't do it.

Well, enough ranting about people taking shortcuts for short-term gain and permanent pain. Let's get back to our SEO "experts" who are gaming the LinkedIn search algorithm. Figure 8–11 on page 64 shows us the profile of the top-ranking SEO expert on LinkedIn.

I'm assuming the gentleman in the figure is a Facebook marketing, internet marketing, SEO "expert," and social media manager. His current and past employment consists solely of fake jobs using only his target keywords. He has 16 Recommendations, but they look very suspicious and are very light on details. He is smart enough not to let us see his 500+ Connections because I would guess many of them are fake LinkedIn members. When I look at the profiles of some of his Recommendations, their profiles are very light in content and substance and every person is from a different country.

Red flags are flying everywhere. This is a classic example of keyword stuffing and a violation of the LinkedIn terms of service. In case you are wondering, I did report this profile to LinkedIn, and you should report profiles like this to maintain the quality and integrity of the LinkedIn community.

You get the point. These guys are promoting themselves as SEO experts by gaming the system. Sure they know how to get the top ranking for their target keywords, but

FIGURE 8–11. The Top Ranking for the Term "SEO"

would you want to hire them to do this to your LinkedIn profile? This is a completely unprofessional approach and you should run the other way if an SEO "expert" with a profile like this approaches you. These guys are the equivalent of ambulance chasers in the legal world, willing to do anything to make a buck. Unfortunately, there are many people who would hire these guys to do SEO work for them because they don't know any better.

CONCLUSION

You now know more about LinkedIn Search and Advanced Search than 90 percent of all LinkedIn members. We just scratched the surface of what you can do with these advanced search capabilities and a database of more than 150 million business professionals. Play around with LinkedIn Search and see what you can uncover in the treasure trove of business intelligence.

I'll show you some more advanced tricks later in the book when I teach you how to use LinkedIn as different user types like students, sales reps, recruiters, and job seekers. For now, take a short break and practice your LinkedIn searching while it's still fresh in your mind. See you in the next chapter, where I will show you how to get found on LinkedIn.

Getting Found on LinkedIn

What do you do when you want to learn more about a product or service? I bet the first thing you do is go to Google and search the internet. With so much data available to us today, search engines are an integral part of our life. When you search Google, you can find information about literally anything in seconds.

The problem with Google is you get a broad search result. If you search for "web marketing consultant," Google doesn't know if you're looking to hire a web marketing consultant or if you're trying to find information on how to become a web marketing consultant. Google isn't smart enough to read our minds yet—but it continues to get better!

When you search LinkedIn for "web marketing consultant," chances are your search result will show you a list of web marketing consultants. By narrowing your search, such as by a location like "web marketing consultant New York," you can generate a targeted list that may give you the result you need.

LinkedIn is a vertical search engine. A vertical search engine shows you very focused results based on the keywords you search for. This is why it's so important to use your target keywords when creating your LinkedIn personal and company profiles.

What are target keywords, you ask? Target keywords are the phrases you enter into a search engine to find targeted results. The more specific your keyword phrases are, the better your search results will be. If someone did a Google search to find you or your business, what keywords would they have to enter?

Optimizing your LinkedIn profile is similar to optimizing your website or blog so you can rank highly in Google. Optimizing your LinkedIn profile not only helps people find your profile through the search function, it helps LinkedIn recommend people to connect with, companies you may be interested in, or your perfect job. LinkedIn scans your profile and uses your keyword phrases to make targeted recommendations for you. The more targeted your profile is, the more targeted the LinkedIn suggestions will be. Once your LinkedIn profile is fine-tuned, you will see targeted recommendations in your sidebar every time you log in. The LinkedIn algorithm is a very powerful artificial intelligence tool.

KEYWORD SELECTION

The most important component of search engine optimization is keyword selection. Search engines use keywords and phrases to find and rank websites. The crawler or spider-based search engines—so called because they sift through websites and add keywords to their databases—sort through millions of websites by following an algorithm, or set of rules.

The algorithms for the various search engines are not exactly the same, which is why a search of the same keyword brings different results. However, they follow very similar processes. Most of the search engines rank websites based on where and how often a particular keyword is used on the website. They will rank a website higher if, for example, the keyword is used in the title, placed near the top of the page, and if it is used often.

LinkedIn has its own search algorithm, which ranks user profiles on a number of factors including your keywords.

Take time now to use the questionnaire in Figure 9–1 on page 67 to create a list of at least ten keyword phrases that best describe you and your expertise. The more focused your keyword phrases are, the more your profile will stand out.

LINKEDIN SEO TIP

To increase your chances of having your LinkedIn profile rank highly, use your keywords in these sections of your profile:

- Profile Headline
- Current Work Experience
- Past Work Experience
- Summary
- Specialties

Think about these questions while creating your list of keyword phrases:

1. What are your skills? _____

   _____

2. What is your expertise? _____

   _____

3. What job titles best describe you or the job you are looking for? _____

   _____

4. What makes you different from your competitors? _____

   _____

5. What makes you better than your competitors? _____

   _____

FIGURE 9–1. Keyword Worksheet

If you are like most people, you have a hard time describing your skills and areas of expertise, so you're struggling to come up with your keyword list. If you're struggling to come up with a list of what you're really good at, ask your friends or colleagues. They'll be glad to tell you what you're good at (and what you're not so good at, if you're brave enough to ask!).

COMPETITIVE ANALYSIS

One of my favorite ways to compile keyword lists is to look at my competitors' and colleagues' profiles to see what keywords they use to make their profiles stand out.

Let's say you're a certified public accountant in San Francisco and you want to see which keywords are being used in the profiles of the top search results. Start by doing an Advanced Search in LinkedIn, then entering CPA as your keyword, and your ZIP code in the Location field. Start with 25 miles in the "Within" box, so you get a variety of profiles to view. Leave the rest of the search boxes empty and click on Search as shown in Figure 9–2 on page 68.

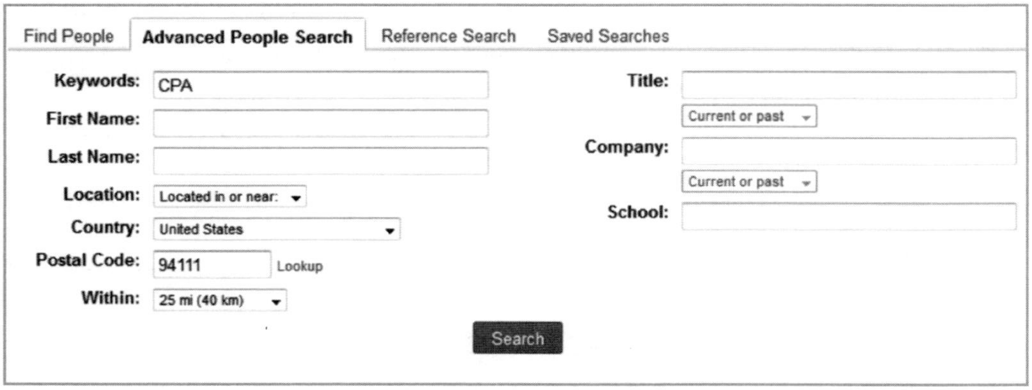

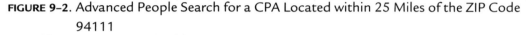

Find People | **Advanced People Search** | *Reference Search* | *Saved Searches*

Keywords: CPA
First Name:
Last Name:
Location: Located in or near: ▾
Country: United States ▾
Postal Code: 94111   Lookup
Within: 25 mi (40 km) ▾

Title:
Current or past ▾
Company:
Current or past ▾
School:

Search

FIGURE 9–2. Advanced People Search for a CPA Located within 25 Miles of the ZIP Code 94111

When your search is complete, change the Sort by option to Keywords and the View to Expanded. This highlights every instance of the keyword "CPA" in each profile so you can see where they strategically placed "CPA" to get high search rankings.

Change the Sort by setting to all of the other options and compare the search results. The LinkedIn Advanced Search will rank the search results based on each sort criteria as you see in Figure 9–3.

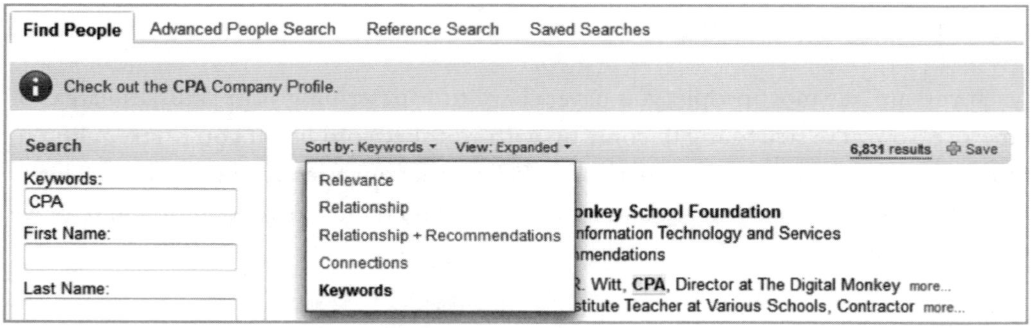

Find People | Advanced People Search | Reference Search | Saved Searches

ⓘ Check out the **CPA** Company Profile.

Search
Keywords:
CPA
First Name:

Last Name:

Sort by: Keywords ▾   View: Expanded ▾

Relevance
Relationship
Relationship + Recommendations
Connections
Keywords

6,831 results   ✪ Save

onkey School Foundation
nformation Technology and Services
mendations

. Witt, **CPA**, Director at The Digital Monkey more...
stitute Teacher at Various Schools, Contractor more...

FIGURE 9–3. Your Available Sort Settings

The Relevance sort is based on a variety of factors. Relevance is a proprietary LinkedIn algorithm, which is constantly improving so they can provide optimal search results based on the searcher's activity on LinkedIn, the Profiles returned by the query, and other members who have made similar searches in determining the sort order.

You can search for people you are connected to using the Relationship sort. The Relationship search results will be displayed by first-degree, second-degree, and third-degree connections, and then groups.

FIGURE 9–4. Sort by Connections Search Result

The Relationship + Recommendations sort is displayed by the degree of your connection and the number of recommendations. A second-degree connection with 20 recommendations will appear before a first-degree connection with no recommendations.

Figure 9–4 shows us the Sort by Connections search results in respect to your connection to that person and the degree of the connection.

The Keyword sort displays your keyword in yellow highlights.

LinkedIn engineers create new experimental applications in the LinkedIn Labs, which is located at http://linkedinlabs.com. One of their tools, Swarm (http://swarm.linkedinlabs.com), is a rotating cloud of the top keywords searched on LinkedIn Today. The cloud shows the most popular keywords in categories like Today's Most Searched Titles, Today's Most Searched Companies, Today's Most Popular Job Searches, Today's Most Searched Companies in different industries.

The categories automatically refresh so you get a continuous stream of relevant keywords from today's LinkedIn search activity. The larger the word is in the cloud, the more popular it is. On a daily basis you can instantly see the hottest jobs, most popular job titles, top companies, and the leading upcoming industries.

THE GOOGLE KEYWORD TOOL

Another great way to find keywords for your profile is to use the Google Keyword Tool, which is located at https://adwords.google.com/select/KeywordToolExternal.

You may be wondering why I'm teaching you how to research the most popular keyword phrases on Google in a book about LinkedIn. First of all, if a search term is popular on Google, it's usually a popular search term on Yahoo, Bing, and LinkedIn because people tend to use the same thought process when using search engines. Second, LinkedIn profile information—including keyword phrases—frequently appears on Google search results, often near the top. That means if you use keyword phrases that are popular on Google in your LinkedIn profile, there is a good chance your profile will appear on the first page of Google searches for that keyword phrase. This is because Google considers LinkedIn to be a reputable authority site so profile information from LinkedIn can rank higher than other website content that isn't as highly regarded by Google. It's another case of "who you know," not "what you know."

Keyword research has always been a frustrating task because there is no source that provides the actual search data. Every keyword tool, including the Google Keyword Tool, provides only estimated values, which are "guesstimates" at best. I'm sure Google knows the exact numbers but they are infamous for not sharing the exact numbers for competitive reasons.

While the Google Keyword Tool is meant for pay-per-click advertising research, it's also a vital tool when performing keyword research for search engine optimization. The Google Keyword Tool provides a ballpark estimate of the number of searches for specific words or key phrases, which is still valuable information. Knowing which keywords or keyword phrases are most popular can give you a huge advantage over your competition.

If you don't have a Google AdWords account, you can access the Google Keyword Tool at https://adwords.google.com/select/KeywordToolExternal. If you already have a Google AdWords account, you can access the Keyword Tool under the Tools and Analysis tab in your account.

Let's try some keyword searches, so you can see how to use the Google Keyword Tool effectively. If you go to the keyword tool and search for "web developer," "website design," and "web design," you'll receive a listing similar to the one shown in Figure 9–5.

Search terms (3)				
Keyword	Competition	Global Monthly Searches ⑦	Local Monthly Searches ⑦	Approximate CPC ⑦
☆ web developer	Medium	1,000,000	301,000	$8.43
☆ website designer	High	3,350,000	1,000,000	$7.56
☆ web design	High	7,480,000	2,240,000	$7.00

FIGURE 9–5. Web Developer Search

The first column lists your target search terms. The next column, Competition, tells you how competitive your keyword phrases are. The next two columns, Global Monthly Searches and Local Monthly Searches, tell you approximately how many times those keyword phrases were searched. These results are averaged over the past 12 months. If you are a local business or service provider, you want to focus on the Local Monthly Searches column. If you are doing Google AdWords pay-per-click advertising, the last column, Approximate CPC, tells you approximately how much you will pay per click for your keyword phrases.

Now let me show you a little trick that will give you more accurate results from the Google Keyword Tool. By default, Google gives you the number of searches based on a broad match type. Google lets you filter your search results based on three different match types: broad, phrase, and exact.

Broad Match

Broad, the default match type, refers to the number of searches that involve each word in the phrase. For example, it's giving you search volume numbers for the keyword "web developer," as well as search volume for all the other peripheral keywords, such as "web," "developer," "web designer," and "web hosting," which may not match your original search phrase 100 percent.

Phrase Match

Phrase match refers to keywords in which the exact phrase of your keyword is used, including within the phrase. For example, using the phrase match type while searching "web developer" might give you search volume for other keywords like "*best* web developer" or "*online* web developer." It would not search "online developer" or "best developer," however, because the original phrase has been broken up.

Exact Match

In this case, only the *exact* keyword phrase is entered in the search. Using the previous example, if you were to search for "best website developer in San Francisco," the search results will only display results containing the exact phrase "best website developer in San Francisco."

Underneath the search field is a checkbox with the option labeled "Only show ideas closely related to my search terms." Make sure this is checked, or you will receive a large list of keywords that are unrelated to your keyword phrase.

Next change the Match Type from Broad to Exact and do another search. Here are the results for exact match searches, which are much lower than the broad match results.

Search terms (3)					
Keyword	Competition	Global Monthly Searches ⑦	Local Monthly Searches ⑦	Approximate CPC ⑦
☆ [web developer]	High	40,500	9,900	$8.62
☆ [website designer]	High	14,800	4,400	$8.41
☆ [web design]	High	301,000	60,500	$8.73

FIGURE 9–6. Exact Match Search Results Are More Accurate

As you see in Figure 9–6, these results are much more accurate than the Broad match results.

The Google Keyword Tool is powerful and can provide a lot of great information about the best keywords to use in your LinkedIn profile. We don't need to go into the advanced features of the Google Keyword Tool, since you are just trying to get a high level overview of the most popular keyword phrases to use in your LinkedIn profile.

Some tips for finding the best keyword phrases to use:

- Try to find keyword phrases that have a fair number of monthly searches, especially local searches, if you are a local business or service provider. The more searches per month, the higher the competition. Your best keyword phrases are medium competition with a fair amount of monthly searches, so you have a good chance of appearing near the top of the Google search results.
- You can add the highly competitive keywords from Google as Skills in your LinkedIn profile, so they appear in LinkedIn searches. It's much easier to rank well in LinkedIn right now because very few people know how to optimize their LinkedIn profile. Since you are reading this book, you are among the 10 percent of LinkedIn users who do know how to optimize their profile, so you have a huge advantage.

CONCLUSION

Use your target keyword phrases frequently when you fill out your LinkedIn profile, but don't overdo it. Figure 9–7 on page 73 shows us the search results for the term "Search Engine Optimization." This person, who will remain anonymous because she's gaming the LinkedIn search algorithm, ranks on the first page of a LinkedIn People Search for "Search Engine Optimization." Would you hire this person to do SEO for your website?

In the next chapter, I'll show you the best way to give and receive LinkedIn Recommendations, which are an essential part of your LinkedIn profile.

SEO Training★SEO Trainer★SEO Solution★**Search Engine Optimization** Expert★**Search Engine Optimization** Solution★SEO Strategy

Toronto, Canada Area │ Information Technology and Services

Current	**SEO, Search Engine Optimization, Training, Trainer, Expert, Specialist, Strategy** at **SEO, Search Engine Optimization, Training, Trainer, Expert, Specialist, Strategy**
	SEO, Search Engine Optimization, Training, Trainer, Expert, Specialist, Strategy at **SEO, Search Engine Optimization, Training, Trainer, Expert, Specialist, Strategy**
	SEO, Search Engine Optimization, Training, Trainer, Expert, Specialist, Strategy at **SEO, Search Engine Optimization, Training, Trainer, Expert, Specialist, Strategy**
	see all ▾
Past	SEO, **Search Engine Optimization**, Training, Trainer, Expert, Specialist, Strategy at SEO, **Search Engine Optimization**, Training, Trainer, Expert, Specialist, Strategy
Education	Michigan State University - The Eli Broad Graduate School of Management
Connections	**500+ connections**
Websites	Search Engine Optimization
	SEO Training
	SEO Trainer

FIGURE 9–7. A Profile Optimized for "Search Engine Optimization"

Giving and Receiving LinkedIn Recommendations

The evolution of the internet and social media has changed the way we make decisions. Social proof existed long before the internet, but the ability to submit and view online reviews for products and services has revolutionized our purchasing behavior. In a matter of minutes, we can tap into the collective opinions of hundreds—even thousands—of people who have already purchased a product or service and know exactly how they feel about their purchase. You can see how many raving fans are gushing about the product or how many disgruntled customers want their money back. With the evolution of mobile apps, we can scan a barcode on a product with our mobile phone to receive comparative pricing as well as product reviews while standing next to the product in the store.

Today, there's no hiding if you're offering an inferior product or service. If you read a lot of negative reviews, you probably won't complete the purchase. On the other hand, when you read a lot of positive reviews, you feel comfortable purchasing that product or service and won't hesitate to spend more for the more advanced version of the product if others recommend it. Also, your chances of buyer's remorse diminish significantly because social proof justified the purchase in your mind.

In case you're not familiar with social proof, it's when we make decisions based on what others recommend, whether it's really the best option or not. What happens when you drive by a new restaurant and see a long line out the door? You assume the food is great, so you quickly park your car and jump in line. The food may be no better than your favorite restaurant, but the fact that so many others are waiting to get into this new restaurant makes you have to join the crowd. You will probably love the food, even if it's only average, because you're caught up in the moment and the excitement of the crowd. If the crowd loves the restaurant, you love it too so you can be part of the "in" crowd.

In the past, social proof was primarily word-of-mouth or through print media, so word spread slowly. Today, a good or bad review can be seen or heard by millions of people around the world instantaneously. The internet spawned many new forms of social proof that I'll get into in a minute. First, I'll offer some background about the evolution of social proof.

Let's go back a few years, so I can show you an example of social proof before the era of online reviews. Your best friend went to a movie last night and she can't stop raving about it. She's gushing with enthusiasm and wants to tell you every detail of the movie, but she resists because she doesn't want to ruin the movie for you. You can tell from her actions that it was one of the best movies she's seen in years. She's so excited she can't sit still and she's chomping at the bit to tell you more.

Based on your best friend's actions and opinion of the movie, will you go? Of course you will—probably tonight! This is classic old-school social proof.

When someone you trust tells you she likes a movie, you want to see it as soon as possible. If your trusted friend tells you the movie sucks, you won't see it and you'll probably tell your other friends to avoid it as well—even though you haven't seen it. Negative social proof spreads exponentially based on what people say, even if they didn't have a negative experience themselves.

The key to social proof is that you act on someone's advice—without question—if you trust that person. If you don't know the person well enough or don't trust her, you'll probably take the advice with a grain of salt and seek advice from a trusted source. We all have our trusted circle of friends and colleagues that we depend on when we need to make decisions. The bigger the decision, the more trusted opinions we will seek. We all want to feel comfortable that we are making the right decision. So we like to bounce ideas off of people we trust. Discussing the issues with others makes us feel confident, even if they just listen to our concerns.

Today, online social proof has evolved from online forums to popular websites like Yelp, where you can post reviews about local businesses. On Yelp, the business owner doesn't have control over the reviews posted by customers. A few positive reviews can send your sales through the roof. An angry customer can write a scathing review about a business and damage the reputation of that business. The business owner can respond to that criticism online, but the negative comments remain. These un-moderated comments make social proof more credible because everyone knows that every business has unsatisfied customers occasionally. When you see a series of negative reviews, a red flag should go up in your head telling you to avoid that business. Chances are, the business won't survive if the company doesn't address the negative comments head-on and change its business practices.

Facebook created its own form of social proof with the "Like" button. You "vote" for comments, pictures, and companies that you like on Facebook. Unlike Yelp, which posts positive and negative comments, Facebook only registers positive votes. Facebook "Likes" have taken off, and it has become a significant measurement of success if your Facebook Company Page receives a lot of likes. It has the same effect as great reviews on Yelp.

Google recently implemented its +1 button, which is the equivalent of the Facebook Like. You click the +1 button when you like something on Google-related pages. The +1 button isn't as popular as the Facebook Like, but you can be sure Google is doing everything in its power to increase its popularity.

So what does social proof have to do with LinkedIn, anyway? Well, actually social proof has a lot to do with LinkedIn. Essentially you are marketing and selling yourself on LinkedIn. Your profile, job experience, skills, expertise in the Answers section, and Recommendations are your marketing collateral that people read to get to know your product—which is you!

HOW CAN SOCIAL PROOF GET YOU HIRED IN TODAY'S ECONOMY?

You and a few million other people are looking for jobs these days. You can spend hours every day on Craigslist and hope you can be one of the first to submit your resume when a new job listing is posted. If you don't submit your resume within a few minutes, your resume will go unnoticed because often hundreds of people apply in the first hour.

You can spend the rest of your day searching Monster.com or other job websites and pray that your resume will be noticed. You can apply for hundreds of jobs and rarely will you receive any acknowledgement that they even received your resume.

It's so frustrating, especially when you know you are qualified for these positions, but you can't cut through the noise and get noticed. You have to resort to making one of those crazy YouTube videos to catch their attention, but still, your chances of getting the job are minimal.

Finding a job online is very similar to cold calling. You are a complete stranger to each company, so getting past the gatekeepers is a huge challenge. You need to get very creative to get your resume in front of the hiring manager, which seems nearly impossible.

Now let's look at the other side of the coin. You work in the human resources department and you've posted some jobs online. Within minutes, you have more than 100 resumes for one open position. You scan through a few of the resumes and very few people are qualified for the position, even though you clearly spelled out the job qualifications in the job posting.

People are so desperate that they're applying for any job—even if they aren't qualified. They hope to catch the attention of the human resources department or the hiring manager, so maybe they can get hired for a more appropriate position. The human resources department is overwhelmed and spends hours digging through the hundreds of resumes to find a handful of people to interview. There has to be a better way!

So how do you find good candidates in today's economy with millions of qualified workers looking for a job?

Most jobs are filled through word-of-mouth recommendations, not by sifting through hundreds of resumes. When a job is posted online, hundreds of resumes are submitted which makes finding your perfect candidate like finding the proverbial needle in a haystack. It's much easier and more reliable to hire someone who comes highly recommended by one of your trusted colleagues. The old adage "it's not what you know, it's who you know" is more powerful than ever today, and you can get to know the "right" people by leveraging social proof.

Again, the key is building your network of trusted resources and keeping in touch with them on a regular basis so they are there when you need them. Once you establish your network of 100 to 150 trusted people, you can reach out to them and tap into their expertise or into their network of resources to solve your problem, or, if they can't, they'll introduce you to someone else who can. If you don't have a stable professional network and you suddenly lose your job, you have to spend months building up your professional network and gaining their trust before you can reach out to them for help.

You build a strong professional network by creating a strong online reputation with a lot of social proof. When someone searches Google for your name, you want a lot of very positive social proof to appear. When people see pages and pages of positive social proof about you, they will be pursuing you to join their professional network. You will be the one in demand and your professional network will be full of A-list players.

WHAT ARE LINKEDIN RECOMMENDATIONS?

LinkedIn created its own version of social proof called LinkedIn Recommendations, which is a reputation manager for professionals. When people write LinkedIn Recommendations for you, it's the online version of the written recommendations you used to receive from your instructors and former employers. The good news is that you have control over the recommendations that are posted on your LinkedIn profile, so you won't see negative comments.

Recommendations are not just for the person receiving the recommendation. The person writing the recommendation can display the recommendations they write on their own profile. This adds value to your credibility when you write strong recommendations for others because it shows LinkedIn members that you have strong people in your professional network.

You can think of LinkedIn as a reputation engine for business professionals. Your LinkedIn activity builds a complete picture of you and your business. Your LinkedIn profile is more than an online resume with a list of your past and present jobs, your education, and your accomplishments. Your professional reputation includes whom you associate with, the groups you belong to, the associations and clubs you belong to, and how much you interact with your network. I like to combine all of these things and think of them as your LinkedIn image.

If you are a small-business owner looking to hire new employees, recommendations can help you determine if a potential employee will be a good fit for your business. Recruiters and hiring managers at large companies do read recommendations and take them into account, but it's unlikely that a recommendation would make or break a LinkedIn member's chance of getting hired. Recommendations add value to your overall LinkedIn profile, but usually they are not evaluative since most recommendations are solicited. Later in this chapter, I will show you some sample recommendations that are so powerful they can influence a manager's decision to hire a person. These are the type of recommendations you want to look for when you are searching for new employees.

Savvy LinkedIn members can tell if you are actively networking and reaching out to others or if you are a passive LinkedIn member with a static profile and no networking activity. If you are not active on LinkedIn, it doesn't mean you are not good at what you do. It just means you are not actively building your professional network as well as you could be. In today's economy, no one's job is safe, given the constant corporate mergers, reorganizations, and restructuring. You need to spend a few hours every week networking on LinkedIn so you can quickly land on your feet if you're unfortunate enough to lose your job.

The way the market has been and how industries and positions seem to come and go, chances are you will have to change jobs or careers in the next few years. The 20-year career I had as a network engineer in the 1990s doesn't exist today and I had to learn new skills. Now I manage Google AdWords, social media, and do search engine optimization for a living. None of these jobs existed in their current form 10 years ago. A few years from now, Google AdWords will evolve into some other form of online advertising, social media will have a new name, and who knows if search engines will even exist in 2020.

By keeping my LinkedIn profile current and participating in LinkedIn Groups and Answers, potential employers can learn more about me than they ever could by just reading my resume. The icing on the cake is the LinkedIn Recommendations, which provide third-party verification of my skills. Each online activity is like a piece of a puzzle and recommendations are the glue that holds the puzzle together. When you are using LinkedIn to find new employees for your company, you want to look for LinkedIn members who have a complete, updated profile with lots of great recommendations.

LinkedIn Recommendations are a huge part of your LinkedIn image. Obviously, it's good to have a lot of recommendations—but it's much better if they are *quality* recommendations. In this age of online deception, it's possible to hire offshore workers to write fake recommendations for you. You can have hundreds of hollow recommendations in a matter of days for less than a hundred bucks. It's better to have a dozen high-quality reviews instead of hundreds of low-quality, suspicious reviews.

WHY DO I NEED LINKEDIN RECOMMENDATIONS?

Great question! People rarely provide written recommendations when they apply for jobs these days, so why bother getting recommendations on LinkedIn?

First of all, your LinkedIn profile will not be complete until you have at least three recommendations. Getting to the 100 percent complete mark on your profile is a huge accomplishment and adds a lot of credibility to your LinkedIn profile.

The second reason you want LinkedIn recommendations is because the recommendations are the only way you can verify your LinkedIn profile and accomplishments. You enter your LinkedIn profile information, including your education, work history, and accomplishments. There is no way for others to verify this information by reading your profile. When people recommend you on LinkedIn, it's a written testimonial of your work history, education, or accomplishments. It's very important to have that third-party verification of your LinkedIn profile, especially if you are a consultant or independent service provider.

Did you know the keywords in your LinkedIn recommendations show up in search results and help your LinkedIn search ranking? Many factors determine your search ranking on LinkedIn and every little bit helps.

While we are on the subject of LinkedIn search rankings, did you know the more recommendations you have, the higher you can rank in LinkedIn searches? If your recommendations contain the same keywords you want to rank for, your search ranking should rise as your recommendations increase. You don't want to get recommendations full of your keywords just to increase your search ranking. Be genuine and nurture good recommendations, and your search results will take care of themselves.

If you are a small business, consultant, or service provider, your potential customers expect to see recommendations in your profile. Recommendations and your complete LinkedIn profile are the way they judge you to determine the quality of your work and your expertise before they'll hire you or trust your product.

HOW MANY LINKEDIN RECOMMENDATIONS SHOULD I HAVE?

There is no right or wrong answer for this question. I see some LinkedIn profiles with a few excellent recommendations that go a long way highlighting the expertise of a person. I see other profiles with page after page of recommendations, but they don't convince me that this person is an A-lister who is worthy of being part of my professional network or someone I would hire. The recommendations seem hollow and they're not convincing.

How many recommendations are right for you? I would recommend at least one recommendation for every year you work at a job. If you've been at your current company for five years, I think you should have at least five recommendations for that company. I have no scientific proof that you should have one recommendation per year of work, but don't you think you have at least one great accomplishment at work every year?

When you accomplish something great at work, you need to have someone who benefited from that accomplishment write you a recommendation. When you benefit from someone else's accomplishment, write that person a LinkedIn recommendation and don't wait for them to ask you. Just do it!

WHAT MAKES A LINKEDIN RECOMMENDATION GREAT?

People want to read relevant recommendations that are clear, concise, and add value to their assessment of a person's professional skills and capabilities. Recommendations are a form of social proof that expresses your personal and/or professional opinion of the person you are recommending.

Recommendations should go beyond letting people know you are a whiz at Excel or a social media aficionado. Every recommendation should be personalized and detail why you think this person is worthy of your recommendation. When you recommend a person, it impacts your reputation as much as hers. If you create a bunch of meaningless recommendations for people who are not worthy of your recommendation, it negatively affects you and your reputation.

Say your friend Joe calls you up one day asking if you know a good plumber who can quickly fix a leaking pipe. The last time you hired a plumber he didn't do a very good job for you, but he's the only plumber you know. You give Joe the plumber's name and the plumber goes out to Joe's house to fix the leaking pipe. Instead of stopping the leak, the plumber breaks the pipe, causing a huge flood at Joe's house. Joe is furious at the plumber and he wonders why you recommended this inadequate person. Your reputation has taken a huge hit with Joe and it could end your friendship.

Recommending people on a professional level is no different. If for any reason you don't feel comfortable recommending someone, then you shouldn't write a recommendation. Remember, your reputation is at stake here, too. If one of your connections hires someone based on your written recommendation and it doesn't turn out well, then your connection is going to lose faith in you and your credibility suffers.

You need to carefully craft your recommendations so you are always telling the truth and not exaggerating. If they are the "best of the best" in their field, you can say that. If they are not the best, then you shouldn't "highly recommend" them. You can phrase your recommendation in a different way, so you are not stretching the truth but you are highlighting their strengths and giving them a positive recommendation.

WHAT TO SAY IN YOUR RECOMMENDATIONS

Here's a sample recommendation I found underneath a profile of one of my connections:

Joe is always a pleasure to work with! He is extremely knowledgeable, personable, communicative, and highly effective.

So what do you think about that recommendation? Are you going to hire Joe? Do you even know what Joe does for a living or what he is extremely knowledgeable at? Since Joe is my friend and I know that he is very good at what he does, I know this recommendation is completely true.

If you don't know Joe, this recommendation isn't going to help you decide if Joe is the right person to hire for your project. You know Joe is a pleasure to work with, which is always a good trait if you are looking to hire some help. What did Joe do for this person when they worked together? What skills did he use? Was it a big project or a small project? How many times did Joe work with this person? What challenges did he overcome while working on the project? These are the things you need to mention when writing a review for someone, so you can paint a complete picture for the person reading the recommendation.

Unfortunately, the above recommendation doesn't help Joe nor does it help the person who wrote it. If you are going to take the time to write a recommendation, make sure you write a thoughtful, thorough summary so others will know exactly what kind of person you are recommending.

Now, take a look at this recommendation.

Melanie has been one of the biggest influencers on me in my career. I knew the first time I saw her speak at a conference that she was someone I needed to meet and model myself after. She's incredible at seeing the big picture in order to make the necessary changes needed to create a well-oiled machine out of an organization, program or process, while still understanding the details of the minutia involved.

We were at different enterprise-level companies with the same challenges when I met Melanie, and the things I learned from her about how the organization needs to be set up for success, properly measuring success, creating accountability, getting the right pieces in place for all moving parts to work together to get to an end goal, and getting around the bullshit were fundamental *insights for me, that truthfully, I just didn't hear from other people in the industry.*

She's a born leader, she's bright, she's quick, she's motivated and *she's fun to be around. One of the true top players in the entire industry, who I will always intend to continue to learn from. —April 17, 2011*

—Laura Lippay, Director of Technical Marketing, Yahoo!

Wow! Now *that* is an incredible recommendation. What do we learn about Melanie from just one recommendation? She had a big influence on Laura's career and Laura wants to meet her because Melanie is her role model. (My guess is that Melanie has a big influence on many careers!) We know that Melanie has the unique skill of being able to see the big picture while understanding the details of minutia. It's rare to see one person with both skills.

Laura was encountering the same problems in her organization as Melanie was in hers, so they had a lot in common. By connecting with Melanie, Laura learned how to change the direction of her organization by modeling what Melanie did.

The last paragraph sums up Laura's opinion of Melanie: a born leader, bright, motivated, and fun. With all those attributes, it's no wonder Melanie is one of the top players in her industry. From my personal experience, I would second what Laura said about Melanie and she definitely is one of the top players in the search marketing industry.

Laura's entire recommendation was only 186 words, but look at what we learned about Melanie in just three short paragraphs. Wouldn't you love to have a powerful recommendation like this in your LinkedIn profile? Melanie has dozens of other recommendations in her LinkedIn profile just like this, which provides a ton of social proof that Melanie is an A-list player in the search marketing industry. There's nothing more powerful than your peers writing glowing recommendations about you to build up your reputation and let others know you are a true leader in your field.

WHO SHOULD I RECOMMEND?

The best way to get started with LinkedIn Recommendations is to recommend others. If you work for a company, recommend co-workers whom you respect and appreciate.

You can also write recommendations for your boss if you want to score some brownie points—just kidding! Don't ever write a recommendation for your boss just to suck up. Write one only if she is a mentor to you and if you really respect the work she does.

If you own your own business, you can write recommendations for your customers or the vendors you do business with. When your IT consultant comes in and fixes your server that was down and affecting your entire business operation, take a few minutes and write him a glowing recommendation on LinkedIn. Tell the story how he responded to your call for help in minutes, isolated the problem in no time, and had your business up and running in less than an hour. Highlight his responsiveness, troubleshooting skills, and beaming personality in the recommendation. He will appreciate your thoughtfulness in taking the time to do this, as it will do wonders for his business. Someday, he may do a favor for you when you least expect it.

If you are a consultant, write favorable recommendations about other consultants you work with. Let's say you're a web designer and you work with a graphic designer who creates the beautiful graphics you turn into a website. You can talk about the different projects you've collaborated on and highlight her design skills, creativity, timeliness for completion, and passion for the work. Provide as many details as you can in the project, so you can fully demonstrate the range of her talents and expertise.

The best time to write a recommendation for someone is right after you've completed a successful project that you worked on together. You know that fantastic feeling of accomplishment that you have after you've finished a long project. You and your co-workers work long days for many months, riding the emotional highs and lows of a difficult project. Some days you don't think the project will ever end and then you suddenly have a breakthrough that takes you to the next stage. The breakthroughs come when you work together, combining all your strengths to create a powerful team.

It's easy to write a recommendation for someone after struggling through a long project together. You know their strengths, emotions, leadership ability, and motivation. As we saw with Melanie's recommendation from Laura, you can write a very powerful recommendation in less than 200 words. If you write the recommendation while you're still riding the high of the project completion, it will be authentic and very meaningful, which has a powerful effect on the reader. I don't know this for sure, but I would guess that Laura wrote Melanie's recommendation shortly after seeing her speak at an event while she was still feeling the emotional impact of the speech.

When you are ready to write a recommendation for a colleague, you can simply click on the Recommend link next to her profile. You must be connected to a person before you can recommend her. Once you click the Recommend button, you will see this screen as shown in Figure 10–1 on page 85.

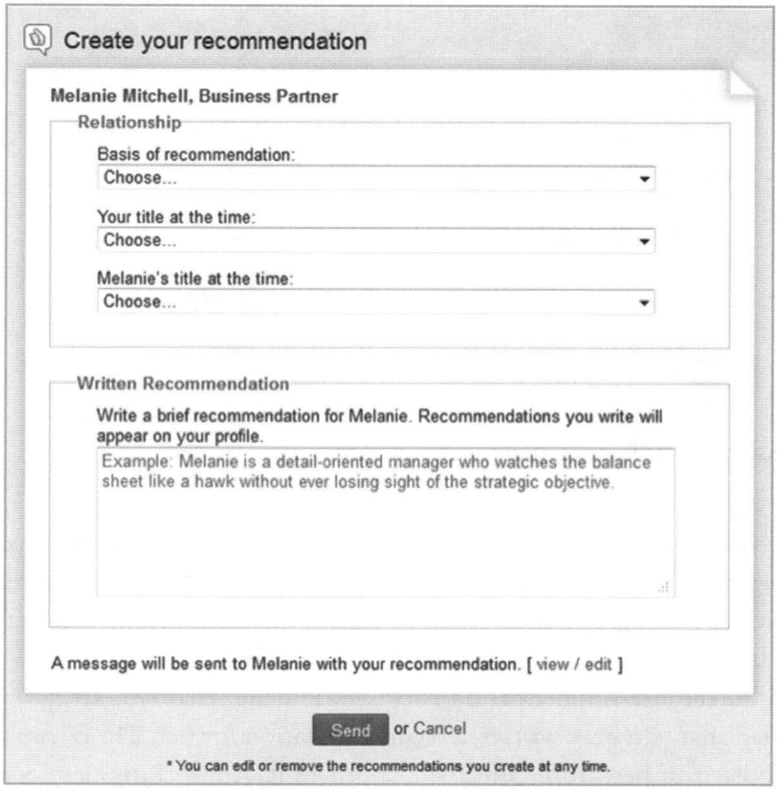

FIGURE 10-1. Creating a Recommendation

Choose the appropriate option and you will be prompted with a few questions to help customize your recommendation. The first prompt, "Basis of Recommendation," gives you a list of choices where you identify whether you worked for the person, she worked for you, you worked as peers, and a few other options. This shows up in the recommendation, so the reader will know the professional relationship between you and the person you are recommending.

The second prompt is "Your Title" at the time of the recommendation. The dropdown list will display all the titles you have listed in your LinkedIn profile.

The third prompt is "Her Title" at the time of the recommendation. The dropdown list will display all the titles she has listed in her LinkedIn Profile.

Below the Relationship section of the form is the actual Recommendation area, where you can enter your formal recommendation. Remember to make your recommendation clear and concise. Don't make it too short—as in Joe's example—and don't make your recommendation too long or people will stop reading it and miss some key points.

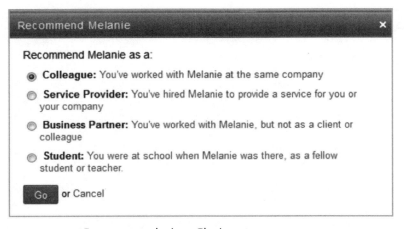

FIGURE 10–2. Recommendation Choices

If you choose "Service Provider," "Business Partner," or "Student" from the list shown in Figure 10-2, you will need to select from a different set of relationship options, which are tailored to each category. Again, this relationship will appear in the recommendation when it's posted on their LinkedIn profile.

After you enter the recommendation, click Send and the person you are recommending will be notified that you have written a recommendation for her. The recommendation will not be posted in her profile until she approves it. A few things can occur at this point, all of them fairly common: She can send it back to you for revision if she would like you to change it; she can approve it as is; or she can reject it, if she doesn't want a recommendation from you for some reason. Remember: Your professional reputation is at stake here, so you don't need to accept recommendations just for the sake of having a lot of recommendations. If you were feeling as if you should reject a recommendation from someone, then it's probably a sign that you shouldn't be connected with that person on LinkedIn.

After you recommend someone, LinkedIn will ask that individual if she wants to recommend you. There's an ongoing debate about reciprocal recommendations by many LinkedIn experts. Some contend that reciprocal recommendations have less value than one-way recommendations. They compare it to sharing website links on the internet. To rank highly in Google, you need a lot of links from high-quality websites to your website. In the past, webmasters would trade links so both websites benefited. Eventually Google learned people were sharing links to improve their search rankings and lowered the value of the links on both sites because they worked out a deal to share the links.

Some LinkedIn experts say sharing recommendations has the same effect on your LinkedIn reputation. Since LinkedIn automatically prompts you to reciprocate the recommendation, they feel you can get a lot of recommendations by writing a lot of recommendations. They feel this isn't natural to have one-to-one recommendations and devalues them. Sometimes I feel like someone recommended me just so I would write a recommendation for them. Most of the time I know if they are sincere and writing a recommendation for me because they value the work I do for them. I do know some people who are not sincere and are just looking for recommendations for themselves. After working with people, you get to know them and you know who is sincere and who isn't.

Other LinkedIn experts feel that a good recommendation is a good thing whether there is a reciprocal recommendation or not. If someone feels you are worthy of a recommendation and they take the time to write it, then that adds value to your LinkedIn reputation.

I'll leave it up to you whether you want recommendations only from people who you haven't recommended or if you want to do reciprocal recommendations. Personally, I write recommendations for people I feel are worthy of my recommendation. It doesn't matter to me if they ask me to write a recommendation for them or if it's a reciprocal recommendation.

I frequently receive requests from former employees to write a letter of recommendation for them and I gladly write a letter for them. With the evolution of LinkedIn Recommendations, people don't ask for written letters of recommendation as often as they used to. I will write them a recommendation on LinkedIn, which appears in their profile under the company we worked for at the time. Again, if I don't feel they were a good employee or not worthy of a recommendation for the work they did for me, I politely decline the invitation.

HOW TO ASK FOR RECOMMENDATIONS

Personally, I don't ask people for recommendations. It's not that I'm afraid to ask for them. If I were going to ask someone for a recommendation, it would be from someone I worked closely with and respected a great deal. I would have a close professional relationship with this person and she would be among the 150 people in my network with whom I keep in touch on a regular basis. I would write a strong recommendation for this person not because I want a recommendation from her, but because I strongly respect her professional ability. Most of the time I receive a strong recommendation in return. If the individual doesn't reciprocate, I don't take it personally; I just assume she doesn't have time to write recommendations on LinkedIn.

If you want to ask someone for a recommendation, you need to ask in a professional way. Don't use a standard request message in LinkedIn; instead, write a thoughtful message and explain why you are asking for a recommendation at this time. You can say you are looking for a new job and you would appreciate a recommendation. Don't ask for a recommendation from someone you don't know well or haven't worked with in a long time. A recommendation about your technical skills from a co-worker from 1990 isn't going to be relevant today and will have very little impact on your LinkedIn Profile. If that coworker is now a chief technology officer at a large company, you could ask them to write a recommendation for you that is focused on your customer service skills or your work ethic. That type of recommendation would carry a lot of weight in your profile.

When you ask for the recommendation, mention a specific project or job you worked on together. Explain why you think that project succeeded and how well you worked together. Tell the connection what you think her strengths were on the project and ask her what she thinks you did well. Also ask her to mention the specific skills or traits you demonstrated on that project and others on which you worked together.

You need to be very clear when you ask someone for a recommendation. Tell him or her exactly what position you are applying for and what skill set and experience it requires. You can even include a link to the job description if you don't think they may be interested in the job, so she can write a recommendation that fits the requirements of the position you are pursuing.

For example, if you are applying for a position as a software project manager that requires Scrum experience and knowledge of LAMP, ask the person writing your recommendation to include those skills and knowledge in the recommendation if they are familiar with your skill set. Obviously you should not ask someone to write a recommendation for you if she isn't familiar with your specific skills. Have her focus the recommendation on the skills they know you excel at.

Here is an example of a recommendation for a director of development for an internet business. Notice how the person writing the recommendation highlighted Michael's project management skills, software development skills, and technical programming language skills. This recommendation clearly demonstrates Michael's well-rounded skill set.

I worked with Michael at GS1 Canada. Michael is an excellent development director with in-depth knowledge of current software development technologies and keen sense of how to apply technology to maximize business applications. I worked with Michael on several projects. Michael is very capable at any level of software development: analysis, design, development, and support. Michael has excellent knowledge of .Net and Java development environment. At GS1 Canada, Michael made significant contribution to several strategic projects, including GDSN integration with 1SYNC. I would highly recommend Michael for any Development Director role.

See how the person writing the recommendation focused on two skills: his knowledge of the products in his industry, and the ability to form partnerships to develop new streams of revenue. It's clear this person worked with Michael and knows his strengths and skills.

If you want great recommendations like this, don't be afraid to reach out and ask for what you want. When you ask for a recommendation, you have more control over what the person will write when you specify what you are looking for in the recommendation. Unsolicited recommendations are usually thin in content and are written in very general terms. I think I just convinced myself to change my personal policy of not asking for recommendations and start asking for *great* recommendations!

CONCLUSION

As you see, LinkedIn Recommendations can be a very powerful addition to your LinkedIn profile. I strongly suggest you focus on a smaller number of quality recommendations instead of large quantity of lower quality recommendations. Get at least three quality recommendations for each position you've held. Take time to recommend co-workers and colleagues, too, which adds credibility to your LinkedIn profile. Recommendations are a form of social proof, validating your work history and expertise.

In the next chapter, I'll show you how to connect with others on LinkedIn so you can build a powerful professional network.

Connecting with Others

How many connections should you have on LinkedIn? I'm asked that question frequently, and there isn't a magic number that works for everyone. LinkedIn isn't a popularity contest where the person with the most connections wins. LinkedIn is not like Twitter, where Lady Gaga has more than 17 million followers but has no idea who those followers are. LinkedIn is about building relationships and connecting with others, which is very different than the monologue communication of Twitter.

There are two distinct approaches to networking on LinkedIn. The first, which is used by most LinkedIn members, is called *strategic networking*, where you focus on quality, not quantity. Strategic networkers usually have less than 500 people in their network and keep in touch with about 100 to 150 people in their network. They have a deep connection with a small number of people.

The other approach, which is often used by sales representatives and recruiters, is called *open networking;* this is where you cast a very wide net. Open networkers often have thousands of connections in their network because their business is a numbers game. The more people in your network, the easier it is to find someone to fill an open position or outreach customers for a sale. As an open networker, you have a limited connection with a lot of people.

STRATEGIC NETWORKING

How many people do you think are in your professional network now? Most people know hundreds of people and often have more than 500 contacts in their online address book. The question is: How many of those contacts do you correspond with on a regular basis? Some people apply the 80/20 and think they correspond with about 20 percent of their professional network on a regular basis. The reality is that you don't have time to correspond with 20 percent of your professional network on a regular basis if you have more than 500 people in your network.

A number of studies—such as "Psychology, Ideology, Utopia and the Commons," by Dennis R. Fox, and "Sorry You May Have Gone Over Your Limit of Network Friends," by Carl Bialik—have been conducted over the years trying to determine the optimal size of a professional network. The studies vary dramatically, with some concluding we can only maintain a stable social network of 100 people, while others suggest we can maintain stable social networks of up to 300.

Maintaining a stable social network means we know everyone in our network and maintain regular contact with each and every individual. To maintain a larger social network requires more restrictive rules, laws, and enforced norms so essentially you are almost being forced to maintain these relationships, which is not natural.

A widely accepted study by Robin Dunbar in 1992 resulted in Dunbar's Number, which suggests the theoretical cognitive limit to the number of people with whom one can maintain stable relationships is between 100 and 230. Dunbar does not specify an exact number because there are so many variables, but the generally accepted number is 150. Dunbar concluded, "This limit is a direct function of relative neocortex size, and that this in turn limits group size . . . the limit imposed by neocortical processing capacity is simply on the number of individuals with whom a stable interpersonal relationship can be maintained."

Do you maintain a regular relationship with 150 people? If you work for a medium to large-sized company and count your co-workers, you probably do maintain a regular relationship with that many people. If you work for a small company, you may not have regular communication with 150 people in your network. If you own your own business, you should be communicating with 150 people on a regular basis to generate leads or find opportunities.

The average number of connections for LinkedIn members is around 60 people, according to a Nielsen study. While many LinkedIn members have less than 60 connections, I see many members with more than 500 connections. When you view their profile you will only see 500+ connections. Once you are connected with that person, you will be able to view a list of their connections and can connect with anyone on the list because you have a second-degree relationship with them. A great way to expand your network is by connecting with appropriate second-degree relationships. Use your invitations wisely because LinkedIn gives you 3000 invitations, after which you have to request more. It shouldn't be a problem, since you're trying to keep your network manageable.

OPEN NETWORKING

Open networkers on LinkedIn are often called LIONs (an acronym for "LinkedIn Open Networkers"). LIONs seek to actively increase their connections by sending out and accepting connection invitations. LIONs, in general, accept invites from anyone, so it's relatively risk-free to invite a LION into your network.

Most LIONs take pride in touting their specific number of connections; it's similar to the way celebrities compete to have the most Twitter followers. The majority of LIONs believe bigger is better and that large networks lead to more opportunity.

How Do I Become a LION?

There is no official LinkedIn designation for a LinkedIn open networker. It's an unofficial designation coined by people willing to connect with anyone to grow their network as large as possible. The official LinkedIn response in the LinkedIn Help Center is:

> LION *is a designation used by several user-created groups and individual LinkedIn members to indicate a high level of interconnectivity to other LinkedIn members. This term is not endorsed by LinkedIn. As a reminder, only connect to people you know and trust and only join groups you want your name associated with. If you need additional information regarding any group's purpose and/or philosophy, contact the identified group owner in the Groups Directory.*

If you want to be recognized as a LinkedIn LION, you can add LION to the end of your name in your profile or in your profile headline as you see in Figure 11–1 on page 94.

Being a LION can have its drawbacks. Unfortunately, with any website or online tool that gets popular, people start abusing its popularity. We're seeing it on Twitter with people automating their Tweets, so they send an endless stream of Tweets 24/7. We're also starting to see a steady stream of Tweet spam where people are creating thousands of fake Twitter profiles that automatically re-Tweet Tweets from popular Tweeters. These automated programs begin with the legitimate Tweet, but then re-Tweet it thousands of times through fake profiles and fake links that lead to automated blogs, which in actuality are intended to sell affiliate products. You can see this Tweet spam when you follow a popular celebrity Tweeter because you will see a hundred re-Tweets in a few seconds from hundreds of fake profiles that are all using the same profile picture.

FIGURE 11–1. How to Identify a LION

We're now seeing similar tricks on LinkedIn with fake LinkedIn profiles. Be careful if you receive an invitation from:

- Someone who has no LinkedIn connections. LinkedIn now warns those who don't have connections or if they are new to LinkedIn.
- Profiles with no profile picture—one of my pet peeves, the incomplete profile
- Profiles with company logos as their profile picture, which is a violation of the LinkedIn Terms of Service
- Profiles with company names instead of a person's name. We connect with people, not companies, on LinkedIn!
- Profiles that use partial names or symbols in their names so it looks machine generated
- Profiles that have an SEO-optimized name, a phone number, email address, or their website URL
- Keyword-stuffed title or summary

Do not connect with these people because it's probably a machine-generated profile or someone who is not on LinkedIn for the right reasons. If someone is not willing to provide their complete name and fill out their complete profile properly, they are not fit for your network.

POP QUIZ

Let's say you are into social media and you connect with a lot of social media managers on LinkedIn. It's always good to network with others who share the same type of job so you can bounce ideas off each other.

One day you receive an invitation from this person, who has internet marketing, social media marketing, and community manager in his job title; this looks inviting to you because you are in the same field. The person owns his own business just like you do and has 206 connections. On first glance, this looks like a good fit for your network and connecting to this person will get you closer to 206 other people who are probably in the same field as you.

Should you connect with this person after reading the Profile Headline in Figure 11–2?

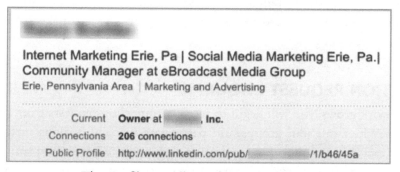

FIGURE 11–2. The Profile Headline of an Internet Marketing Person

This Profile Headline gives you the impression that the individual is an expert in internet marketing, social media marketing, and community management. If you said "no," good for you! Let's take a closer look at this person's profile, shown in Figure 11–3, and I'll show you why he probably isn't a good fit for your network.

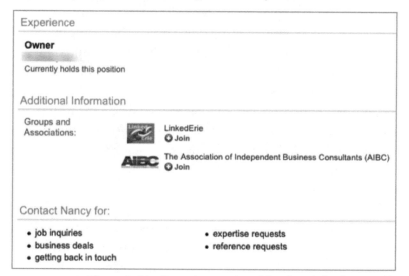

FIGURE 11–3. There Is No Experience Listed in the LinkedIn Profile

This is an example of a SEO-optimized profile that contains very little information about the individual. It's clear this person is an internet marketing and social media marketing consultant in Erie, Pennsylvania, and he created this LinkedIn profile to help his Google and LinkedIn search results. There are no recommendations, no summary, no education, and nothing that would make me want to hire this person to help me with my internet or social media marketing. If the person were a legitimate internet marketing consultant, he would claim his LinkedIn personal URL, add a summary with keywords, add his skills, and get at least a dozen recommendations. This person is gaming the system. I highly recommend ignoring or declining requests like this. Better yet, you should report them as spam so we can keep LinkedIn as professional as possible.

CONNECTION REQUEST ETIQUETTE

As your network grows, you will begin to receive connection requests from people you don't know. When you join groups and participate in conversations in that group, people will reach out to you with an invitation to connect. What should you do?

You have six options when you receive an invitation request. Your options are:

1. *Accept.* The person will immediately become a first-degree connection in your network.
2. *Reply.* You can reply to the person who invited you to connect if you are not sure you want them to become a first-degree connection with you at this time. If you just met someone at a networking event or in a LinkedIn group but you don't know much about him, you can reply to the invitation and set up a meeting or phone call to get to know each other. I also review the profile in detail to see if he will add value to my network. After reviewing their profile and speaking with him, I will know if I want to add him to my network as a first-degree connection.
3. *Delete.* If I don't know this person, never corresponded with him in a group, and have no mutual connection with our networks, I delete the invitation—unless he will somehow add value to my network. I vet each thoroughly before accepting the invitation to connect. If I recognize the person and they recently joined LinkedIn but haven't connected with anyone yet, I will accept their invitation if I know they will add value to my network.
4. *Archive.* If I receive an anonymous invitation, I will review the profile to see if he is a fit for my network. If I don't think he is right at this time but may be a fit at some time in the future, I will add the invitation to the Archive. This lets me review the invitation at a later date and accept the invitation when I believe he will add value to my network.

5. *Ignore.* This is similar to adding the invitation to the Archive, but you have two options: You can select "I don't know them" or "Report as spam." This sends a message to LinkedIn flagging the person as being a spammer or as someone not using LinkedIn appropriately.

6. *Forward.* Sometimes I receive an invitation from a high-quality person who may not be a fit for my network, but is a great fit for one of my connections. I will forward the invitation to my connection, suggesting that she connect with the high-quality person. This is kind of a blind recommendation since I don't know the person and I'm referring him, but I can get a sense from the profile that he is an A-list player and worthwhile for my connection.

REMOVING A CONNECTION

Sometimes you can connect with a person thinking, *She would be perfect for my network!* but it turns out she's not a good fit. Sometimes your connections will be overzealous with constant invitations to webinars or live events they're conducting. Don't get me wrong. I love to see people actively promoting their business and events. I don't mind occasional invitations, if the events are interesting and related to my current position. I do mind people inviting me to events weekly and sometimes every day—especially if the events are not related to my current job.

If you are connected with someone who you feel is taking advantage of your LinkedIn relationship and sending too many invitations, contact her and ask her to slow down or even remove you from her invitation list. Most of the time these individuals get the message and stop sending frequent event invitations. Unfortunately, there are those who won't get the message and keep spamming you with invitations, so you have to remove them as a connection.

You can remove a connection by going to the Contacts tab, Connections, and click on Remove Connections. This will remove the connection from your network and it will not notify them.

CONCLUSION

You now know the essentials to connecting with others on LinkedIn. It's up to you to now decide if you will build a smaller, high-quality network or become a LION and build a massive professional network. You have the ability to vet your connection requests so you can build a professional network that best suits your business needs.

In the next chapter, you're going to learn about LinkedIn InMail, a powerful tool that will help you connect with people who are not in your first- or second-degree networks.

Using LinkedIn InMail
to Reach Out

There are several ways to contact people through LinkedIn and each has its nuances, depending on whether the individuals are in or out of our network. LinkedIn is built to respect users' professional privacy, so people can pick and choose who becomes part of their network and avoid being barraged by spam or people who will disrupt you or your business. Of course, the site does want to encourage positive connections, and has devised a number of tools, such as InMail and Introductions, which allow users to communicate without invading anyone's privacy.

LINKEDIN INMAIL VS. INTRODUCTIONS

Introductions are free to all users. If you want to contact someone who is two or three degrees away from you, you can request an introduction through one of your connections who is a first-degree connection with that person.

You get a total of five introductions per month with a Basic (free) account and no more. If you need more introductions, you can upgrade to the Business account where you will be allowed to have up to 15 outstanding introduction requests at a time. The Business Plus account allows you to have up to 25 outstanding introduction requests and the Executive account gives you up to 35 outstanding introduction requests at a time. This means you can use as many introduction requests as you want, as long as you don't exceed the maximum number of outstanding introduction requests. There is no monthly maximum number of introduction requests for paid accounts.

LinkedIn has a number of features to help you connect with people outside of your network. The best way to connect with someone outside of your network is via an introduction by someone already in your network. A virtual introduction increases your chances of connecting with that person because there is a level of trust between you and your connection and a level of trust between your connection and the person you want to meet. The trust is essentially passed from connection to connection.

WHAT IS INMAIL?

When you send email to someone you don't know, it can be perceived as spam or inappropriate if you aren't careful. Reaching out to people who don't know you through normal email channels usually has a very high failure rate. How do you respond when you receive an unsolicited email from a stranger who wants to meet with you? I rarely respond to unsolicited emails, unless I see something in the subject line or first sentence that catches my eye. There has to be some benefit to me to make me respond to that unsolicited email.

Reaching out to someone you don't know in a trusted community like LinkedIn is a different story. LinkedIn is a trusted network where most members are reputable business professionals. You don't expect people to bother you with unsolicited emails unless they can provide value to you. Even though LinkedIn is a trusted network, LinkedIn understands not all members will respect others' privacy and may abuse the privilege of being able to reach out to each other. They created InMail so members can reach out to each other while protecting their privacy.

It's not always possible to have one of your contacts broker an introduction for you, but there are other ways for you to connect with a person. One option is to use InMail: These are private messages that enable you to contact—or be directly contacted by—another LinkedIn user, while protecting the recipient's privacy. InMail is a paid feature that can be purchased individually or as a part of a premium account.

If you have a Basic (free) account, you don't receive any InMail credits but you can purchase up to 10 InMail credits. If you have a premium account, you receive a certain number of InMail credits available based on your premium package. The Business account gives you three InMail credits per month, the Business Plus account gives you 10 InMail credits per month, and the Executive plan gives you 25 InMail credits every month. If you want more credits than the number you've been allotted, you can always purchase up to 10 more.

What Are the Benefits of InMail?

In addition to helping you outreach and connect with people while respecting privacy, InMail offers several valuable benefits:

- It helps you reach out to passive job candidates. For example, let's say you're looking for a new network engineer for your company and you read some great responses from a really sharp network engineer in the Answers section of LinkedIn. You want to contact this guy because he'd be a perfect fit for your company. He's not actively looking for a new job, but you see that he has Career Opportunities listed in the Contact Settings section at the bottom of his member Profile. He's not in your network and you don't have any connections in common, so you can't connect with him. You can still reach out to him with a personal message using InMail to see if he'd be interested in your network engineer position. The personal message can compliment him on some accomplishments that you found in his profile, so he'll feel honored that you know so much about him. This will make him more responsive to your InMail.

- You can reach out to active candidates who listed Career Opportunities in the Contact Settings section at the bottom of the member Profile, or have written that they are actively looking for a new opportunity. If they have Premium Job Seeker accounts, this will be noted by badges in their profiles so you know to reach out to them using InMail.

- You are writing an article about social media and you were looking for social media experts to interview. You search for social media experts on LinkedIn and find a few seem to fit your criteria. You have no connections in your network to make introductions and they are not in any groups with you. Even if you were in a group with them, they don't allow emails from other group members unless you are already connected with them because they value their privacy. You can use InMail to reach out to them even though you have not actually had a "face-to-face" relationship with them.

- You have a huge project starting tomorrow and your front-end developer is unavailable because of a family emergency. You need to find a great front-end developer who can start on the project immediately. You find the right developer, but she's not in your network; however, she is connected with your friend Joe. You email Joe and ask him for a LinkedIn Introduction, but he doesn't respond because he's out of the country. You can use InMail to reach out to the front-end developer so you don't have to wait for Joe to respond or rely on a long chain of contacts using LinkedIn Introductions.

■ You don't have to be a premium member to receive or respond to InMails. A few times people have reached out to me using InMail to see if I was interested in an opportunity. I didn't know the people contacting me, but it didn't feel intrusive because they had included some personal details like "I see you actively participate in the Social Media Managers group." It's important to break the ice in the subject line or in the first line of the email to create a level of trust or familiarity.

■ There is a seven-day guaranteed response. If the person doesn't respond to you within seven days, your account will be credited with an InMail on the eighth day. It's like a "no questions asked money back guarantee," so you don't lose your InMail if there is no response from the person you send the message to.

Purchasing and Sending an InMail

You can send an InMail by clicking the Send InMail link in the upper right of a member's profile page or from search results. If you have a Basic (free) account and you don't have any InMail credits, you will be prompted to upgrade your account when you try to send an InMail. If you don't want to upgrade to a Premium account, you can purchase InMail credits from within your profile under Settings. You can also check to see how many InMail credits you have remaining from this screen, as shown in Figure 12–1.

FIGURE 12–1. Available InMails

InMail credits can be used up to 90 days after they are issued. Once they expire they are not renewable, so make sure you don't purchase too many at once.

Remember, you don't need to use InMail to send messages to your first-degree connections. Just click Send a Message in the upper right of your connection's profile and you can send them a message for free. You can also send free messages to other group members, even if they aren't a connection, as long as they accept messages from other group members. If you do not want to receive messages from other group members with whom you are not connected, see how to modify your preferences in Chapter 5, "LinkedIn Privacy Settings." I don't recommend preventing people from contacting you on LinkedIn because the purpose of being on LinkedIn is to connect with others and you never know why someone will want to reach you; it could be an opportunity that would lead to additional revenue.

Here are some InMail facts for Premium account holders:

- InMail credits are issued on the monthly anniversary of your subscription start date. (The number of credits you get each month varies by type of Premium account you have.) For example, if you signed up for a Business Plus account on July 3rd, you will receive 10 new InMail credits on the third day of every month, as long as your Business Plus account is active.

- You can accumulate InMail credits from month to month, but they will expire after 90 days. For Business Plus members, you could accumulate up to 30 InMail credits over a three-month period, but the initial 10 credits expire on the 91st day if you don't use them. To be safe, you would have to use 10 of your InMail credits before the 90th day.

- You can purchase up to 10 more InMails than your account type allows or upgrade your account if you need even more. Let's say you are a Business level account holder where you receive three InMail credits every month and you're paying $24.95 per month for your account. You're looking for a new accountant for your company so you use up your three InMails reaching out to candidates. You could upgrade your account to Business Plus for $49.95 per month and receive 10 additional InMail credits. Once you fill the position, you won't need 10 InMail credits every month and you don't want to spend that amount when you won't be using all the features of the Business Plus account. Instead of upgrading your account, you could purchase up to 10 additional InMail credits at $10 each. You could even purchase the additional InMail credits one at a time until you fill the position, saving you even more money.

If you have a Basic (free) account you can purchase up to 10 InMail credits on your account at once or one at a time.

The guarantee is the same for Basic accounts as it is for Premium accounts. InMails are guaranteed a response by the recipient within seven days. If the recipient doesn't open the InMail within seven days, on the eighth day you receive another InMail to send. If the recipient responds after your account is credited, LinkedIn won't take the InMail credit back. If you send an InMail then withdraw it, you will not receive credit for it—even if the recipient doesn't respond.

What's an InMail Feedback Score?

LinkedIn rates your InMails to prevent overuse and spamming by members. Without the rating system, companies could abuse the InMail system by sending too many InMails, which would degrade the quality of the system and community. Everyone hates being spammed, so LinkedIn created the Feedback Score as a mechanism to monitor the effectiveness of the InMail system.

An InMail Feedback Score shows the acceptance rate of the sender's most recent InMails. Senders are rated on a five-star scale that appears at the top of the InMail message. You can see your own feedback score at the bottom of an InMail before you send it.

INMAIL FEEDBACK SCORE RATINGS

Five Stars	=	At least nine positive responses*
Four Stars	=	At least eight positive responses
Three Stars	=	At least seven positive responses
Two Stars	=	At least six positive responses
One Star	=	At least five positive responses
Zero Stars	=	Less than five positive responses
New	=	The sender has received InMail Feedback less than five times

*Positive response = InMail was accepted by recipient

InMail Rules if You Don't Like Spam

LinkedIn created delivery rules for InMail to minimize the amount of unsolicited emails you receive and to ensure that only emails sent from reputable LinkedIn members will be delivered to you. You can also customize your profile settings to control which InMails will be delivered to you and which will be blocked. The basic InMail rules include:

- InMails will only come to your email address if the sender has three stars or more. This means the InMail will be delivered to the email address you used when you signed up for LinkedIn and to your LinkedIn Inbox.
- InMails from someone with a rating of "New" or lower than three stars will only be seen when you sign in to LinkedIn. The InMail will not be delivered to the email address you used when you signed up for LinkedIn. The InMail will only be delivered to your LinkedIn Inbox.
- You can always select the types of messages you're willing to receive or set the frequency of emails from your Settings page. If you do not want to receive InMail messages, simply uncheck the Introductions and InMail radio button under your Settings, Email Preferences page, as you see in Figure 12–2 on page 105.

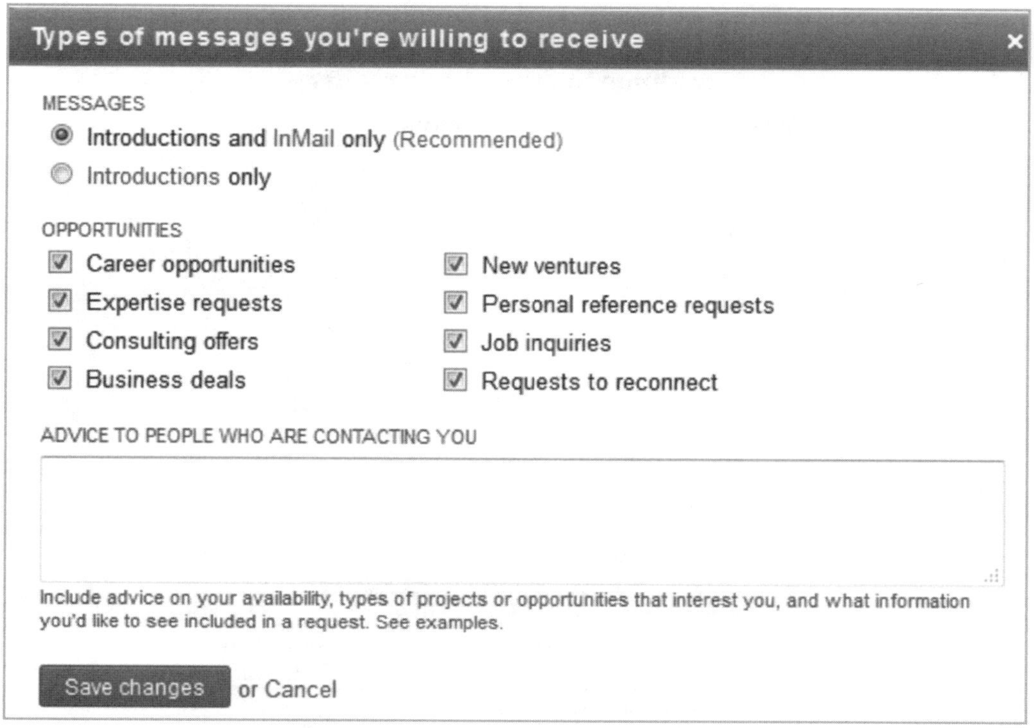

Types of messages you're willing to receive ✕

MESSAGES
- ⦿ Introductions and InMail only (Recommended)
- ◯ Introductions only

OPPORTUNITIES
- ☑ Career opportunities
- ☑ Expertise requests
- ☑ Consulting offers
- ☑ Business deals
- ☑ New ventures
- ☑ Personal reference requests
- ☑ Job inquiries
- ☑ Requests to reconnect

ADVICE TO PEOPLE WHO ARE CONTACTING YOU

Include advice on your availability, types of projects or opportunities that interest you, and what information you'd like to see included in a request. See examples.

Save changes or Cancel

FIGURE 12–2. Types of InMail

TIPS FOR WRITING INMAILS TO INCREASE YOUR RESPONSE RATES

It's important for you to carefully structure your InMail so the receiving person will open it and respond. If she doesn't open your InMail, you get penalized in two ways. First, you're wasting $10 if you purchased the InMail outside of your LinkedIn membership. Second, your InMail Feedback Score decreases, making it harder for you to send InMail.

If you are familiar with email marketing, you understand what I'm talking about except that in email marketing you don't receive a "double penalty" as with InMail. In traditional email marketing, if she doesn't open your email message, there is no penalty except your open rate decreases.

According to a study by Epsilon, the world's largest email marketing firm, and the Email Experience Council, the email marketing division of the Direct Marketing Association (www.the-dma.org), the average open rate of direct marketing emails is around 22 percent and has been holding steady since 2009, as you see in Figure 12–3 on page 106. The open rates vary by industry, but the overall average remains steady at around 22 percent.

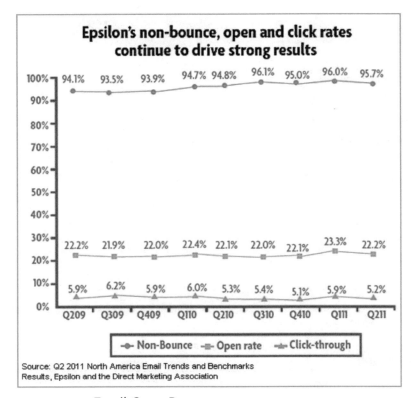

FIGURE 12–3. Email Open Rates

The good news is that LinkedIn InMail open rates are much higher if you structure your message properly. If the open rate of InMails were only 22 percent, it would be a very expensive way for you to reach out to others in LinkedIn. You would have to spend around $40 to get one person to just open your InMail, and opening the message does not guarantee anyone will respond to your request; it is easily possible to spend more than $100 just to get one person to respond.

LinkedIn doesn't provide template options for InMail, which is a good thing. If they did, InMail messages would start to look the same and people would stop paying attention. It's hard enough to get someone's attention these days when everyone is constantly being bombarded with messages and marketing promotions.

As with email marketing, your subject line is the most important part of your message. Some email marketing experts claim that the subject line is 90 percent of your message. If you don't catch their attention in the subject line, they'll never open the email and they'll never see your compelling message. Many copywriters spend more time crafting a powerful subject line than they do writing the email message.

Here are some tips for creating a powerful subject line for your InMail:

- Create curiosity by asking a provocative question.
- Promise answers to a question or solutions to a problem.
- Include a key benefit for the recipient.
- Ask them for advice or their opinion.

You want your subject line to be brief and to the point, catching their attention without giving away the details of your message. On TV, news programs have mastered the technique of piquing our attention about upcoming stories so we don't change the channel. Many times, the actual story is nowhere near as exciting as the teasers they used to pique our interest. The teasers are like subject lines in an email or headlines in sales copy. Their sole purpose is to grab our attention to make us want to learn more.

Remember your goal is to get the recipient to open your InMail so she'll read your message and start a dialogue with you. You want the recipient of your InMail to be so curious she finds herself unable to resist opening your message. You don't want to overhype your subject line or deceive her into opening your InMail, but you want to grab her attention enough to want to open it.

Here are some basic guidelines when composing your InMail to increase your response rates:

- Design your InMail as a conversation starter. You don't ask someone out on a date the second you meet her. You start a conversation first and get to know her before moving to the next level. The same holds true when you're establishing new business relationships. If you are too aggressive, she will naturally back away.
- The goal of sending the InMail is to discuss and explore an opportunity—not seal the deal immediately. Again, don't be too aggressive. Your goal is to get her to open your InMail and reply to you to establish a channel of communication.
- Mention the profile content that prompted you to write. If you were impressed by her education or a specific project she worked on, mention it in the first sentence or paragraph of your message.
- Adopt a conversational, enthusiastic tone. Don't use a form letter approach with boring, scripted text. Be friendly and inviting so she'll want to get to know you.
- Choose words that reflect your personal voice. Write your message in a natural tone like you're speaking with your colleagues. Don't use words you wouldn't use in your everyday conversation because it will sound unnatural.
- Express interest in helping her achieve her goals, rather than your need to fill a position if you're looking to hire her. People are always thinking, "What's in it for me?" so you have to speak to her from that perspective.
- Be brief and to the point so you don't waste anyone's time. If you write a long, drawn out message, she'll lose interest and not want to connect with you.

- Don't share too much. If you do, she may not feel the need to reply. Your only goal is to get a response.
- Focus on finding out her availability and interest in a job or networking opportunity. Express your objective clearly in your InMail so she knows exactly why you reached out to her.
- Give her a reason to reply by asking for advice, opinions, or referrals.
- Don't send a message with something like "Look at the job and tell me if you're interested" in the subject line. Your message will be ignored 99 percent of the time, wasting your valuable InMail credits. A better subject line may be, "Are you interested in joining the #1 consulting company in the world?"

Every InMail you send should be a very personal message to each recipient with a unique subject line. Don't cut and paste subject lines and email content; it's too impersonal and it won't grab her attention. If you are recruiting for a position, it's best to write a personal message mentioning skills or accomplishments you read in her profile and include a link to the job description. Do not include the entire job description in the InMail message.

The same holds true if you are using InMail for networking. Each message and subject line should be unique and let the recipient know your objective in the first sentence or paragraph. Explain what you read in their profile that made you want to reach out to this person. People love it when others notice their accomplishments and bring it to their attention. Play to a person's ego and you'll have a friend for life!

Personally I don't use InMail to network with others. I prefer to use LinkedIn Groups or Answers to connect with others. When I notice an outstanding person, I reach out to him in a group we have in common instead of blindly sending them an InMail. Most of the time, he is very responsive to connecting if we are in a common group.

CONCLUSION

InMail is a great, unobtrusive way for you to reach out to people who are not part of your immediate network. InMail has a very high success rate because LinkedIn's ranking process ensures that people don't abuse the system. If you have a low delivery rate, your InMails will not be delivered, so it's imperative that you take the time to craft meaningful messages to your recipients. InMail is a unique tool that makes it relatively easy for you to connect with key decision makers who are out of your network.

In the next chapter, we're going to learn about LinkedIn Groups, which are niche communities within the LinkedIn community. I'll show you how to effectively connect with subject-matter experts in your industry and how you can become a recognized thought leader in your field.

LinkedIn Groups

When used properly, LinkedIn Groups can be a powerful tool to help you grow your business or professional network. LinkedIn Groups can provide you with the connections you need to reach new industries or regions. In order to create an effective LinkedIn Group, you need to understand how LinkedIn Groups work and determine the purpose for your group. Some companies use LinkedIn Groups to support their products, while others use groups to build a relationship with prospects or to solidify relationships with existing customers.

WHAT ARE LINKEDIN GROUPS?

Groups are forums or discussion boards where LinkedIn members can converse with each other to find solutions to their problems or share relevant information about a product, service, or topic related to your industry or niche.

Groups can be open, allowing anyone to join without approval, or closed, meaning you have to be approved by the group manager before you can participate.

Keeping your group closed keeps the discussions focused on specific topics and cuts down on the unwanted comments that plague many open social networking sites. This allows your LinkedIn group discussions to be higher quality and more relevant to group members, since a group manager must approve all members. The group manager can moderate discussions and remove inappropriate posts or comments, as well as remove people from the group if they are disruptive or out of line.

How Many Groups Should I Join?

This is one of the most common questions I hear about LinkedIn. There are more than 1,200,000 groups on LinkedIn at the time of this writing and you are allowed to join up to 50 groups and 50 subgroups. Interesting new groups appear every day, and you're prompted by the "Groups You May Like" widget in your sidebar, so it's very easy to join a large number of groups without realizing it. The problem with joining numerous groups is that you just don't have time to be an active participant in all of them. Another issue with joining a lot of groups is that you receive daily or weekly email updates from each group. If you belong to 30 groups, your inbox will be full of LinkedIn group updates that you won't have time to read.

It's best to join a few groups and be an active participant instead of joining 30 groups and barely participating. People can see if you are actively participating in a group, which helps build your reputation and searchability in LinkedIn. If you are a member of numerous groups and not participating, it could hurt your reputation because people may perceive you as unfocused or unorganized.

You can join a group if you want to learn about a specific subject and leave the group once you receive the information you need. For example, if you're looking for a new social media monitoring tool, you can join a social media group and see which products the attendees are recommending. Ask a few questions about the different products so you can make an informed decision when it's time to buy. Once you make the purchase and get the software running properly, leave the group since you're unlikely to need to visit the group again.

Finding Groups

You can search for groups using the search box in the top toolbar, by switching the search option from People to Groups. You can also look under Groups in the top toolbar where you will see Groups You May Like and Groups Directory.

LINKEDIN SEARCH TIP

To find the most popular groups on LinkedIn, select Groups from the Search dropdown then search with no query in the search box. This will display the most popular LinkedIn groups, and you have the option of seeing similar groups by clicking on Similar Groups in the search result.

It's easy to find groups related to your job, position, industry, or skill set. If your LinkedIn profile is complete and optimized with your target keyword phrases, LinkedIn will recommend related groups for you in the Groups You May Like section. To see Groups You May Like, locate the widget at the bottom of the right sidebar on your LinkedIn homepage. If you disabled this setting in your profile, you can go to Groups in the top toolbar and select Groups You May Like. LinkedIn will display a list of recommended groups based on the data in your profile, including keywords, job titles of your present and past jobs, industry, company name, and the groups your connections belong to.

If you don't see an appropriate group in the Groups You May Like recommendations, you can do an advanced group search. LinkedIn lets you search for groups by keyword, category, and country, so you can find a very specialized group that may not show up in your recommendations as you see in Figure 13–1. To do an advanced group search, go to Groups on the top toolbar and select Groups Directory.

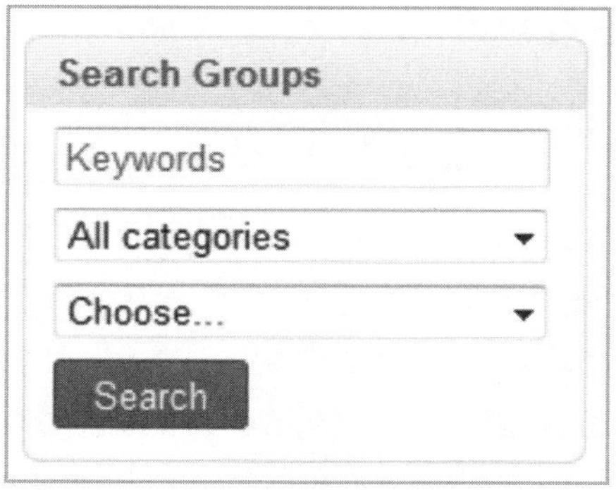

FIGURE 13–1. Search Groups

Simply enter your keywords, select a category, and choose a country if you're looking for a group located in a specific country.

Evaluating Groups

Groups are a very effective way to grow your professional network and demonstrate your expertise. To be effective in your use of groups, you shouldn't just join the first one that looks interesting. When it comes to professional groups on LinkedIn, there will usually be several options to choose from and you need to research the available groups to find the top three to five in a particular area.

First you want to make sure the group is active before joining. See how many members are in the group and check out some of their profiles to see if there are people you know and some you would want to add to your network. It's better to join a small group with the right members than a very large group with people you wouldn't want to add to your professional network.

How often are new discussions started in the group? Do people comment on discussions to continue the conversation or do discussions sit idle with no response? Another pet peeve for me is people starting discussions that turn out to be self-promotions. They aren't trying to add value to the group. They just want to promote their product or service. If most of the discussions are self-promotions, I avoid the group like the plague.

If you see a lot of discussions like these in a group, you may not want to join the group:

Tonight I will teach you the simple way to generate tons of leads. Are any of you interested in taking a very inexpensive (about $27) "how to" or "101" class on LinkedIn (and/or Facebook)? If so, contact me. . . Thanks!

If you see discussions like these, it's probably okay to join the group because people are doing market research or gathering information without obviously promoting their business:

Knowing what you know now about Starbucks, 10 yrs. ago would you have invested in the company? Yes or No

Hey everyone, I just opened Nothing Bundt Cakes in Corte Madera! I wanted to get some feedback so if you have tried my cakes let me know what you think.

There can be a fine line between self-promotion and fact finding so you have to decide for yourself if the group is right for you. If you notice the quality of the discussions isn't up to your expectations, you can always leave the group.

Read some of the discussions so you can get a sense of the group. If you're looking for a group of senior-level web analytics professionals but the discussions are very basic like how to install Google Analytics, the group isn't right for you. You can search for groups using specific keywords that you know will result in deeper conversations. You could search the analytics groups for questions like "How do you effectively measure customer engagement?" which should result in finding discussions by senior web analysts.

Another way you can assess the quality of a group is to review the Group Statistics, which is located at the bottom of the right sidebar when you're viewing the group. You will see tabs labeled Summary, Demographics, Growth, and Activity, as shown in Figure 13–2 on page 113.

The Summary tab shows you a snapshot of the group, including when the group started, the number of members, comments last week, seniority, location, and function.

FIGURE 13–2. Group Statistics for the SEO Hardcore Group

The Demographics tab provides detailed demographics of the group. This screen shows you the seniority of the group, its function, location, and industry. This is very valuable information when you're evaluating a group. If you're looking to connect with network engineers in London but the group is comprised of IT executives located in Japan, you know immediately this isn't the right one for you.

The Growth tab shows you New Members, Total Members, New Members Last Week, and Week Over Week Growth Rate. Its best to join a group that is growing, but the growth rate doesn't have to be significant if there are dynamic discussions between existing members. A fast-growing group doesn't mean it's a quality group, so you have to consider many factors before determining if it's worth joining.

The Activity tab summarizes the number of comments, discussions, jobs, and promotions in a group. You'll also see a graph displaying trend lines for the number of comments and discussions over time. This tab will help you determine if the activity in the group is increasing, declining, or stagnant. You don't want to waste your time joining a group that has stagnant or declining activity; your time is too precious to waste.

As you see, there are a number of factors to consider before joining a group and there is no magic formula. The key is to join a group only if it will benefit you in some way. If you're looking to connect with other network engineers in your local area so you can get together and talk about the latest trends, the group may not have a lot of online activity but could be a fantastic in-person resource. If you work in a very specialized field and don't have access to local resources, you can connect with colleagues around the world in a LinkedIn group, so you can share information and insights. The group may be small but the expertise level will be high. It's comforting to know you can reach out to a group of trusted experts for assistance when you need it.

You can also join groups to receive tech support on products. Large companies like Computer Associates (www.ca.com) have multiple groups dedicated to specific products, so you can get expert assistance instantly from other group members or Computer Associate tech support reps who monitor the group.

Joining a Group

When you find a group you want to join, simply click on the Join Group button located in the group listing. A message like you see in Figure 13–3 will appear, acknowledging your request to join the group and offering you a chance to adjust your settings.

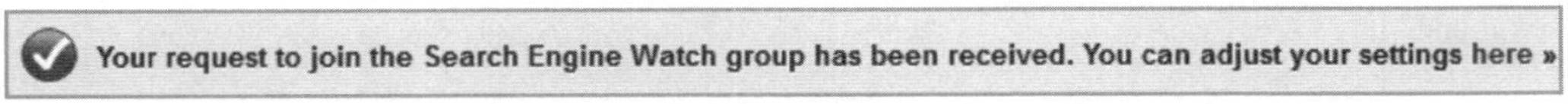

> ✓ Your request to join the **Search Engine Watch group has been received. You can adjust your settings here »**

FIGURE 13–3. Search Engine Watch Group Automated Response Message

This is where you can control where email notifications will be sent, how often you will receive updates, and which notifications will be sent to you.

Posts: Send Me an Email for Each New Discussion

Sometimes you will want to be notified immediately whenever a new discussion is started, so you can contribute quickly. If you are a consultant and want to demonstrate your expertise by answering questions posted by other members, you should select this option. When a new discussion is started you can respond quickly and your comment will appear right after the question, which will give you more exposure. If you are the 20th person to comment on a question, chances are most people will not take the time to read all of the comments and your brilliant response will go unnoticed.

Don't use this option if you are a member of a very popular group, unless you want to receive an extra 500 emails a week for every new discussion.

Digest Email: Send Me a Digest of All Activity in This Group

Delivery Frequency:

No Email—you will not receive email updates from this group

Weekly digest email—you will receive one weekly email update

Daily digest email—you will receive one daily email update

I usually set my email updates to daily digest email for most of my groups and use the weekly digest email updates for groups with less activity. You can always change the frequency of your group updates in your profile settings under Settings, Group, Companies & Applications, and set the frequency of group digest emails as you see in Figure 13–4.

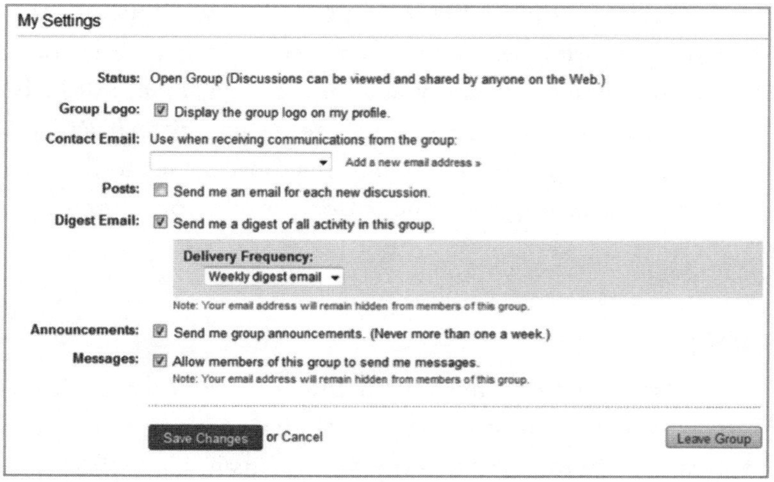

FIGURE 13–4. Email Frequency Settings for Groups

Choose if you want to receive group announcements and if you want to allow other members of the group to send you messages. Once you Save Changes, you will be ready to participate in the group (and receive approval from the group manager, if it's a closed group).

WHAT IS THE BEST WAY TO USE GROUPS?

Visiting and following up on the groups regularly is the only way to effectively use LinkedIn to build up your professional network. You need to make frequent and regular appearances within your group in order to maximize your exposure. One of the best ways to make sure that you are seen within the group is to target the most popular discussions and then be a regular and beneficial contributor to that discussion.

Once you feel comfortable with how groups work, the next step is to start your own discussion. Start with a topic that you are knowledgeable about so you can keep the conversation going. When you start a new discussion you want it to be as engaging as possible. You can look at a few of the extended conversations in your group and see how the discussion started. Starting a discussion isn't always just asking a question. You can ask for advice about a particular scenario or post information that would be useful to the target market you are looking to attract. Once you get the conversation started and others join in, be sure to reply in a timely fashion. You can subscribe to conversations, so you are notified by email when comments are posted.

You want to visit your LinkedIn groups regularly and participate whenever you can add value to a discussion and keep the conversation going. You can follow people in your group if you find them interesting and may want to add to your network. After following them for a while, you can invite them to join your network if they are a good fit.

If you are interested in a particular discussion, you can "Like" it, which lets people know you are interested in that topic. Your profile picture will appear below the discussion showing people you are interested in the topic. Your profile will also appear in the group's latest update widget in the sidebar, giving you more exposure to the group.

CONCLUSION

LinkedIn Groups are a great way for you to connect with other colleagues in your industry to keep up with the latest trends and to share information. The discussions in Groups are usually more focused than the discussions in LinkedIn Answers because the Group members are subject matter experts and industry leaders. LinkedIn Groups is also the perfect place to demonstrate your expertise by participating in the group discussions.

In the next chapter, we are going to explore LinkedIn Answers, a popular discussion forum where LinkedIn members ask and answer questions related to a variety of business-related categories.

Mastering LinkedIn Answers

I f you are old enough, you may remember the days before personal computers and the internet (yes, those days did exist), when we had to use dumb terminals and a 150/300 baud modem to access bulletin board systems, otherwise known as BBSs. We connected our modem to the terminal, dialed the BBS phone number on the keypad of our phone, and stuck our telephone handset into the acoustic coupler to get online. Once we were online, we could scan the BBS forums with topics ranging from car repair to cooking, just like we do in today's online communities. We could post questions or answer questions using our text-based terminal connection at dramatically slow speeds.

As personal computers evolved, services like Prodigy and AOL appeared where we could access online communities using a graphical interface with our dialup connections. These services became very popular, despite the slow dialup modem connections.

Today, the most popular websites continue to be those that allow users to have two-way conversations with other web visitors, just like the original BBS systems. Users can post content or ask questions, while others can respond to that content by adding comments or answering their questions. This is why sites like Facebook, YouTube, Yahoo Answers, Wikipedia, and LinkedIn are among the most popular websites according to www.alexa.com, a web intelligence firm.

The goal of all websites is to get as many visitors as possible, keep them on the pages, get them to return frequently, and encourage them to tell all their friends about it. Allowing two-way conversations and content sharing is the easiest way to accomplish these goals.

Facebook is the king of interactive websites with more than 800 million members. The amazing fact is: More than half of Facebook members log in *every day*. That's over 400 million people logging into Facebook and staying on the site an average of 60 minutes every day.

LINKEDIN'S VERSION OF THE BBS

Imagine having access to more than 140 million business subject-matter experts, 24/7, for free. You could ask any business-related question and receive multiple expert answers within minutes.

I just described LinkedIn Answers to you. It has become the most powerful business intelligence knowledge base on the internet and is LinkedIn's answer to the BBS.

LinkedIn Answers has two distinct modes of operation: asking and answering. First, you can ask questions to receive expert answers and opinions about any business-related subject. The other side of LinkedIn Answers is answering questions as an expert. This lets you demonstrate your expertise to millions of LinkedIn members and, even better, to billions of Google users who may be searching for an expert in your field. LinkedIn Answers, with a summary of your profile, appear in Google search results, giving you lots of exposure.

LinkedIn currently has more than 150 million members, and they are constantly adding features like LinkedIn Answers to keep people on the website for as long as possible and ensure they return every day. Their goal is to keep LinkedIn members engaged on LinkedIn.com with tools and features that improve the quality of the content.

Today, millions of questions have been asked and answered on LinkedIn. The quality of the questions and answers is directly related to the quality of the community. Since LinkedIn is a high quality business networking community, the quality of LinkedIn Answers is generally considered to be very high. Of course, you can have a small number of LinkedIn members posting inappropriate questions or answers but, for the most part, the quality remains high.

LinkedIn does not moderate the Answers section. Instead of moderating the community, LinkedIn prefers to let the community moderate itself. In the past when someone posted an inappropriate question or answer, there was no way to flag it or delete it. Today, LinkedIn has a feature called Report Answer As..., which lets you flag inappropriate posts as an advertisement, connection-building spam, gaming of expertise points, inappropriate content, misrepresentation, or other, where you can enter the details of why you are flagging the content. LinkedIn will review the Report Answer As... request and remove the content if they think it is inappropriate.

The asking and answering techniques you are about to learn can be used in the LinkedIn Answers section as well as in LinkedIn Group Discussions. Both these sections of LinkedIn are great resources for learning about a topic or demonstrating your expertise. LinkedIn Answers lets you ask and answer questions in more than 20 categories, so the conversations can be about very specific topics. When you ask and answer questions in LinkedIn Groups, you can get even more specific because all the group members are usually subject-matter experts in that field or expertise.

ASKING A QUESTION

A well-crafted question that allows subject matter experts to share their knowledge will produce many insightful answers and numerous comments by other users. A not-so-well-crafted question can have the reverse impact and damage your reputation, which means you want to take your time and ask something compelling and thought-provoking. You don't want to ask questions just for the sake of asking questions that will influence your LinkedIn and Google search results.

Before you ask a question in LinkedIn, think about these questions:

- What am I trying to achieve by asking this question?
- Am I really seeking an answer to a question or am I trying to establish myself as a thought leader in my field by asking a thought-provoking question?
- Am I trying to attract the attention a specific person or company? Am I trying to get a job with that company or make a connection that can lead to a big sale?
- Will this question create a lot of responses and an extended dialogue or will it be answered only by a small number of niche experts?

If you ask simple questions on LinkedIn, you will receive a few simple answers and you won't be regarded as an expert. If you ask complex, thought-provoking questions you will be perceived as an industry expert and you'll receive responses from other industry experts and thought leaders. The answers and comments to your question will be deeper in context and thought provoking, leading to extended conversations. Your circle of influence will expand and you will meet many experts in your field with whom you'll want to connect.

You can also ask questions to do market research and find out if there is any interest in a product or service. Let's say you manage Google AdWords accounts for medium-sized businesses on a contract basis and you want to see if small-business owners would be interested in your services to help expand your business. Most of the time large businesses have a full-time staff that manages their Google AdWords accounts, so they wouldn't be interested in your services (but wouldn't it be great to land a huge contract with a Fortune 50 company?).

You could ask a question like, "As a small-business owner, what are your biggest challenges or frustrations with Google AdWords?" Notice how the question begins so it will attract the attention of only small-business owners. If the prospect is not a small-business owner, chances are they won't read the rest of the question, which is exactly what you want. You don't want medium and large businesses to respond. If you are trying to attract the attention of large businesses, just replace "small business" with "large business."

The second half of the question attracts small-business owners who are struggling with Google AdWords. A small-business owner who is using Google AdWords effectively probably won't respond to the question because they aren't frustrated. If they are a small-business owner struggling with Google AdWords, they'll see this as an opportunity to vent. Questions phrased like this often hit a nerve with people who are spending a lot of money but not receiving the results they desire. They'll tell you in great detail what frustrations they're having, which will be a gold mine of information for you. You'll receive answers like "I'm spending a fortune on clicks but nobody is calling my store" or "Google AdWords is so complicated I can't figure it out."

People will be crying for help when they answer your question, which will give you a comprehensive list of the problems small-business owners face with Google AdWords. Once you know what they struggle with, you can create a free ebook that addresses their problems that you can use to build an email list of small-business prospects. You can also write blog posts that answer some of their biggest issues, which will build your credibility. You can even create targeted marketing campaigns around their biggest challenges, so you can easily convert them into paying clients. It's like knowing the answers to the test before the teacher hands it out!

After you ask the question and receive answers from frustrated small-business owners, don't try to sell them your services in your responses. This is the biggest mistake you can make because it will make it look obvious that you asked the question only to get some new clients. If possible, you should give them some free advice in your response.

If they say Google AdWords is too complicated, you could refer them to some helpful articles in the Google AdWords help section or ask them to specify the issues. Get them to tell you why they are frustrated and offer free guidance in the conversation thread. You may not be able to help them with all their problems, but they will appreciate that you tried. Most of the time people will reach out to you if you show interest in their problems and you will probably end up with a new client.

Helping people for free will bring you more paying clients in the future because others will see that you know what you are doing. They say, "The more you give, the more you gain" because people feel obligated to return the favor after you've helped them. It turns out to be a win-win for you and your new clients.

Get Creative with Your LinkedIn Questions

There are many other effective ways to ask questions in LinkedIn Answers, which fall into three categories:

1. *Knowledge*. How do I install the latest version of WordPress?
2. *Experience*. What are the best web hosting companies?
3. *Opinion*. What impact does a Google algorithm update have on your website?

If you want to learn how to do something, ask a *knowledge* question, which results in an answer that provides the step-by-step instructions or links to more resources. Knowledge questions usually begin with, "How do I . . ." or "How can I . . ." You will receive a variety of answers that explain how to accomplish your task, which can be helpful. Some people are better at explaining how to do something than others, so it's good to get different perspectives.

When you are researching products or services, you can also ask *experience* questions. These questions usually begin with "What are the best . . ." or "Who is your favorite . . ." In my example above, "What are the best web hosting companies?," people will share their positive experiences with a web hosting company. I like to include the words "and why?" at the end of my experience questions to solicit more information from the person answering the question. If you don't solicit more information, you may receive one- or two-word answers without any explanation, which may not help you make a decision. Be very clear when you ask a question and make sure you ask for the details you need to make an informed decision.

The flip side of the *experience* question is to ask, "What are the worst web hosting companies and tell me why you think they are the worst." This helps you learn which web hosting companies have a lot of downtime, poor customer service, or are unreliable. This information is often more valuable than learning about the positive experiences people have with companies.

The last type of question, the *opinion* question, lets you hear what people think of product updates or evolving trends in an industry. The answers to *opinion* questions often are not backed up by facts, just the opinion of the person answering the question; these can have philosophical responses. Thought leaders often respond to *opinion* questions, so you can use these questions to attract the attention of the leaders of your industry. These questions often start with "What do you think of . . ." or "Who do you think is . . ." Even though the answers to these questions may not be fact-based, you can see what the consensus of opinions is for evolving trends in an industry.

Tips for Asking Questions

You may notice that some questions receive a lot of responses while others remain unanswered. Other LinkedIn members flag some questions as inappropriate. Here are some guidelines to help you ask questions that will generate a response and also prevent your questions from being flagged by other LinkedIn members.

1. Make sure you select the appropriate category when posting your questions. There are more than 22 categories in LinkedIn Answers ranging from Administration to Using LinkedIn. You can also ask and answer questions in more than a dozen languages, making LinkedIn a truly international resource.

2. Answers is not intended to help you recruit, advertise, or announce your job search. These questions will be flagged and removed.

3. Your question will immediately appear:
   - Listed under the Answers tab
   - On your profile
   - On the LinkedIn homepage of your connections
   - In email, if you sent your question to any specific connections

4. You can also ask your question privately. If you choose to do so, your question will not appear publicly on the LinkedIn the site; instead, it is delivered as a message to the specific connections you chose.

5. LinkedIn limits you to only ten questions every month to prevent people from abusing the Answers section. Don't post questions just to post questions. Carefully plan your questions and have a clear purpose for asking questions. Your questions appear for others to see, so they can reveal your level of knowledge by the quality of the questions you ask.

ANSWERING QUESTIONS

Why should you take the time to answer questions on LinkedIn? I know you are very busy and don't have a lot of spare time to answer other people's questions. If you took just a couple of minutes every week to answer a few questions, millions of business people would see that you are an expert in your field. Where else can you reach millions of business people around the world in just a few minutes a week for free? You would have to pay millions of dollars to reach 140 million people and they still wouldn't get to know you as well as they would from your answers on LinkedIn.

Before you start answering questions in LinkedIn Answers, make sure your LinkedIn Profile is complete. When people like your answers, the first thing they will do is check out your profile to learn more about you. Remember, you are on LinkedIn to grow your network and answering questions will attract more people to your profile. There's nothing worse than being impressed by someone on LinkedIn and then finding an incomplete profile when you're trying to learn more about her. Some people view an incomplete LinkedIn profile as unprofessional because its purpose is to make connections. If you can't take the time to fill out your own profile completely, it sends the message that you're either too busy or careless to add value to others' personal networks. I would never hire or refer anyone who has an incomplete LinkedIn profile.

LET'S PRACTICE

If you've never answered questions on a forum or on LinkedIn, take some time to read some of the questions and answers in your area of expertise. LinkedIn Answers organizes the questions into more than 20 categories, so you can easily find questions in your niche.

Let's say you are in marketing and sales and you want to see some sample questions and answers. Start by going to the More tab on the LinkedIn toolbar and select Answers. From the Advanced Answers Search tab, you can select Marketing and Sales in the Category section, leave the Keyword box blank, and click on Search. This will give you a list of all the questions and answers in this category. You will be able to sort the search results by All Questions and Open Questions as you see in Figure 14–1.

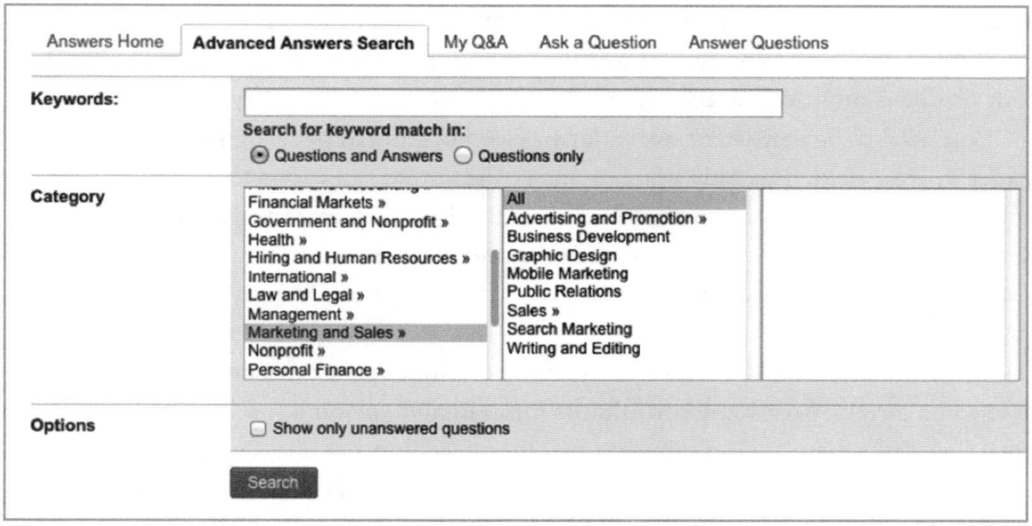

FIGURE 14–1. Advanced Answers Search Options

When you are comfortable with answering questions, you can save time by entering specific keywords and checking the Show Only Unanswered Questions box in order to see specific open questions that you can answer.

As you are reading the questions and answers posted by other LinkedIn members, notice the different approaches people take when using LinkedIn Answers. See if you can find questions posted using the three previously discussed categories of *knowledge*, *experience*, and *opinion*. How do people phrase knowledge-type questions and how do others answer them? Are there more knowledge, experience, or opinion-type questions in your area of expertise? Are the opinion-type questions controversial with spirited debates?

If you are just getting started answering questions in LinkedIn, I don't recommend jumping into a heated debate right away. I suggest looking for a few "softball" questions that you know you can answer quickly and correctly. It's best to start slowly, building your confidence and credibility.

MAKE A PLAN

Figure out which categories and keywords make you most comfortable. You are an expert in your field, but it's best to focus on your strengths when answering questions. Every question you answer will remain on LinkedIn for others to see so you want to leave a positive, lasting impression.

Decide how you want to use LinkedIn Answers. Do you want to be a thought leader in your industry or do you just want to pick up a couple of consulting contracts? This will determine how many questions you want to answer on average every week. Some weeks there will be lots of questions you can answer and other weeks there may not be many good questions. You don't want to just answer questions so your answer total in your profile is high. You want to think "quality" instead of "quantity."

You need to be consistent over a long period of time to be recognized as a thought leader in your field. You only want to answer advanced questions that require a lot of knowledge and thought to answer. Yes, LinkedIn does keep score and maintains a leader board for number of questions answered. Leave the basic questions to the people who like to be at the top of the leader board. I'll get into the pros and cons of answering basic questions later in this chapter.

If you are using LinkedIn Answers just to occasionally pick up some new clients, you have to be careful. I see some consultants jump in and answer a few hundred questions until they get a client then disappear until they need another one. Others can view your past answers and see how often you participate. A smart LinkedIn user (like you will be after you finish reading this book!) will be able to detect LinkedIn members who only use Answers for their own well-being and aren't interested in building a strong community. I believe in the theory that "the more you give, the more you gain" and consistently helping others will benefit everyone in the long run. People who are out for themselves usually don't succeed for long in communities.

LET'S ANSWER SOME QUESTIONS!

You've done your research and you have your plan. It's time to answer some questions and build your reputation.

It's best if you can be one of the first to answer new questions. When you are one of the first answers, more people will read your response. Many questions receive more than 20 answers and most people will not read all 20 answers. If you are number 20, chances are someone already said what you were going to say so it's not worth repeating.

If you aren't one of the first to answer a question, you can still add value to the conversation by expanding on a previous answer. Don't repeat what that person wrote, but expand on the answer. If she gave three reasons why you should buy a certain product, you could add more reasons why it's a product worth investing in or expound on the three reasons provided.

For example, if someone asks a question "Which are the best 15 laptops?" and someone answers "I recently purchased the Inspiron 15R and I love it. It's fast and the screen resolution is fantastic," you could continue the conversation by replying "I recently purchased the Dell Inspiron 15R too, and I recommend upgrading the memory from 4 to 8GB for only $60. It's worth the small investment if you want better performance."

The other approach to answering someone's question is to take the opposing view by playing devil's advocate. Disagreeing with someone is a great way to stir up a lively conversation. I'm not telling you to be a total jerk and go off on someone, but you can attract a lot of attention by going against the grain.

If someone asks, "What are the business benefits to moving my business to Michigan?" and someone responds "Moving your business to Michigan can be a great move for your company. The cost of living is low which is a huge benefit to your employees plus you receive a lot of tax incentives from the state," you could respond: "Why would you want to move your business to Michigan? The talent pool is very limited and you'll have a hard time getting anyone to move there. Plus the weather is horrible. Who in their right mind would move their business to Michigan?"

See how being controversial could generate a lively conversation? I'm sure a comment like this would generate a lot of discussion.

The key is to add value to the conversation in a meaningful way. Your answers should be clear, concise, and on-topic. Often I see long, rambling answers that answer the question in the first sentence, but then becomes a short story. Remember: The person who posted the question is busy and is looking for a solution to her problem, not the complete history of the product.

YOUR OPTIONS WHEN ANSWERING QUESTIONS

When you've found a question that you want to answer, you will see four options under the box where the question is displayed as shown in Figure 14–2.

FIGURE 14–2. Question Responses

The Answer Button

As you would expect, the Answer button is where you click to enter your answer. Make sure you proofread your answer carefully for spelling and other potential errors before you post.

If you want to add a URL to a website, you can enter it below your answer as shown in Figure 14–3 on page 127. I don't recommend referring them to your website unless you are referring them to a relevant blog post or article you have written.

If you know an expert who can better answer the question or solve their problem, you can Suggest an Expert. This is an easy way to give referrals to people in your network.

The last option allows you to write a note to the person who wrote the question. Again, don't take advantage and self-promote. If you are sending a note, make it short and to the point. Sometimes I'll send someone a note complimenting a person on her

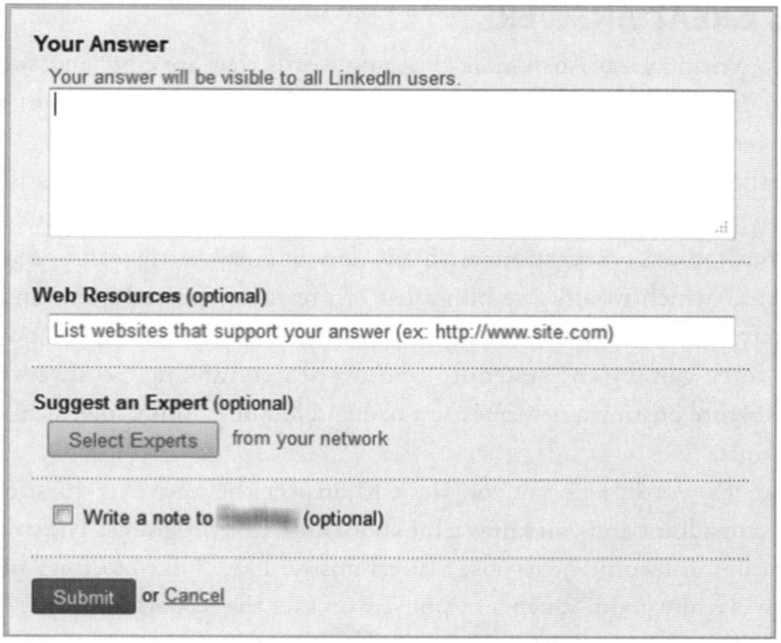

Your Answer
Your answer will be visible to all LinkedIn users.

Web Resources (optional)
List websites that support your answer (ex: http://www.site.com)

Suggest an Expert (optional)
Select Experts from your network

☐ Write a note to ▮▮▮▮▮ (optional)

Submit or Cancel

FIGURE 14–3. Your Answer

question and suggest that she join a specific group or ask if she wants to be a connection on LinkedIn.

Suggest Expert

This is the second button under the Answer box. As I mentioned above, this is a great way to refer people in your network who are more qualified to answer the question or help the person.

Reply Privately

Use this option if you don't feel comfortable replying publicly to a question and would rather send it in private. Remember, replying privately will not appear in your profile and will not count if you are trying to earn expert status.

Share This

Use this option if you want to email the question to a friend or if you want to share the question on the social bookmarking website Delicious.

WRITING GREAT ANSWERS

The secret to writing great Answers is choosing words that are clear and succinct, but with enough detail so that readers understand the solution you are recommending and why you are recommending it.

One of the more popular questions you'll see on LinkedIn Answers is: "What is the best antivirus for my personal computer?" The person who posted it could easily find numerous recent conversations with a variety of answers. Instead of searching for "best antivirus," which would give him a list of previously posted questions, he starts an unnecessary new conversation thread. To savvy LinkedIn users, his post appears ignorant or to be gaming the system to improve search ranking. So always search for your answer before posting a new question to avoid looking dumb, unethical, or a waste of anyone's time.

For what it's worth, let's say you want to answer the antivirus question because you're an IT consultant and you know a lot about antivirus programs. The wrong way to answer that question would be to post a direct answer like, "I like Norton Antivirus," or "TrendMicro is really good." Such a response won't let the readers know why you think your selection is the best antivirus program. These answers are in the *opinion* format and you should be answering in the *knowledge* or *experience* format.

If you want to answer based on your experience you could say, "I've been using Norton Antivirus for over 10 years and I've never had a virus on my computer. My computer runs faster than it did with Symantec Antivirus, and it protects my data, email, and internet browsing."

To answer from the knowledge perspective, you could answer like this expert below:

I use Avira for personal use. They have quite a good free version that seems to contain slightly better "smarts" in the product than most.

I have been a NOD32 and AVG user for many years in the past and find Avira a lot easier to use with more practical functions.

Being a former IT security consultant myself, and having experience with most major firewalls within the Australian Federal Government IT space, and seeing a lot of free-for-home-use products, I'd choose Avira over the rest, also that it was rated the most downloaded product on the website download.com and PC Pro Best Value product online, being the most effective free antivirus package PC Pro has ever seen.

This is the link to the free version: http://www.free-av.com/ and I've also included the link to the company's website if you require more info. Best of Luck!

See the difference between that answer and "I like Avira antivirus"? If you were looking for a new IT consultant, which one would you want to hire?

Tips for Effective Answers

People will judge you and your business based on how you answer questions, so you want to answer questions completely and in a professional way. If someone asks a long, multipart question, make sure you answer all of the questions completely. Don't answer it if you don't feel confident that you can address the entire scope of the question. Here are some tips to help you answer questions like an expert:

- *Always spell check the answers you post.* You are trying to present a professional and expert image and misspellings will diminish your reputation.

- *Don't self-promote in your answers!* You are an expert who is providing unbiased answers to questions, which will enhance your credibility and reputation. Eventually, helping others with no expectation in return will turn you into a thought leader in your industry. This will bring you higher-paying projects or sales than if you self-promote in your answers.

  Think about thought leaders in your industry or other industries. Do you ever hear them promote themselves or their companies when they speak or write white papers? Of course they don't, because they are focused on being thought leaders in their industry and earn more than most people in their industry.

- *Always display the questions, answers, and the expertise you've earned in your profile.* This lets others easily see your expertise. You can enable this under Settings, Edit Profile; look for the Q&A tab near the bottom of the right sidebar.

- *Answer only relevant questions.* If you are a tax attorney and you're trying to appear as a tax expert on LinkedIn, you shouldn't be answering questions in the sustainability section, unless it is directly related to your work as a tax attorney. We all have a breadth of knowledge and could answer questions in many categories, but it's best to focus on your area of expertise.

- *Don't answer too many questions in a short period of time.* LinkedIn displays This Week's Top Experts in each category and often I'll see the top expert answering more than 1,000 questions in one week. To me, this raises many red flags. Either this person is unemployed, desperate for work, or is really comprised of virtual assistants to answer the questions for him. For example, let's say the top expert answered 1,000 questions last week and it takes five minutes to answer each question (a thoughtful answer would take much longer than this, but bear with me). That's 5,000 minutes or 83.33 hours in one week answering questions. That's almost 12 hours a day, seven days a week. When does anyone have time to do his job or complete work for clients?

  Obviously this looks like this person is trying to game the system. They earn a lot of Best Answers so they will receive Expert Status, which looks great in their profile. I'll explain more about Expert Status in a minute, but you see my point about being too active answering questions.

EARNING EXPERTISE

When you see a star on a profile, you know that person has proven her expertise by answering questions that have been chosen as the best answer.

If you want to earn Expert Status, just answer questions in your area of expertise. Remember, private answers won't help you earn this title, so be sure to answer the questions publicly if this is your goal.

Every time the questioner picks your answer as the best answer, you gain a point of expertise. The more points of expertise you accumulate, the higher you'll appear on lists of experts. This will help your reputation significantly if you demonstrate your expertise on a regular basis. Don't forget to display this in your profile so others can see you are an expert in your field.

CONCLUSION

As you see, LinkedIn Answers and Questions are great tools to help you engage with other LinkedIn members. Answering questions posted by others lets you demonstrate your expertise and establish yourself as an industry expert. Asking questions helps you get feedback from a variety of experts.

In the next chapter, I'll show you how to monitor your LinkedIn network so you'll know how large your professional network is and how fast it's growing.

Monitoring
Your Network

As your LinkedIn network grows, you will want to keep track of the new people being added. LinkedIn provides a great tool called Network Statistics, which is located under Contacts on the top menu. You see a snapshot of Your Network of Trusted Professionals which includes the total number of Your Connections, and connections two and three degrees away. With two people joining LinkedIn every second, your network two and three degrees away can grow very quickly. You'll also see the Total users you can contact through introductions.

As you see in Figure 15–1 on page 132, I have 610 first-degree connections, more than 223,500 second-degree connections, and more than 8,660,200 third-degree connections in my network. I can reach almost 9 million professionals through an introduction, which is unbelievable. Where else do you have access to so many targeted resources?

As of December 18th, 2011, 12,991 new people have joined my network since yesterday and I didn't lift a finger! In the famous movie *The Secret*, they talked about the Law of Attraction and learning how to attract new clients. LinkedIn is like the Law of Attraction on steroids, automatically adding new prospects to your network while you sleep.

Network Statistics also breaks down your connections into Regions and Industry, giving you detailed demographic information about your network. You see where your connections are located, additional

Your Network of Trusted Professionals

You are at the center of your network. Your connections can introduce
you to 8,884,400+ professionals — here's how your network breaks
down:

1	**Your Connections** Your trusted friends and colleagues	610
2	**Two degrees away** Friends of friends; each connected to one of your connections	223,500+
3	**Three degrees away** Reach these users through a friend and one of their friends	8,660,200+
	Total users you can contact through an Introduction	8,884,400+

12,991 new people in your network since December 17

FIGURE 15–1. Your Network Connections

locations that can be reached through your network, and which locations are growing
fastest.

If you own a business, the above information helps you figure out how to focus your
efforts and where you can potentially grow your business. LinkedIn makes it very easy
for you to expand into another region by giving you direct access to potential contacts in
other regions. In my Network Statistics, for example—as demonstrated in Figure 15–2—I
can expand to 1,342 additional locations including Miami/Fort Lauderdale, Houston,
and Paris, France.

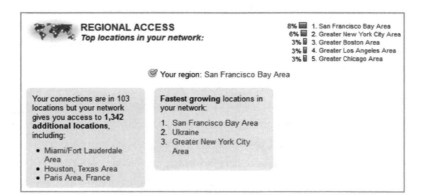

FIGURE 15–2. Expanding to New Regions

Let's say I wanted to expand my business to Miami/Fort Lauderdale. I simply click
on the Miami/Fort Lauderdale link in Network Statistics and LinkedIn shows me the
most relevant connections that can help me expand my business in that area, as you

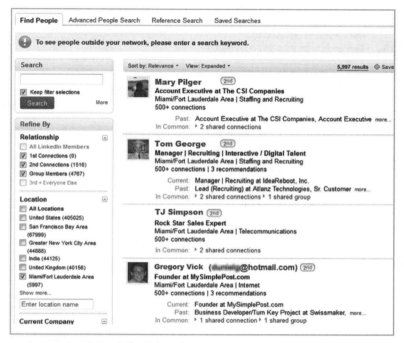

FIGURE 15-3. Search by Location

see in Figure 15-3. This particular search shows me first-degree connections, second-degree connections, and Group members in my network. I can also change the sort from Relevance, to Relationship, Relationship + Recommendations, Connections, or Keywords. One click of the mouse and I receive highly targeted search results in seconds.

I also see my network broken down by Industry, which reveals the fastest-growing industries in my network, the top industries, and additional networks I can reach through my existing connections. If I want to expand into the Market Research industry, I simply click on the Market Research link and I receive a similar targeted search result to the one I received in my Regional search. See Figure 15-4 on page 134 for my industry breakdown.

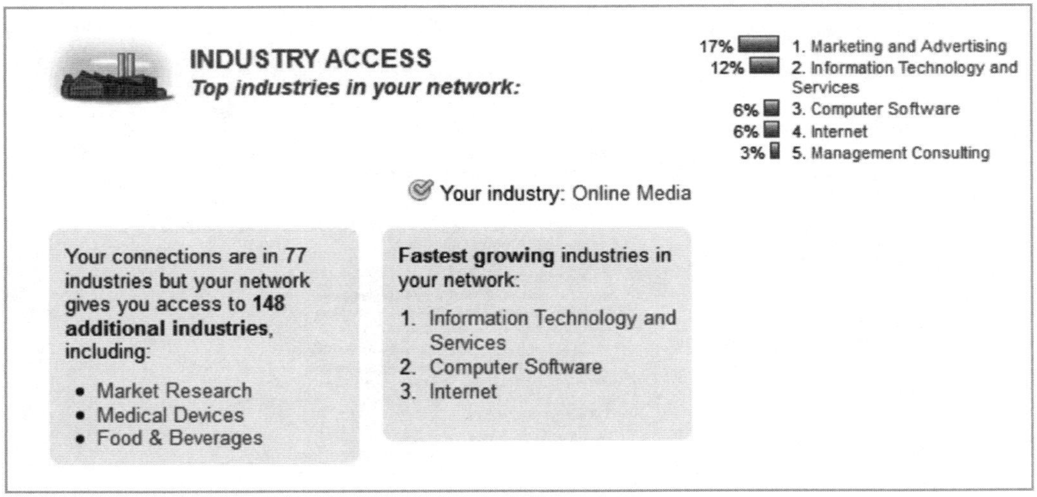

FIGURE 15–4. Connections by Industry

USING TAGS

As you add new connections to your network, you want to keep them organized so they're easy to find when you want to reach out to them. LinkedIn has a feature called Tags, which is located under Contacts, Connections, and Tags. LinkedIn describes Tags as "simple keywords that you can create to organize your connections for quick filtering on LinkedIn. You can use this window to create new tags or delete old ones. Note that you can create up to 200 unique tags."

LinkedIn predefines some Tags, such as colleagues, friends, partners, group members, and classmates. You can create custom tags that are appropriate for your network. Some of the tags I use are search marketers, PPC experts, SEO experts, and programmers.

CONCLUSION

LinkedIn's Network Statistics lets you closely monitor your professional network and gives you analytical tools that help you identify key decision makers who reside in different industries or locations. Tools like Network Statistics are invaluable for mining the massive LinkedIn database as you grow your business and professional network.

In the next chapter, we're going to explore LinkedIn Apps, which are applications that extend your LinkedIn account exponentially.

LinkedIn Apps

The LinkedIn networking site has a collection of powerful tools that let you connect with infinite possibilities on matters of business, moneymaking, and job hunting. However, many people haven't fully realized the power of this site. It has practically all of the tools you need, whether you are an internet marketer or a job hunter. We decided to review eight of the interesting tools, or apps, offered on LinkedIn that you can actually use in job hunting, team management, and business propagation.

TWEETS

Tweets is an application that allows you to display your Twitter stream on your LinkedIn profile. You can choose to have your latest Tweets appear on your Profile page under the Recent Tweets heading and on your homepage. Your Tweets can also appear in your Status updates, if desired.

To install Tweets, go to your Settings, then the Groups, Companies & Applications tab, and Add Applications. Click on the Tweets icon and the app will install automatically. You will be prompted to enter your Twitter username and password and then you will have to authorize the use of the Tweets app in LinkedIn. It's okay to authorize the transfer of your Twitter data to the Tweets app, so you can share your Twitter experience on LinkedIn.

FIGURE 16–1. Manage Twitter Settings

You will also have to decide if you want to display your Twitter account on your LinkedIn Profile. See Figure 16-1 for your options. Some people prefer not to display their Twitter account on their profile, but they will choose to have their Tweets appear on their LinkedIn status by selecting the option under Sharing Tweets. If you add #li in your Tweets from Twitter, they will appear in your LinkedIn status.

You can also configure the Tweets app by going to More on the top LinkedIn toolbar and selecting Tweets. Go to the Settings tab and you can select Display all Tweets or Display only Tweets that include #in.

I discussed these options earlier in Chapter 5, "LinkedIn Privacy Settings," when I showed you the advanced configuration settings. In the past, social media experts recommended connecting all your social media accounts together so you could automate your posting. You post once on Twitter and it blasts the same message to Facebook, LinkedIn, MySpace, your blog, and anywhere else you had an RSS connection.

Today, I recommend creating separate posts for each social media property because your LinkedIn connections are interested in different content from you than your Facebook friends. I don't recommend mixing business and personal conversations online.

If you use Twitter exclusively for business, then it's okay to select the Display all Tweets option as shown in Figure 16-2 on page 137. If you want to display only certain Tweets on LinkedIn, then select the second option and add #in to your Tweets.

Once you are in the Tweets app, you can see an overview of your Twitter account from the Overview tab. This tab is similar to being logged in to www.twitter.com. You see a list of the people you are following in the left column and the Twitter stream of the people you are following on the right side of the screen. You can Tweet directly from the top of the page.

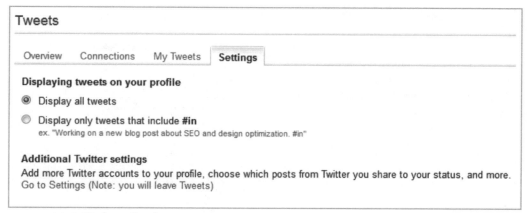

FIGURE 16–2. Twitter Settings

The Connections tab will show you a list of your LinkedIn connections and whether you are following them or not. If you aren't following them, you can follow them from this screen. You can also create custom Twitter lists from this screen so you can easily follow your LinkedIn connections on Twitter.

The My Tweets tab will display a list of your Tweets. The advantage of the My Tweets tab is that you can see a complete history of your Tweets that you cannot see on Twitter because Twitter limits your history due to capacity issues.

SLIDESHARE PRESENTATIONS

SlideShare Presentations is a website and an online application that lets you share your PowerPoint slide show presentations on the internet. SlideShare has quickly become the world's largest community for sharing presentations online. The LinkedIn SlideShare app lets you easily share documents and presentations with your LinkedIn network. You can upload portfolios, resumes, and PDFs, and display them on your LinkedIn profile. You can also embed YouTube videos in your presentations or add audio to make an online seminar presentation.

The SlideShare app is very easy to use. There is an upload button that lets you upload PowerPoint, Microsoft Word, Keynote, and iWork files. You can also upload and display videos through your Slideshare app if you have a Premium LinkedIn account. After you upload content, you can share the content with your network using the share button. Once you share your documents, your network can view and comment on your presentations. Figure 16–3 on page 138 shows your SlideShare App configuration options.

You have the ability to customize your Slidespace to feature specific presentations and videos. You can also display your content as thumbnails so viewers can easily scan

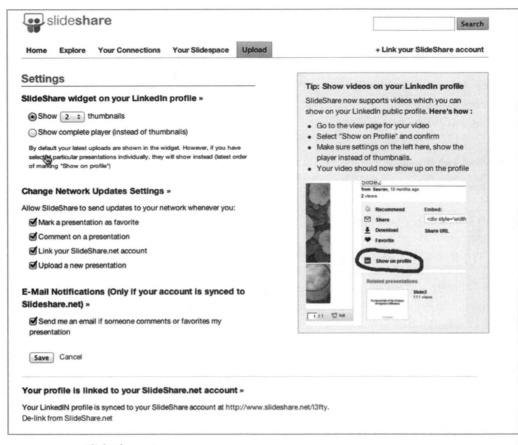

FIGURE 16–3. SlideShare App

all your content. SlideShare and the LinkedIn SlideShare app are powerful tools that let you easily demonstrate your expertise to LinkedIn members.

GOOGLE PRESENTATION

The Google Presentation application is similar to the SlideShare app where you can share PowerPoint-type presentations with your network. You can upload existing PowerPoint presentations to your account or you can create a new presentation from within the app using the Google Docs application.

The Google Presentation app lets you showcase your work portfolio to potential employers or to potential clients, if you own a small business. Many sales professionals use this app to upload sales presentations to prospective customers.

The Google Presentation app is limited to PowerPoint or Google Docs presentations. It does not let you upload videos, Word documents, or Excel spreadsheets.

CREATIVE PORTFOLIO DISPLAY

The Creative Portfolio Display application by Behance.com is great for artists, designers, and professionals to showcase their work. You can create an online portfolio and gallery of your work that is accessible through the LinkedIn app by your connections and synced to your online account at www.behance.com.

You can upload unlimited multimedia projects including images, text, audio, and video to your online portfolio through the Creative Portfolio Display app. Once you upload your media, it appears in your LinkedIn profile and on the Behance website. The Behance website is also designed so you can easily share your portfolio using Twitter, Facebook, and on Behance-powered galleries which are embedded into websites. This network is designed to be social-media friendly, so it's very easy for visitors to share their favorite portfolios throughout the internet.

The Behance Network gets 15 times the traffic of all other leading portfolio sites combined; that amounts to millions of visitors every month. The Behance Network includes top creative companies such as Apple, Adobe, Nike, and Google, so your portfolio will receive a lot of attention.

E-BOOKSHELF

E-Bookshelf is an application that lets you download and read e-books about business, management, motivation, entrepreneurship, sports, and many other topics. If you are not familiar with e-books, they are short, electronic versions of books that are usually very focused on one subject. The idea of an e-book is to give you a brief but detailed overview of a subject or topic. E-books are not intended to give you in-depth knowledge of a subject. Their sole purpose is to give you a high-level overview of a topic so you'll have a working knowledge of a subject. You can usually read an entire e-book in less than an hour, making them attractive to busy executives.

E-Bookshelf is a LinkedIn app that lets you purchase e-books using credits. Once you purchase an e-book, you can start reading it immediately within the E-Bookshelf app or save it on My E-Bookshelf to read later.

Credits for E-Bookshelf are very affordable and will not expire. See Figure 16–4 on page 140 for your pricing options.

WORDPRESS

Blogging is a great way to share your thoughts and ideas with your network and helps develop your personal brand. Bloggers are often considered thought leaders in

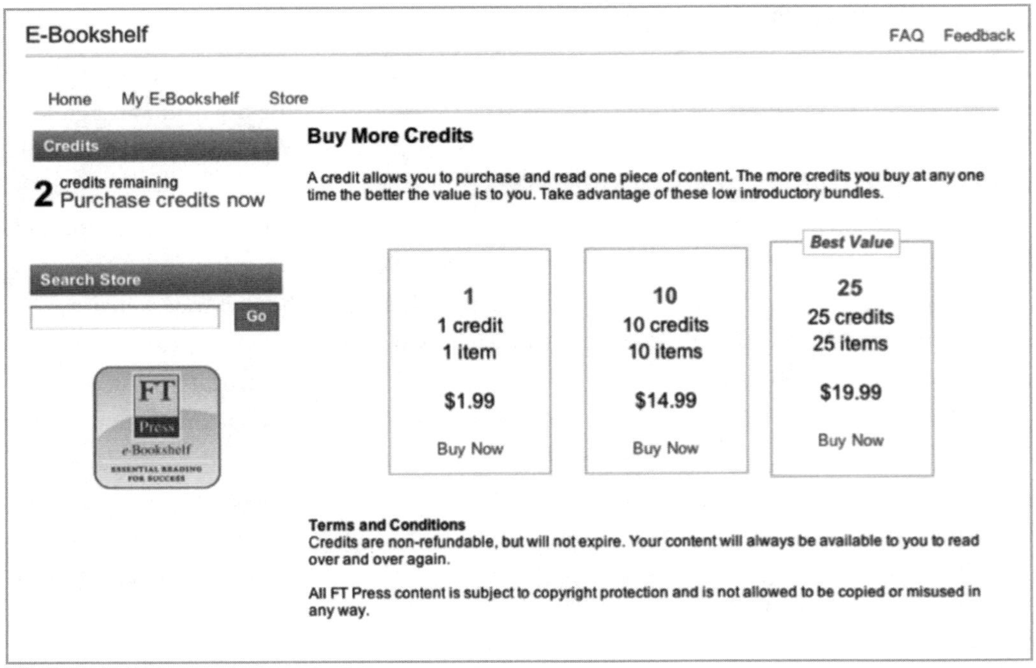

E-Bookshelf   FAQ   Feedback

Home   My E-Bookshelf   Store

Credits

2 credits remaining
Purchase credits now

Buy More Credits

A credit allows you to purchase and read one piece of content. The more credits you buy at any one time the better the value is to you. Take advantage of these low introductory bundles.

Search Store

[   ] Go

FT Press e-Bookshelf
ESSENTIAL READING FOR SUCCESS

Best Value

1	**10**	**25**
1 credit	10 credits	25 credits
1 item	10 items	25 items
$1.99	$14.99	$19.99
Buy Now	Buy Now	Buy Now

Terms and Conditions
Credits are non-refundable, but will not expire. Your content will always be available to you to read over and over again.

All FT Press content is subject to copyright protection and is not allowed to be copied or misused in any way.

FIGURE 16–4. E-Bookshelf Credits

their industry because they're sharing their insights to a worldwide audience via the internet.

WordPress rapidly became the most popular blog and content management software because it's free and very easy to use. There are more websites and blogs built with WordPress software than any other software platform.

The WordPress LinkedIn app lets you display your blog posts on your LinkedIn profile and on your LinkedIn homepage. You can display all your blog posts on your LinkedIn profile and HomePage or you can choose to display select blog posts by adding a tag, "LinkedIn," to the blog posts you want to appear on LinkedIn. If you don't add the "LinkedIn" tag to your blog post, it will not appear on your LinkedIn homepage. This is a handy feature in case you write personal blog posts that you wouldn't want to share with your business network.

To configure the WordPress app to display your blog, simply enter your blog URL in the application settings while you are installing the WordPress app. In Figure 16–5, you can choose whether you want to display your blog on your profile and/ or your LinkeIn homepage and you're done!

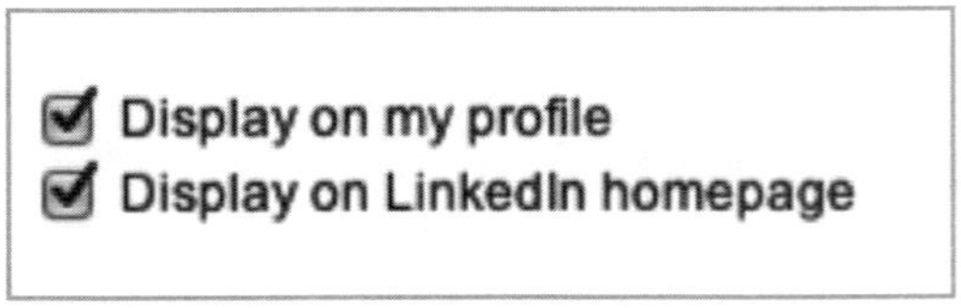

☑ Display on my profile
☑ Display on LinkedIn homepage

FIGURE 16–5. WordPress Options

BLOG LINK

Blog Link is another LinkedIn app that lets you display your blog posts on your LinkedIn profile and homepage. Blog Link gives you more flexibility in case you don't use WordPress as your blogging platform. Blog Link lets you add your WordPress blog and it also supports other blog platforms, such as TypePad, Vox, Blogger, and LiveJournal.

Blog Link also displays blog posts from all your LinkedIn connections that have blogs being displayed on LinkedIn. This seems like it would be a nice feature, but if you have a lot of LinkedIn connections that have blogs being displayed on LinkedIn, it can take a long time for the page to load and often it never finishes loading. This is frustrating to viewers and makes this feature unusable. Unfortunately, you can't select just a few blogs from your LinkedIn connections, which would increase the usability of this app.

To display your blog and blogs from your connections on your LinkedIn profile and homepage, just enter the blog's URL in the application settings and you're ready to go.

PROJECTS AND TEAMSPACES

Projects and Teamspaces is a virtual workspace you can use for managing team projects. This tool is helpful for: recruiting projects, tracking your sales lead generation process, managing fundraising campaigns, and a slew of other group-related activities. This tool is specifically designed for teams of employees working together on projects.

You can assign a work task to a team member, send a message, or manage the tasks that are assigned to you. Projects and Teamspaces has free unlimited workspaces and eliminates the need for you to use multiple software programs to manage your team projects.

Projects and Teamspaces integrates with your personal Google accounts, so you can add task deadlines to your Google Calendar and use Google docs to create and store project documents created by you and your team members.

As project tasks are assigned, updated, and completed, Projects and Teamspaces shows the entire team when and who updated project tasks and projects documents in a user-friendly dashboard. I was very surprised at the ease of use and the comprehensive project management tools available in this free application and I highly recommend trying it out for managing your team projects. If you are managing very large-scale projects, Manymoon—the creator of Projects and Teamspaces—offers upgraded versions of the app with advanced project management features at a reasonable cost.

EVENTS

The Events app in LinkedIn lets you search for networking and educational events by geographic location or by industry. Once you install the Events app, you can create your own events that will be displayed to the target audience you choose.

You can see what events your professional network is attending and find events recommended to you based on your industry and job function. The Events app will help you connect with prospects at the next industry event in your area or reconnect with old friends.

The Events app lets you learn more about conferences and seminars. You can read comments about events, see who's attending, and find out who's interested. When you decide to attend, you can add important conferences to your profile and let people know when you are attending and/or presenting.

READING LIST BY AMAZON

The Reading List by Amazon application lets you share which books you are reading with your LinkedIn network. The app also lets you see what other people in your industry are reading.

You start by adding the books that you want to read, are reading right now, and have already read. The application then finds matches and displays the books that people on your network are reading. It also lets you follow other people's reading lists and notifies you when they update them.

The Reading List by Amazon app is divided into four categories:

1. Your Reading List
2. Network Updates
3. Industry Updates
4. All Recent Updates

Your Reading List shows everyone which books you are currently reading, which ones you want to read, and those you have finished reading. Once you finish a book, the app will prompt you to Recommend the book to others if you enjoyed it and add your personal comments. When you search for new books to read you will see which LinkedIn members have read the book, their recommendations, and their comments, so you can decide if the book is for you. You can also follow the reading list of other LinkedIn members from the book detail screen, in case you have similar interests as other members.

The Network Updates tab shows you what other people in your LinkedIn network are reading if they have the app installed. This is a good way to get to learn more about your LinkedIn network members' interests. If you see a lot of people in your network are reading about certain topics, you could create a product or service related to them since you have uncovered a common interest.

The Industry Updates tab shows you what people in your industry are reading. You can see the hot topics in your industry and keep up with the latest trends. If you are looking for a job, letting people know you are well-informed shows potential employers that you are proactive and well-educated.

The All Recent Updates tab shows you the current reading list of everyone on LinkedIn who has installed the Reading List app. This is a great way to meet new people who have common interests with you. When you see someone on LinkedIn who is reading books about subjects that you like, it gives you something to use when you reach out to them to connect. You can say something like: "I noticed you read a lot of books about business development in your Reading List on LinkedIn. I also love to read about business development and I just finished reading *Jack: Straight from the Gut,* by Jack Welch. I would highly recommend it if you haven't read it yet. I didn't see it on your reading list."

MYTRAVEL

The MyTravel application is a great tool for those who travel for their jobs. The MyTravel app lets you tell people you know when and where you are traveling for work. This lets you sync your travel plans with your network, so you can get together if you are in the same city at the same time. If you are attending a conference or considering it, you can post it in MyTravel to let others know. You can also see who else in your network is going to the same conference.

This application is very easy to use. All you have to do is upload a PowerPoint presentation from your computer or you can also use Google's free document processor in making a presentation.

GITHUB

GitHub is an application for people in the coding community. It is a tool that programmers can use to showcase their GitHub projects right in their LinkedIn Profile. You can also choose to follow other GitHub users and watch their projects. GitHub is a useful tool for connecting with other coders in LinkedIn.

POLLS

The Polls application lets you leverage the wisdom of millions of business professionals on LinkedIn. You can create simple polls that consist of one question and up to five

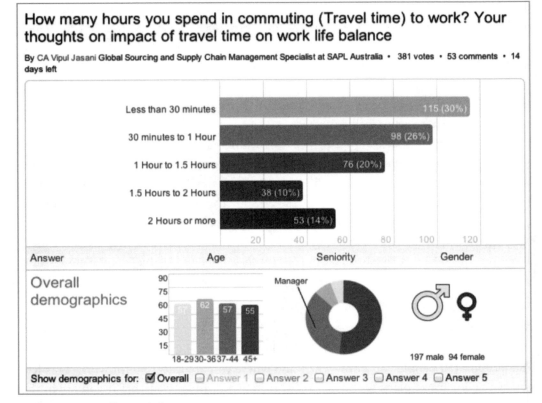

FIGURE 16–6. Poll Breakdown

multiple-choice answers. You can control how long the poll question is open, and closed polls are available for review by everyone.

Your poll questions will be distributed to your LinkedIn connections and millions of other professionals on LinkedIn. You can also share your Poll through the Facebook or Twitter integrations, or embed the voting module on your own website or blog.

A nice feature of Polls is that you get very detailed results, including the number of responses, a detailed breakdown of the answers, comments, and the demographics of the people who responded. See Figure 16–6 to see a sample poll breakdown. You'll know the age, seniority, and gender of the people who responded. You can also break down the demographics of the people who responded by each answer in your poll, which is invaluable information.

REAL ESTATE PRO

Real Estate Pro is an application for real estate professionals who want an easy way to stay informed about their local real estate and office space marketplace. The most common use of Real Estate Pro is to find office space listings for lease and property for sale. The app lets you follow and connect with active brokers and professionals, track new property listings, and see the latest deals in your market.

If you are a real estate professional, you can use Real Estate Pro to feature your property listings and promote client transactions on your LinkedIn profile. Real Estate Pro lets you easily share your work and completed deals with your business connections, track your market, create a following, promote your expertise, and develop new business.

LAWYER RATINGS

Lawyer Ratings is an application for attorneys that helps justify the credentials they post in their LinkedIn profiles. The application is from Martindale-Hubbell® Lawyer Ratings, an independent ratings firm.

The Martindale-Hubbell® Lawyer Ratings Application provides an opportunity for attorneys to support their stated credentials in their LinkedIn profile by prominently displaying the Martindale-Hubbell® Client Review and Martindale-Hubbell® Peer Review Ratings. When people are searching for attorneys on LinkedIn, the Martindale-Hubbell® Review adds credibility to the attorneys who are reviewed and approved by this service.

Martindale-Hubbell® is the authoritative resource for information on lawyers. For more than 140 years, the Martindale-Hubbell® Legal Network has evolved into a database of more than one million lawyers and law firms in more than 160 countries, helping to connect you with other lawyers and with buyers of legal services. There are two services they provide: Martindale-Hubble® Client Review Ratings™ and Martindale-Hubbell® Peer Review Ratings™.

Martindale-Hubble® Client Review Ratings™

This service confirms a firm or an attorney's communication ability, quality of service, responsiveness, and value for the money on specific matters. It also includes an optional overall recommendation by the client and narrative feedback. The attorney then has an opportunity to respond to the narrative feedback to provide a broader picture of how she does business.

To initiate the client review process, the attorney submits at least five client nominations and surveys are sent out to those clients. Alternatively, clients can visit the attorney's Lawyers.com or Martindale.com® profile and click the "Review as a Client" button.

Martindale-Hubbell® Peer Review Ratings™

This service is an objective indicator of a lawyer's credentials based on reviews by peers. To be rated, lawyers must meet the "very high" General Ethical Standards

Rating and also be rated on their Legal Ability. Legal Ability Ratings review five key areas:

1. Legal knowledge
2. Analytical capabilities
3. Judgment
4. Communication ability
5. Legal experience

Any subscribing lawyer can initiate a peer review. There's a minimum of 18 nominations—attorneys and/or judges outside your organization—and a maximum of one set of nominations per year.

The Lawyer Ratings app helps build credibility for attorneys while providing a valuable tool for potential clients looking for reputable attorneys.

BOX.NET

The Box.net application helps you manage and share files within your LinkedIn profile. Box.net lets you easily upload files from your computer into your LinkedIn profile, so that your LinkedIn connections, potential clients, and co-workers can view and download them. If you are looking for a job, you can easily share your resume or work portfolio online. If you are an employer who is looking to hire new employees, you can post job requisitions in your profile. Freelancers can post their work portfolio for potential clients to review.

Box.net not only lets you upload and share files with your LinkedIn connections, it also allows you to view files posted by your connections. The application is user-friendly and easy to install.

CONCLUSION

Applications or apps have been the rage since Apple introduced them with the iPhone in 2008. Apps continue to evolve in literally every consumer electronic product. LinkedIn released their version of apps in 2010, expanding the functionality of the LinkedIn platform. LinkedIn apps are a collection of incredible tools and services that are underutilized by LinkedIn members. I invite you to explore LinkedIn apps to see how they can improve your LinkedIn experience.

In the next chapter, we'll explore LinkedIn Tools that are applications developed by LinkedIn in their LinkedIn Labs.

Chapter 17

LinkedIn Tools

Some people use the terms *tools* and *apps* interchangeably. Don't worry if one author calls a LinkedIn add-on a tool while another author calls the same add-on an app. In this book, I will refer to LinkedIn tools as apps that are developed by the LinkedIn Labs, not by independent developers. LinkedIn makes it easy for developers to create new apps and tools that extend LinkedIn, and you can learn more at http://developer.linkedin.com.

In this chapter, I'll introduce you to a few of the most popular LinkedIn tools. All of these tools are free to download and will enhance your LinkedIn experience.

LINKEDIN MOBILE

LinkedIn developed mobile applications for the iPhone, Android, BlackBerry, and Palm smartphones. The app is free to download and connects you seamlessly to your LinkedIn account from your phone. See Figure 17–1 on page 148 to see what LinkedIn Mobile will look like on your smartphone.

The app is well-designed, fast, and easy to use. The app lets you check messages in your InBox, invite people to connect, review updates, and send messages to your connections.

FIGURE 17–1. LinkedIn Mobile

The app is simplified so you navigate by selecting one of four buttons:

- *Updates*. View the latest updates from your contacts.
- *You*. View the updates you've posted and add an update in a matter of seconds.
- *Inbox*. Check out your LinkedIn email with one click or touch.
- *Groups & More*. Check out Groups you belong to and see the "People You May Know" suggestions from LinkedIn.

CARDMUNCH

CardMunch is a LinkedIn app that lets you take a picture of a business card with your iPhone; this contact information is saved in the app on your phone. LinkedIn recently released the much-improved version 3 of their CardMunch app for the iPhone. They reduced the entire application to three intuitive and easy-to-use screens: Card capture, Contact list, and Contact details/LinkedIn profiles. Currently the CardMunch app is only available for iPhones in the United States.

Every card you scan is saved in an online Rolodex on your phone. It takes a few minutes for the image to be digitized, and you will receive a push notification when the process is complete. You can enter personalized notes for each contact you scan, so you know when and where you met this person.

If you are not connected to that person on LinkedIn, you can click Connect to send an invitation after scanning their business card. The downside of connecting automatically with the Connect button is that you can't personalize the invitation.

Once you are connected with a person, you will be able to pull up their entire LinkedIn profile from within the Contacts section of the CardMunch app. You can also save their full contact information to your iPhone address book with just one click, as well as email the person or forward their contact information to others from within the app.

As your database grows within the CardMunch app on your iPhone, you can scroll through a well-designed display that lets you swipe through virtual business cards of all your contacts. To see virtual images of the cards you've scanned, simply turn your iPhone sideways while you are in the CardMunch app.

CardMunch is a convenient app that shows a lot of promise as it matures. CardMunch isn't perfect, but it's worth a look because it's an easy way to enter contacts into your iPhone address book and to connect with them on LinkedIn. Figure 17–2 shows you the CardMunch dashboard.

FIGURE 17–2. CardMunch

LINKEDIN LABS

LinkedIn offers their employees one day a month to work on their innovative ideas. These special projects, known as Hackdays, are an outlet for individuals to brainstorm and create new, experimental applications. These apps are meant to be low-maintenance, so they have limited functionality and may have some bugs. Some experiments become popular and/or useful and eventually move into production to work out the bugs. Many experiments disappear from the lab because they aren't popular or the team doesn't have time to work out the bugs.

Some LinkedIn Lab Apps to Consider

In honor of Veterans Day 2011, a number of new apps were developed to honor the United States military veterans. The winning app, which was called Veterans, was designed to help veterans reconnect with each other on LinkedIn. You can see the Veterans app at http://veterans.linkedinlabs.com.

The MOCHA app is The Military Occupational Classification Hack for Advancement and can help military personnel in their transition to the civilian job market by matching skills relevant to their military occupation with jobs in the civilian market. You can see the MOCHA app at http://mocha.linkedinlabs.com.

Another interesting app, SpeechIn, reads your LinkedIn Today headlines to you on your mobile phone or through your Chrome browser. This app lets you catch up on your LinkedIn Today headlines while you are driving to work.

The Swarm application shows you a rotating cloud of keywords from various categories. The cloud shows the most popular keywords in categories such as Today's Most Searched Titles, Today's Most Searched Companies, and Today's Most Popular Job Searches in different industries. The categories automatically refresh so you get a continuous stream of relevant keywords from today's LinkedIn search activity. The larger the word is in the cloud, the more popular it is. This is a fantastic tool to help you with your keyword research. You can play with Swarm at http://swarm. linkedinlabs.com.

One app that has officially been moved into production from LinkedIn Labs is the Signal application. You can see Signal under News in the top toolbar on your LinkedIn homepage. Signal shows you a timeline of your connections status updates with the ability to search for specific information in the timeline. You can search for keywords, by network (your status updates, first connections, and second connections), by company, by location, by industry, by time, by school, by group, by topics, by seniority, and by update type (shares, groups, profiles, answers).

Let's say you wanted to see what executives were talking about on LinkedIn related to social media ROI. You can enter "social media ROI" in the search box, select Senior and Director under the Seniority tab, and select Shares, Groups, and Answers under Update Type. The search result will show you every discussion on LinkedIn related to "social media ROI." If there are too many results, I like to exclude the Shares update when doing this kind of research because people often post self-promoting links in the Shares. When they Tweet or promote a new blog post, it will appear under Shares and it's hard to filter out the quality blog posts from the low-quality self-promotions. I also filter the Time to Last Day or Last Week if there are too many posts.

If you want to see some of the experimental apps being tested in the LinkedIn Lab, visit www.linkedinlabs.com. LinkedIn Labs hosts a small set of projects and experimental features built by the employees of LinkedIn. These experimental apps are meant to be demonstrations and to solicit feedback. They are not intended to be production-ready applications.

CONCLUSION

LinkedIn Tools can also be considered apps and are powerful extensions to the LinkedIn platform. As LinkedIn expands its API (application program interface), developers will be able to build even more powerful tools and applications, extending the LinkedIn platform further. This will be beneficial to all LinkedIn members as the community grows larger and larger.

In the next chapter, I'll show you how to set up your LinkedIn groups and optimize it to give your company a strong presence on LinkedIn.

Creating and Managing LinkedIn Groups

LinkedIn Groups are an easy way for you to start an online community for your company. If you already have a lot of customers and prospects who are members of LinkedIn, starting a LinkedIn Group for them is a smart thing to do.

HOW TO START A GROUP

Before you start your own group, you need to determine if you are willing to make the time commitment to make the group a success. Starting a group is easy, but growing it and keeping it active can take a lot of work, especially in the beginning. I highly recommend you create a team of people who can share in the management and promotion of your group. As your group grows, you can invite a few of the most active people in the group to become facilitators. Most of the time, they will feel honored if you invite them to facilitate the group.

The topics you choose to be the focus of group discussions will determine how appealing your group is to others and how many members will be willing to join. Before starting your group you should research topics within your niche that generate interest and choose the top two or three as the basis for your group.

When you start a new group you will need to fill out a profile. You need to create a description of the group, which includes keywords that will help to generate interest in the group. Look at some popular LinkedIn groups and see how they worded their descriptions, so you know what to say in your group description.

Here is the group description for The Recruiter Network:

Recruiter: #1 LinkedIn Recruitment & Career Networking Social Media Group. Network with recruiters, find a job or headhunter. Read recruiting, HR, staffing, & employment news. Recruit talent, find jobs, careers, executive, alumni, and professional connection. Members in US UK Europe Canada India USA

As you see, they clearly state they are the top LinkedIn recruitment group, which catches your attention immediately. They go on to describe the benefits of joining the group whether you are looking for a job, looking to get to know recruiters, or looking to hire new employees. They capture the essence of the group in a just a few sentences.

GROUP SETTINGS

LinkedIn offers many options for configuring how your group will function in the Group Settings section under Manage. It's important you consider all of these when configuring the Group Settings.

First you'll want to make sure you check the Enable the Discussions and News features, which is on by default. You have the option to conduct group Polls and display Promotions and Jobs. You have to determine if you want to allow your group members to post their own polls, move discussions to the Promotions area, and post Jobs. There are pros and cons of each option, so I recommend only allowing moderators and managers to use these functions until you get to know the group members. Many group managers disable the polls, promotions, jobs, and subgroups initially to help members focus on creating quality discussions and not be distracted by the other options. You want to enable your group members as much as possible, but I believe it's best to start slow and add features as the group matures. Your Group Settings options are shown in Figure 18–1.

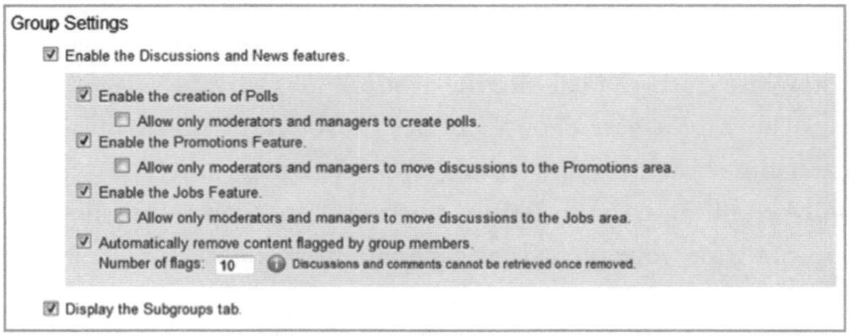

FIGURE 18–1. Group Settings

PERMISSIONS

The Permissions section allows you to control how group members can post new content. I recommend setting the Permissions to the first setting, Free to post (discussions, promotions, jobs, and comments), as you can see in Figure 18-2. When the group is just starting you don't want to frustrate users by limiting their access. If they create a new discussion or want to comment on a current discussion, they want to see their content immediately. If they have to wait for the group manager to approve discussions or comments, they will get frustrated and limit their participation.

I see no reason to ever change this setting because everyone in your group is a professional. If someone is posting inappropriate discussions or comments, the group manager should address the offending member and remove them from the group if they continue violating the group rules.

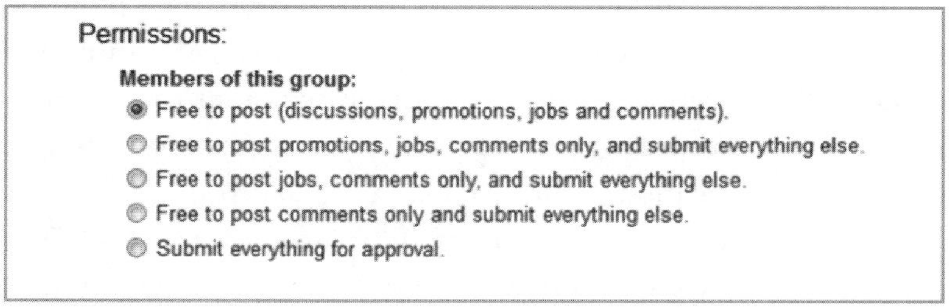

FIGURE 18-2. Group Permissions

RESTRICTIONS

You have the ability to temporarily moderate new group members, new LinkedIn members, and members with few or no connections who are usually spammers. Figure 18-3 on page 156 shows your options as a moderator.

If someone is new to LinkedIn or has few or no LinkedIn connections, I wouldn't approve their membership to the group because they wouldn't be able to provide much value. Once they become established on LinkedIn, they would understand how groups work and be able to contribute. The only time I would admit a person who just joined LinkedIn to my group is if I knew the person, or if that person was recommended by someone I trusted.

MEMBERSHIP

You have two membership options with your group. You can automatically approve all members if you want your group open to everyone, or you can keep your group closed so everyone has to be approved.

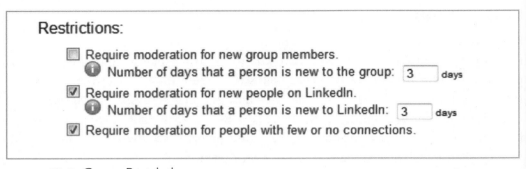

FIGURE 18–3. Group Restrictions

From my experience, open groups that serve large audiences can become unfocused if the group manager or moderator doesn't participate actively. Even when the group manager is an active participant, it can be hard to keep thousands of group members focused on the group topics. A good group manager can keep the group focused on her topic by starting new discussions, featuring popular discussions that are relevant to the group, and privately contacting members who are posting discussions that are off-topic. It also helps to have multiple moderators for a large, open group.

If you are starting a group that you know will be large, it's much easier to keep the group open so you don't have to manually approve every member. If you are starting a group for a popular product such as Adobe Photoshop, you know the group will be large, active, and focused. Products like Photoshop have many highly engaged online communities where users ask questions and get support from other Photoshop users and moderators from Adobe.

Currently, the Adobe Photoshop group on LinkedIn has more than 40,000 members. It adds almost 500 new members every week and averages more than 10 new discussions and 100 comments per week, making it a fairly active community. Since it's an open group, the group manager can focus on moderating discussions and promoting the group, instead of manually approving new members.

Starting the Discussions

The discussions in product-related communities are amazingly focused and on topic. You don't see many people asking questions about other Adobe products or competitors' products in the Photoshop communities because the members are knowledgeable enough to keep the discussions focused. If someone does start a discussion that is not relevant to the group, a group member or moderator will often respond to that member and suggest a better place to post that question. These communities are often self-policing and self-supporting, which makes the community much stronger and more vibrant.

Closed groups by nature will be smaller and more focused, since every member is manually approved by the group manager or moderator. You usually don't have as many new discussions or comments, but the discussions are very focused. You also have a small community of experts who are very knowledgeable about specific products or topics.

Not all closed groups are small and focused. For example, the Media Professionals Worldwide group is closed, but they have more than 161,000 very active members. The group averages almost 600 new discussions and more than 300 comments every week. The group also adds almost 2500 new members every week.

It's up to you to decide if your group will be open or closed. You can start your group open and close it anytime you want or vice versa. Groups often start out open or closed and later decide to switch. Here are some questions that may help you decide how to structure your group:

- What is your group's purpose (i.e., building loyalty, providing support, networking)?
- Is your product or service mainstream or is it a niche product/service?
- How many members do you estimate your group will have? If your company has 2,000 current customers, you wouldn't expect your group to have 10,000 members.
- How many group managers or moderators will you have?
- How many new discussions and comments per week do you expect?
- How fast do you expect your group to grow?
- How are you promoting your group?

There are a lot of factors that come into play when deciding how to structure your group, and it's imperative that you have a plan and a goal before you begin. The reputation of you and your company are on the line when you create a group; if it's unfocused or unmanaged, it will reflect poorly on you.

Identify the purpose of your group, allocate resources, and create a detailed plan, so your group will thrive and provide value to your company.

Group Membership Options

When creating your group, you always want it to be listed in the Groups Directory unless you are creating an exclusive, private group for your customers. Also allow members to display the logo of your group in their profiles to help promote your group in LinkedIn. Your Membership options are displayed in Figure 18–4 on page 158.

After you configure your group settings, make sure you add some valuable content and information before you promote the group. Get some co-workers and a few of your

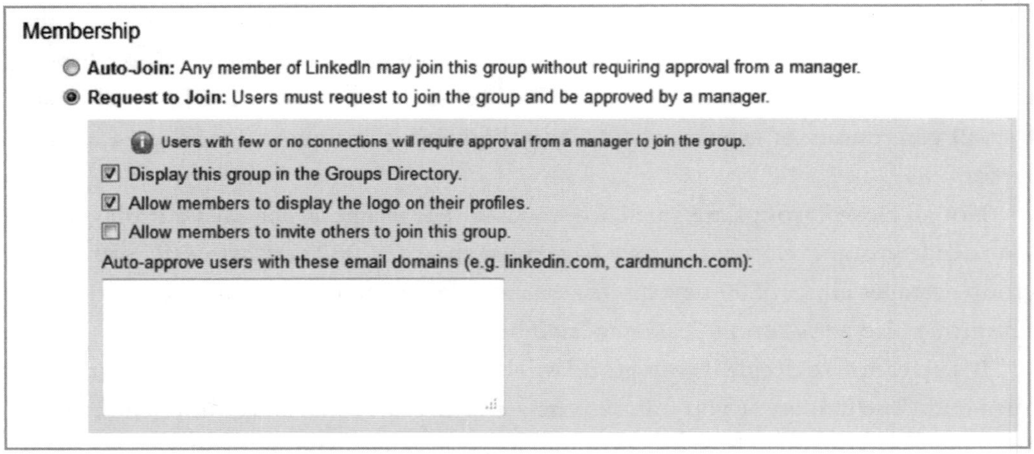

FIGURE 18–4. Group Membership

better customers to join the group and ask them to start some discussions and comment on each other's discussions. You want to show some activity and quality content before you start promoting your group. If you invite people to join your group and there are no active discussions, they probably will not join.

Using an RSS feed, you can automatically populate your group with a steady stream of content from your blog or an industry news blog. Use the "Manage news feeds" feature to add the RSS feeds for your blog or other blogs to the News section. New posts will become automatically available to the members of your group for reading and discussion. Once you are getting enough content from your members, you may want to remove the feed and manually update the news section with a variety of content.

Once you show some activity and quality discussions, you can start promoting the group by inviting your network to join. Have your co-workers invite their network, too. If you feature some of your customers in the group discussions, they'll likely join the group and promote it to their customers.

Promoting the Group

Once you've seeded the group with some stimulating conversations, you can start promoting the group to your network and through social media. Never, ever send group invitations using the Send Invitations tool under Manage Group. This tool looks useful—it allows you to send a mass email invitation to your entire network and to contacts outside of LinkedIn—but it's not a good idea. When you send a mass, automated invitation the recipient may not remember how you are connected and

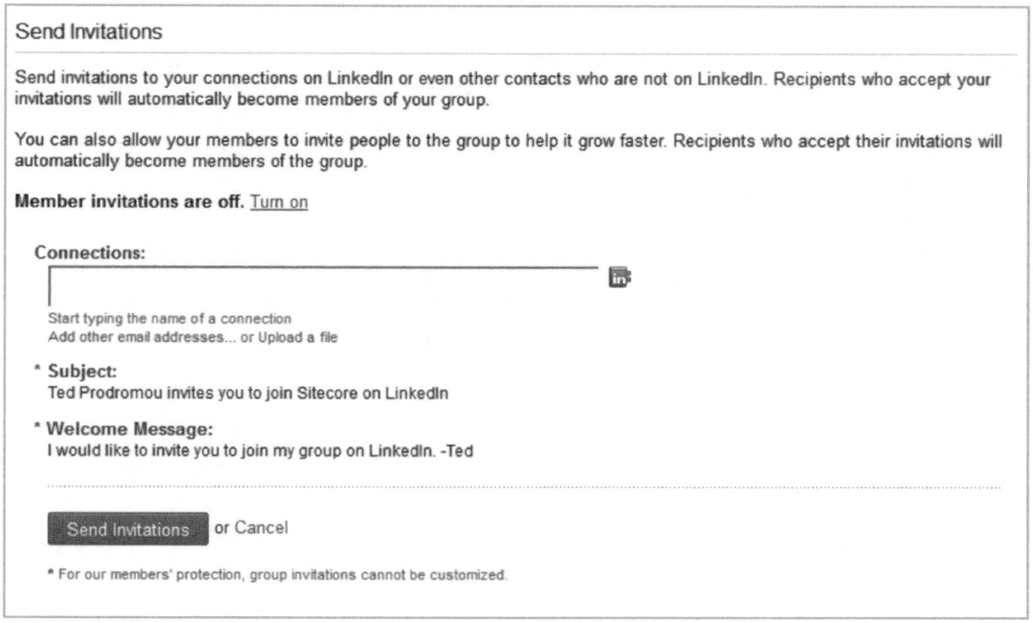

Send Invitations

Send invitations to your connections on LinkedIn or even other contacts who are not on LinkedIn. Recipients who accept your invitations will automatically become members of your group.

You can also allow your members to invite people to the group to help it grow faster. Recipients who accept their invitations will automatically become members of the group.

Member invitations are off. Turn on

Connections:

Start typing the name of a connection
Add other email addresses... or Upload a file

* **Subject:**
Ted Prodromou invites you to join Sitecore on LinkedIn

* **Welcome Message:**
I would like to invite you to join my group on LinkedIn. -Ted

[Send Invitations] or Cancel

* For our members' protection, group invitations cannot be customized.

FIGURE 18–5. Send Group Invitations

how they would benefit by joining your group. Also the automated invitation is very impersonal as you can see in Figure 18–5.

The best way to invite others to join your group is by sending an invitation with a personal message to let them know who you are and why you want them to join the group. Figure 18-5 shows the Send Invitations Wizard with the Subject and Welcome Message, which you cannot edit.

Make sure "Member invitations are off." If you turn this feature on, your group members can send automated invitations to their network and all recipients are automatically added to the group.

You can easily lose control of who is added to your group if you allow your members to invite others using the automated tool.

It is acceptable to encourage your group members to invite their friends to join the group, if they use personalized messages. You will then be able to approve or decline new invitations as you see fit.

If you want to grow your group quickly, you can start promoting it via social media. You can Tweet links to your group, post an invitation on your Facebook wall, and blog about your new group. Encourage people to join your group and invite their friends. You can also run ads on LinkedIn to promote your group. I'll show you how to create effective LinkedIn ads in Chapters 21 and 22.

MANAGING THE GROUP

Consistent group management is really the key to a strong group. LinkedIn provides a powerful toolkit of resources to help managers facilitate their groups and members. A good manager will use the LinkedIn group management tools to monitor, facilitate, and grow their group.

I highly recommend creating rules for your group and posting them under Group Rules and in a Featured Discussion in your LinkedIn group. Establishing the guidelines for posting and displaying them prominently are easy ways to help new members get acquainted with your group. Such guidelines generally provide users with community contacts, encourage them to post only relevant information, and specify conduct that can get them banned. (These include items such as spamming, excessive self-promotion, verbally abusing other group members, and other rules that will keep your group safe for all members.)

Here is an example of a well-crafted Group Rules from The Recruiter LinkedIn Group:

> *The Recruiter LinkedIn group is managed by Recruiter.com, the global recruitment platform. Join Recruiter to network with recruiters, find jobs and find recruiters, and connect with both corporate recruiters and recruitment agencies.*
>
> *http://www.Recruiter.com*
>
> *The Recruiter LinkedIn group is the largest group on LinkedIn for recruiters. In order to maintain a quality forum and resource for the recruitment industry, we ask that you read and follow these four easy rules:*
>
> 1. *Share only discussions that are related to recruiting and the general recruitment industry. Linking to your own blog or articles is ok, if it's highly relevant to recruiting and HR.*
>
> 2. *Post jobs in the jobs area only—please make sure they are "real" jobs.*
>
> 3. *Promotions are fine, as long as they are placed in the promotions area and are highly relevant to the Recruiter group.*
>
> 4. *Lastly, be kind to one another and don't get personal, even when involved in a heated debate.*
>
> *Members that violate these rules will have their Recruiter membership revoked without notice.*
>
> *Thank you and enjoy the group!*
>
> *Recruiter.com*

As you see, the rules of the group are clear and simple. If you violate the rules, you will be removed from the group. This is a great example you can use to create the rules for your LinkedIn Group.

When a new member is added to your group, LinkedIn automatically emails them the Group Rules. If someone violates those of a group I'm running, I send the person a copy of the group rules and point out how they are violating them. If they continue to commit violations, I remove them from the group and block them from being able to reapply for membership.

As a group manager, you also have the responsibility of getting discussions started and helping to keep them going. This requires that you actively follow the conversations within your group, so you can promote the popular discussions using the Manager's Choice feature if you feel they are stimulating conversations.

A great way to encourage group discussions is to feature members who are top contributors. When group members see others being recognized as top contributors, they'll want to be recognized as well and will start participating more. LinkedIn also shows a graph in the sidebar, showing the group who is contributing the most. The graph is like a public scoreboard so everyone knows the top contributors at all times.

LinkedIn has a new moderation toolkit that helps you moderate the group discussions in the following ways:

- Managers and moderators can now delete inappropriate posts right from their email box using the new option "Send me an email for each new discussion" in More > My Settings.
- Managers and moderators can now delete inappropriate comments right from their email box by clicking "Delete" within any followed-discussion email alert.
- Members can also flag items as inappropriate, which will then enter the moderation queue; or, if you choose, as manager you can delete the content outright after members have created a number of flags. You can adjust the number of flags required to move an item to the moderation queue. You can adjust this in your Group Settings, under Manage, Group Settings in the Enable the Discussions and News features section.
- The moderation queue will allow group managers to decide how many member flags can delete a thread or a comment.
- Managers can now restrict the Move-to-Jobs capability to themselves. Users will still be able to "Flag-as-job" to move an item into the moderation queue.
- Very-low-connection users will now be flagged as such in groups' request-to-join queues.
- Very-low-connection users will no longer be admitted directly to open-access groups, but routed to the groups' request-to-join queues.

Excessive Self-Promotion

One of the biggest complaints about LinkedIn Groups is when members join simply to promote themselves or their business. Every discussion they start or comment on comes off as a self-promotion. They aren't showing an interest in engaging with others, which can have a negative impact on your community.

One way to manage self-promoters is by creating a Subgroup for group members to promote their service offerings. Members are only allowed to post self-promotions and service offerings in this subgroup. This keeps the low-quality content away from the main discussion area, ensuring that your group discussions are useful to your members.

Group Etiquette

Most LinkedIn members joined to expand their professional network, gain social influence, and increase the visibility of their business. For this reason, people generally follow the rules of groups in order to present a professional image to their peers and prospects. As group manager you are empowered to resolve difficulties with any members who decide they do not want to follow the rules. You need to act quickly to resolve issues and ensure that your members have an enjoyable experience as a part of your LinkedIn group.

As group manager, you set the tone for the discussions on your group. If you do not want to see a certain kind of language used in the discussions, you need to make it clear in the group rules that it will not be tolerated. The ideal tone of discussions within a group—especially business-related—should be professional. Most of the time this is the case, but there will be occasional exceptions. If you see inappropriate conduct in your group, remove the post immediately and contact the offender. Explain why his post was offensive and remove him from your group if he refuses to obey the rules.

CONCLUSION

Remember: The image of your group reflects directly upon you and your company. You need to maintain a high standard and maintain a high-quality reputation for you and your company.

If you are not the group manager, it is also important to respect the role of the group manager. If both group managers and members follow the rules of social etiquette, the LinkedIn group experience can be rewarding for all.

In the next chapter, I'll show you how to use LinkedIn to recruit new employees for your company.

Recruiting
New Employees

LinkedIn has become a gold mine for recruiting firms and in-house recruiters. Nowhere else can they find more than 150 million business professionals in one place prominently displaying their job experience, skills, education, recommendations, and expertise. A simple search on LinkedIn can give them multiple qualified candidates in seconds. As LinkedIn grows, the available talent pool multiplies, allowing companies to pick and choose from among the very best business professionals in the world. No longer is a talent search limited to your local area.

Recruiting new employees isn't limited to searching for unemployed professionals or recent graduates entering the workforce. According to a survey from The Adler Group, 18 percent of employed professionals are active candidates pursuing a new opportunity. Another 60 percent of all employed professionals are open to listening to new opportunities. That means 78 percent of all employed professionals are willing to listen to you if you have an interesting opportunity for them. Knowing that fact, you have a pretty good chance of landing some quality candidates for your open positions. Don't they call it "shooting fish in a barrel" when the odds are stacked in your favor?

Knowing that up to 78 percent of all employed professionals are willing to listen to your opportunity, how can you find these candidates?

When you do find them, how can you narrow your search to approach the very best candidates?

In Chapter 8 we covered LinkedIn Search and Advanced Search in great detail. Let's take a moment to refresh your memory on LinkedIn Advanced Search, so you'll know how to find your ideal candidates in seconds.

Let's say you are an in-house recruiter at a biotech firm and you are looking for a director of quality to create, implement, and oversee quality systems in your company. You minimum job requirements are:

1. Minimum eight years of experience in quality assurance for a human or animal drug company
2. Substantial knowledge of cGMP requirements for multiple dosage forms along with prior experience in supplier qualification.
3. Additional experience in GDPs and/or GLPs (preferred)
4. Excellent communicator and team player with the ability to proactively address and lead resolution of compliance issues internally and with external partners and contractors
5. Willingness to travel

I have no idea what most of these requirements mean, but I'm sure they are key skills for a director of quality in a biotech firm.

So let's go to LinkedIn Advanced Search and find some candidates. On the right side of your LinkedIn toolbar or menu, make sure you are set to People Search. Click on the Advanced link, which is next to the magnifying glass to the right of the search box. For this search we want to modify the search parameters as follows:

1. In the Title field, enter "Director of Quality" if you are looking for someone who currently holds that position or held that position in the past. You can change the dropdown to choose Current or Past.
2. Change the Industries from All Industries to just Biotechnology.
3. Change Seniority Level to Director. This option is only available to LinkedIn Premium members, so I highly recommend upgrading your account if you are going to use LinkedIn for recruiting.
4. Leave all the other options at their default settings.

Figure 19–1 on page 165 shows you what your Advanced Search should look like to get your first pass search results. If you want to narrow your search to your local area, you can change the Location to your local area or within 50, 100, or 150 miles of your location.

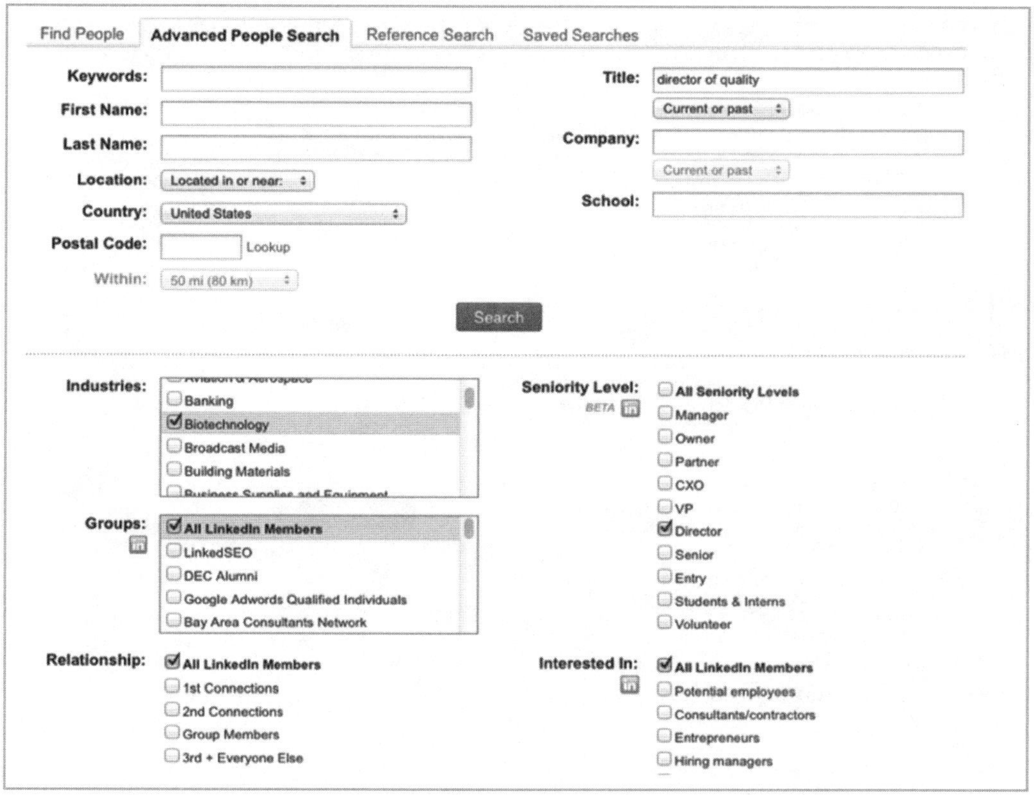

FIGURE 19–1. Advanced People Search

Of course, you can modify your search parameters to narrow or widen your search, but take a look at these preliminary search results. As you see in Figure 19–2 on page 166, you have a list of 976 directors in the biotech field with just one search! Not all of these people are looking for a job, but I bet at least a few of them would be open to listening to a new opportunity if the situation sounded interesting.

Before we start reaching out to some of these directors, let's narrow our search a bit to see if we can find better-qualified candidates. Remember: Your qualifications included 8+ years of experience and substantial knowledge of cGMP requirements for multiple dosage forms, so let's add "cGMP" to our search criteria in the Keywords field.

Now we have only 37 candidates, which is much better than digging through 976 candidates. The next step is to start looking at the profiles of these remaining prospects to see if they are actively looking for work, which would be displayed in the profile headline. You can also look near the bottom of their profile where it says "Contact *name*

FIGURE 19–2. Biotech Search Results

for:"; one of the options is Career Opportunities. You can add or remove the reasons for people to contact you in your Profile Settings. Select Edit Profile under the Profile tab on the LinkedIn menu and scroll down the page until you come to the "Contact *name* for:" section and Edit to change your preferences.

If your search returns some LinkedIn members who are interested in Career Opportunities, you have a few options:

■ You can send them an InMail to introduce yourself. Don't start out by asking them if they are looking for a new position or you may scare them away—even though their profiles say they're interested in Career Opportunities. Tell them you came across their profile on LinkedIn and saw something that caught your attention. Find something unique, like an award they won, interesting certifications, schools they attended, etc. You can ask them about these things or congratulate them. Try to establish a relationship, so you can get to know them and see if they are a fit for your organization. If you mention things you have in common they will be more apt to respond to you.

■ Find Groups they belong to and join that Group, so you can reach out to them by sending them a message. At the beginning of your message state that you both belong to the same group and you thought they may be interested in an opportunity at your company. If you are a recruiter, I highly recommend joining groups related to your industry (such as in biotech) and participate frequently so people become familiar with your name. If they see your name regularly in the forum, they are more likely to respond to your messages even if they've never corresponded with you in the past. This is a very effective and inexpensive way for small businesses to recruit new employees.

■ If they are a second-degree connection of yours, find out whom in your network is a first-degree connection between you and ask for an introduction. You can also ask your first-degree connection what they think of that person to help determine if they would be a good fit for your company.

■ If they are part of the LinkedIn OpenLink Network, you can send them a regular message without having to use an InMail. People who are members of the Open-Link Network are open to people reaching out to them with job opportunities. As I've said many times before, you joined LinkedIn to be found, so take full advantage of all the tools available to gain more visibility. Most people join LinkedIn to be found so they can grow their professional network. Unless your company requires you to limit the visibility of your profile, I highly recommend being as visible as possible. No matter how happy you are at your current job, there are always bigger and better opportunities out there, so be open to the possibility and let LinkedIn help you!

In Chapter 9, "Getting Found on LinkedIn," we went into great detail about the importance of keywords when searching on LinkedIn and how to find the best ones. Now is a good time to review that section of the chapter and create a list of keywords that will help you find your ideal candidates. Once you create a search demographic that returns quality candidates, don't forget to save the search in Saved Searches, so you can use it over and over to fill open positions.

TIPS TO HELP YOUR RECRUITING EFFORT

For great recruiting tips, have a look at the LinkedIn recruiting blog at http://talent. linkedin.com/blog. The various LinkedIn blogs teach you more about the solutions LinkedIn provides and new features and tools as they are released. LinkedIn does a great job communicating and teaching on their blogs. Here is a summary of some recruiting tips from various blog posts:

■ If you are the recruiter looking for talent on LinkedIn, make sure your own profile is in order. Check to see that your profile is 100 percent complete, including your three recommendations. When you reach out to candidates, they are going to check out your profile to get to know you and your company, so you want to give a great first impression.

- Make sure the employees in your company complete their profiles, including their recommendations. When a candidate researches your organization, you want to present a professional image from top to bottom. It also makes a great impression on a candidate when they see a lot of recommendations on your employees' profiles. Encourage your teams to get as many glowing recommendations as possible so your candidates see that your company hires only top-notch employees. Make sure your employees get a variety of recommendations from past and current positions, not just from current co-workers, which can look suspicious.

- Create a company page on LinkedIn and fill it out completely. Active candidates will visit your company page to get to know your company and its culture. You can set up a company page for free or invest in a Premium account in order to add additional features to your company page. Learn more about LinkedIn company pages at http://learn.linkedin.com/company-pages/overview/.

- Join Groups related to your business and industry. Be an active participant and have other employees of your company do the same. When someone sees a lot of employees from one company engaged in stimulating discussions in LinkedIn Groups, they will get a good impression of your company and the quality of your employees.

- Search LinkedIn Alerts, Groups, Answers, and Profiles to find the best candidates. Use the Advanced LinkedIn Search features when you can and save your best search templates in Saved Searches. Again, if you are recruiting new employees on a regular basis, invest in a Premium LinkedIn account so you can save your searches in the Saved Search of your profile.

- All these tips are effective whether you are an in-house recruiter or work for a staffing firm. You always want to be on the lookout for quality candidates and keep your pipeline full. The key to success is consistency—whether it's searching through profiles, Groups, Answers, or Companies, or building your LinkedIn professional network—so you are always just one invitation away from a candidate or hiring manager. As a recruiter, you want to build your network as large as possible to help cast a wider net that is less focused than the network a business professional would build. It's all about quantity when you are recruiting, but you also want to build a network of quality contacts who can send you referrals or introduce you to potential candidates.

LINKEDIN RECRUITING SOLUTIONS

LinkedIn also has a number of paid solutions for companies who do a lot of recruiting and for staffing agencies. The LinkedIn Recruiting Options include:

- LinkedIn Recruiter Corporate Edition
- Recruiter Professional Services
- Referral Engine
- Talent Direct
- The Jobs Network
- Jobs for You
- LinkedIn Career Pages
- Work With Us
- Recruitment Ads
- Recruitment Insights

Now you see why LinkedIn has become the premier place to post your jobs, track down the best candidates, and find a job when you're looking for new opportunities. Let's explore these premium options in more detail, so you can see how they can help you build a premier organization with the very best employees.

LINKEDIN RECRUITER CORPORATE EDITION

This premium subscription is designed for corporate recruiters in large companies who are constantly searching for the best talent. Some of the benefits of the LinkedIn Recruiter Corporate Edition subscription include:

- You get unlimited access to names and full profiles of potential candidates. When you search for talent using your free LinkedIn account, you won't see the full profile of many LinkedIn members and the number of search results is limited. With this subscription you will see the complete profile of every LinkedIn member and up to 1000 search results, which is a huge advantage over your competitors who aren't using this premium-recruiting package.
- You receive Advanced Search Features that are not included in the free version of LinkedIn Advanced Search. With the LinkedIn Recruiter Corporate Edition subscription, you can filter your searches by Industry, Company Size, Education, Company, Years in Position, and Years of Experience. This lets you find the ideal candidates for your open positions.
- You can contact candidates directly using InMail. You receive 50 InMails per month per seat to contact any candidate you like in the trusted LinkedIn

environment. When you send an InMail and it isn't answered within seven days, you get the InMail credited back to your account. In other words, this is like having 50 replies to your InMails per month guaranteed. This is a great benefit because InMails have proven to have very high response rates since LinkedIn is such a trusted professional network. Being able to contact up to 50 prospective candidates per month is a tremendous boost to your recruiting efforts.

■ You can receive up to 50 search alerts per day when you are targeting candidates for an open position. This means you can queue up searches for specific jobs and you will be automatically alerted when a prospective candidate is found. You can quickly reach out to this candidate before your competition, giving you a huge advantage. You can also send 1-to-Many InMails using saved InMail templates, enabling you to contact more candidates faster. Finding the best talent is about beating your competitors to the punch, and these LinkedIn tools help you automate many of your recruiting functions, freeing you up to personally reach out to a greater number of people.

■ You can use shared Project Folders to stay on top of each search. When you have a team of recruiters working together to source candidates, these tools help the recruiters coordinate their searches and eliminate duplicate efforts. Team members get visibility into their colleagues' projects, notes, and communication history with candidates, increasing the efficiency of your recruiting team.

■ You can set reminders on specific profiles so you can follow up with candidates of interest in a timely manner. Without these automated tools, you might forget to follow up with key candidates and lose them to another recruiter.

■ The sourcing activity and history of a recruiter does not disappear when they leave your company. You can just reassign their activity to another team member. LinkedIn Recruiting subscriptions also support your OFCCP compliance efforts.

■ You are assigned your own account manager to help you get the most from your subscription. You also receive help from LinkedIn training experts who will help you get the most from LinkedIn.

RECRUITER PROFESSIONAL SERVICES

This package is designed for professional staffing or recruiting firms. It is very similar to the LinkedIn Recruiter Corporate Edition package with a few differences that benefit outside recruiters. Many of the features of this package enable your recruiting teams to work together and function more efficiently. The features of the Recruiter Professional Services subscription include:

- Your team's sourcing activity is tied to your company's Recruiter license, including saved profiles, notes, jobs, and InMail history. This lets your team share information so they are more efficient and don't duplicate efforts. You can access a team member's activity if they leave your firm and you can reassign the intelligence to other team members.

- You can see more profile information than LinkedIn members with free accounts or lower-tiered paid accounts. You'll see first and last names on all profiles within your third-degree network, unlike most other LinkedIn members. You'll also gain access to expanded profiles across the entire network so you know more about potential candidates.

- You receive the very best search tools available on LinkedIn. You can dig very deep into the LinkedIn database using the free version of Advanced Search, but with this subscription you can dig even deeper. The advanced filters let you narrow your search results down to criteria such as Industry, Company Size, Education, Company, Years in Position, and Years of Experience, which saves you a lot of time when you're searching for candidates for your open positions. Most of the time employers are looking for very specific job skills and experience, and using these advanced search filters lets you find qualified candidates quickly and efficiently.

- Just like the LinkedIn Recruiter Corporate Edition package, you can contact candidates directly using InMail. The same rules apply in this package. You receive 50 InMails per month per recruiting team member to contact any candidate you like in the trusted LinkedIn environment. When you send an InMail and it isn't answered within seven days, you get the InMail credited back to your account. In other words, this is like having 50 replies to your InMails per month guaranteed. This is a great benefit because InMails have proven to have very high response rates since LinkedIn is such a trusted professional network. Being able to contact up to 50 perspective candidates per month is a tremendous boost to your recruiting efforts.

- You can empower your team to work faster and smarter using the 1-to-Many InMails. Using your saved templates to send 1-to-Many InMails helps you contact more candidates faster. You also receive up to 50 daily search alerts that notify your team when new candidates who fit your exact requirements are found by the automated LinkedIn searches. Finding qualified candidates and contacting them in a timely manner gives you a huge advantage over your competition.

- You receive unlimited project folders, so you can manage your pipeline as a team. Everyone has access to the team data so everyone knows the hot open positions and who the hot candidates are. You can set reminders on the profiles of the top candidates to follow up at the right time.

- Team collaboration is a breeze when you use Saved Profiles in shared project folders. The shared project folders let all recruiting team members see more names and full profiles. These easy-to-use collaboration tools keep your team on the same page with the shared searches, profiles, notes on candidates, and communication history. Your team can work more effectively, even if they're not in the same office, by accessing your shared project folders remotely. For example, if you find a talented candidate who is not quite right for one job, you can look at colleagues' open projects for a better fit.
- Your dedicated account manager and LinkedIn training experts will help you become a master at finding the best candidates on LinkedIn.

REFERRAL ENGINE

The LinkedIn Referral Engine is a new option for the LinkedIn Recruiting Solutions packages. The idea behind the Referral Engine is unique because it's designed to let your current employees know about your current job openings and in turn they can refer qualified candidates, if they know of any. The concept centers on the idea that if an employee isn't aware your company is looking for someone with a specific skill set, the employee can't refer anyone. It makes perfect sense, given that many companies don't proactively notify their employees when there are new openings.

Let's look at how the Referral Engine works. Your company has a new opening for a chief marketing officer and your in-house recruiter posts the job on the Referral Engine. At that point the Referral Engine notifies your employees on LinkedIn about the new job opening. The employee can then search her LinkedIn networks to see if one of her contacts is a match for the job. If one is found, she can contact that potential candidate to see if she is interested in the position. If she is interested in the CMO position, the employee can refer the person to the in-house recruiter.

This automated approach helps employers find word-of-mouth referrals quickly, which helps fill positions quicker with well-qualified candidates. Word-of-mouth candidates are usually the best, since there is a personal connection between the candidate and the referring employee. This is a win-win for the company and the employee, since many companies offer financial incentives to employees when they refer qualified candidates who end up getting hired.

TALENT DIRECT

Talent Direct is a "done for you" sourcing service from LinkedIn. Instead of you searching for qualified candidates and reaching out to them via InMail, LinkedIn does it all for you. Here's how it works:

1. Give LinkedIn the attributes of your perfect candidate, including your recruitment message. LinkedIn uses their unique targeting capabilities to find the best candidates. LinkedIn targets candidates using the same advanced search criteria you would use if you were to manually perform an Advanced Search. LinkedIn searches for your candidates using the title, seniority, industry, company, region, job function, and other specified search criteria. You create the message LinkedIn sends out to attract top talent and let them know about your opportunities.

2. LinkedIn sets up and launches your InMail campaign using the message you create to attract your ideal candidates. LinkedIn members receive your message, which is displayed prominently at the top of their LinkedIn homepage. InMail messages have a high open rate, so there is a good chance your message will be received by many qualified candidates.

3. You get highly qualified leads because of the advanced targeting used by LinkedIn. You can create an active talent pipeline for existing and future opportunities, as well as for building lasting relationships with desirable candidates. Letting LinkedIn do the targeting for you ensures you get the best candidates for your openings.

THE JOBS NETWORK

The LinkedIn Jobs Network is the fastest-growing job network on the internet. Nowhere else on the internet can recruiters find more highly qualified candidates for their open positions. For job seekers, targeted jobs are displayed on the sidebar of their LinkedIn homepage and other LinkedIn pages as they browse LinkedIn Answers or participate in Groups. LinkedIn scans your current and previous job titles, companies you've worked for, and the keywords in your profile to automatically match you up with potential jobs. These targeted jobs are displayed in your sidebar in the Jobs You May Be Interested In widget, as shown in Figure 19–3 on page 174.

As I mentioned earlier, an average of 18 percent of employed workers are actively looking for a new job. Another 60 percent of employed workers are willing to listen to new opportunities even though they aren't actively looking for a new job. By using the LinkedIn Job Board, companies can expand their search for candidates to passive candidates using the Jobs You May Be Interested In widget. Letting LinkedIn members see what other opportunities are out there in a subtle manner catches their eye so they explore the new opportunities. This creates a phenomenon where your job postings find the best candidates instead of putting the burden on your recruiters.

With job openings constantly but subtly being displayed on the LinkedIn sidebar, we can't help but notice and become curious when we see certain job titles or companies

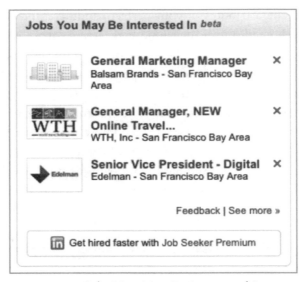

FIGURE 19–3. Jobs You May Be Interested In

we may want to work for. It's sort of like subliminal advertising in a way, because the jobs don't appear in the center of our screen; however, they are just off to the side enough that we notice them out of the corner of the eye. As we see jobs that may interest us, we click on them to see if any of them are interesting enough to investigate further. If we aren't interested but we know a friend or colleague who may be interested, we can forward the job to her LinkedIn InBox—assuming she is a LinkedIn connection—or we can share the job opening on Facebook and Twitter. This gives companies a huge benefit by allowing their job openings to go viral on the internet, at no additional cost to the company who posted the job opening. Your job openings can be seen by millions of people on LinkedIn, Facebook, and Twitter, increasing the chances you will find an outstanding candidate.

Companies that post jobs in the LinkedIn Jobs Network have the ability to measure the impact of their job postings through LinkedIn's job analytics. The LinkedIn job analytics is the equivalent of Google Analytics for your websites. When you use Google Analytics to monitor your website, you learn how many visitors you have, how long they stay, what pages they visited, and what they downloaded or purchased. In addition, you can find detailed demographic information like what country, state, city, or ZIP code they live in. This information is invaluable to a website owner. LinkedIn job analytics helps companies understand exactly which types of candidates your jobs are reaching and lets you see who's viewing your jobs by role, company, geography, and more to ensure you're reaching the best professionals. If you are not reaching the right people with your job postings, you can adjust the title of your open position, change the wording in the job description, or reconfigure whom you are targeting in the job search. Without these analytics, you would only know you are not attracting the right candidates because their skill sets or experience aren't right for your job, but you wouldn't know why the posting is attracting the wrong candidates. Knowing who, when, and where the candidates are coming from will save you a lot of time and help you fill your positions faster with better candidates.

Show Up in LinkedIn Career Pages

In addition to the sidebar widget, your job postings will also appear on the LinkedIn Career Pages, covered more in depth on page 176. You can purchase a recruiting program called the LinkedIn Job Slot, which allows you to do all of the following:

- Change your job posting as often as you like—even daily, if necessary.
- Easily renew and keep a position open on LinkedIn for longer than 30 days.
- Receive up to 50 real-time candidate recommendations per post.
- Streamline the job posting process with integrated third-party job distributors so your job listing gets maximum exposure on the internet.
- Pull job postings from your website into LinkedIn automatically through job wrapping, which is an additional cost. Job wrapping is a proprietary technology created by LinkedIn that automatically keeps your job postings in sync on your website and LinkedIn.
- Send applicants straight to your Applicant Tracking System from LinkedIn. LinkedIn has developed many APIs and plug-ins that let you easily connect your recruiting systems with LinkedIn. You can find out more about the LinkedIn development tools at https://developer.linkedin.com/.
- You can also add a third-party tracking URL to your job posting so you can track your results with your own analytics system. This allows you to easily track the success of your recruiting campaigns.

Jobs for You Web Ads

Jobs for You Web Ads is a LinkedIn service that automatically pushes your jobs to the most qualified candidates, wherever they go online. This lets you distribute your jobs to thousands of websites across the internet, automatically. LinkedIn doesn't provide details how this is done, but it looks like they are using a new technology called *ad retargeting.*

Ad retargeting is a relatively new technology, where you can place an ad on a website that will follow the web visitor for a period of time, usually 30 days. A retargeting ad contains special code that places a cookie in your web browser when the ad is displayed to you on the initial website. You don't have to click on the ad. It just has to be displayed to you in order to have the cookie placed in your browser. The ad reappears automatically on certain websites that you visit over the next thirty days. It appears that the ad is following you, which is what it's doing, but the ads will usually stop following you after 30 days. Retargeting ads will appear only on certain websites that accept banner ads from ad networks, such as Doubleclick or ReTargeter, and will only be re-displayed to you around five to ten times over the 30 days, so you aren't overwhelmed by ads from one company.

As I said earlier, LinkedIn doesn't explain the technical details about how Jobs for You Web Ads works, but here's a stab at explaining how it works:

1. You post a job on the LinkedIn Job Network.
2. Select the exact audience you want to target, including job title, seniority, years of experience, skills, education, or any of the other targeting options we described earlier in this chapter.
3. LinkedIn will place LinkedIn-branded ads on external websites that accept banner advertising. The headline of the 300 x 250 pixel ad will say Jobs at *Your Company Name* and will feature your job listings in the ad widget. Your job openings will only be displayed to those candidates who meet your targeting criteria. The ads will follow that candidate and appear periodically on other websites they visit that accept banner ads.

This is a very effective way to reach passive candidates who aren't actively searching for a new position but are open to the possibilities of changing jobs. LinkedIn uses a combination of your targeting criteria and data from a person's LinkedIn profile to display your ads to the most qualified candidates. For example, engineers will see only your engineering jobs, and sales professionals will see only your sales jobs—even if they're reading the sports section of an online newspaper.

LINKEDIN CAREER PAGES

Every organization needs a company page on LinkedIn where you can post company update messages, provide information about your products and services, post job openings and view detailed analytics information about the people who have visited your company page.

Another important feature of company pages is the ability for people to "follow" your company. What is "follow your company," you ask? Following a company on LinkedIn is very similar to clicking the Like button on a company or personal page on Facebook. The more people that Follow you on LinkedIn or Like you on Facebook, the better because it adds credibility to your company.

When someone Follows your company, it lets them keep up-to-date on job opportunities, personnel changes, and new product or services at that company. Once someone Follows your company, any company updates, job openings, or new product announcements posted on your company page will appear automatically on their LinkedIn homepage. It is less intrusive than emailing them to let them know about new developments at your company.

One of LinkedIn's premier recruiting packages is called the Career Page. Subscribing to the Silver or Gold level Career Page subscription provides many enhancements to your company page that will improve your recruiting experience and build a loyal following for your company. Your Career Page, alongside your company profile, is a powerful tool to educate and inform active and passive job candidates. As potential candidates explore your company page to learn more about your company, they will see your current job openings on the same screen. You have the ability to display customized content for each visitor, based on his or her LinkedIn profile data. If a software engineer visits your Career Page, specific content related to software engineers will be displayed, including open positions that the visitor may be qualified for. This targeted content helps convince candidates that you are the right company for them.

Upgrading to the Careers Page will give your more flexibility and let you customize your LinkedIn Company page. Some of the features of the Careers Page include:

- Your messages dynamically adapt to the viewer based on information from their LinkedIn profile.
- Targeted job postings appear for each viewer.
- You can feature employees in the Employees Spotlights module so viewers can get a sense of what type of people work at your company.
- You can add a custom video to your page so viewers get to know your company better.
- You can display a list of benefits of working at your company.
- You can link to additional information on your company website.
- Viewers can contact your recruiters directly.
- You can create three additional customizable modules so viewers can learn more about the culture of your company.

You also have the ability to set up ads that run on LinkedIn to drive people to your company page to learn more about your jobs or products and services. You can also prevent ads from other companies from appearing on your company page if you choose the Gold Careers Page package.

The LinkedIn Career Page can help you position your company as an "employer of choice" by providing insight into your company culture and your community of

"Followers." Candidates are more likely to respond to your recruiting messages when they are familiar with your company and products. The Career Page enhancement also acts a mini-web portal that lets you drive traffic to other vital web destinations, such as your company website, blogs, and social media communities.

WORK WITH US

This is not only one of the simplest LinkedIn recruiting and advertising solutions, it's also one of the most effective. How do you feel when you are looking at the LinkedIn profile of one of your colleagues and you see a huge ad from one of your competitors in the sidebar? Doesn't it drive you crazy when you see your competitors invading your company's space? In the past no one had any control over this, but now we do.

The LinkedIn Work With Us ads let you display your advertising on your employees' profile pages and your company pages. Here's an example of a competitor's ad being displayed on the profile page of one of the founders of our company in Figure 19–4. That's a very effective ad for our competitor, grabbing that much real estate on the profile page of a company founder. When people research companies, they often review the profiles of the founders and executive team so it's important to protect that real estate with your own advertising.

To run Work for Us ads, just contact LinkedIn, provide them your creative material, and they will automatically place your ads on all of your employee profile pages and your company pages. If you are only going to run one marketing campaign on LinkedIn, this is the one you need to do to protect your brand.

Figure 19–5 on page 179 shows you an effective Work for Us ad displaying my name and profile picture as ING Investment's newest employee. These are very effective ads

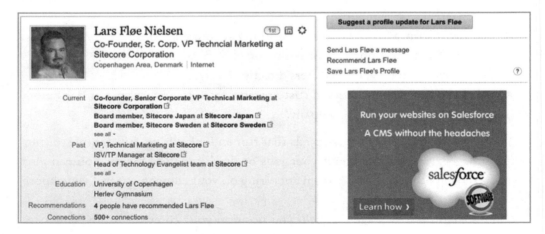

FIGURE 19–4. Competitor's Ad on Employee Profile

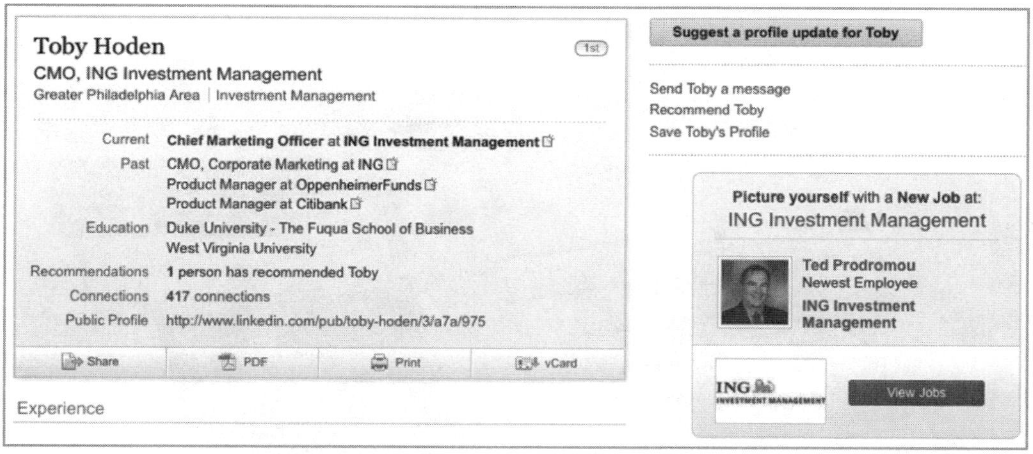

FIGURE 19–5. Work for Us Advertisement

because the potential candidate sees herself as an employee of your company and she can easily browse your job openings to find the job that is right for her.

RECRUITMENT ADS

LinkedIn Recruitment Ads are the large career ads you see in the sidebar of your LinkedIn homepage and on other pages throughout the LinkedIn website. These are 300 x 250 pixel banner ads that are primarily displayed on your homepage, since that is the page that we spend the most time on when we're visiting LinkedIn. See Figure 19–6 on page 180 for an example of a Recruitment Ad in from the LinkedIn website.

As you can see, your ad is prominently displayed on LinkedIn homepages, keeping your company and career opportunities top-of-mind for LinkedIn members actively pursuing new career opportunities. Placing your career opportunities in front of LinkedIn members also helps attract those "not actively looking but open to new opportunities" candidates. It's important to always have a full talent pipeline, so you hire the very best candidates for your company.

LinkedIn Recruitment Ads use the same proprietary ad-targeting algorithm as other LinkedIn advertising options. This ensures your ads are only shown to the appropriate potential candidates. This ability to target your ads with precision gives you a competitive advantage when you are recruiting new employees.

When you are ready to start your LinkedIn Recruitment ad campaign, just describe your perfect hire including the targeting options you desire, send LinkedIn your ad text or banner ad, and they will set up and monitor your ad campaigns. It doesn't get any easier than that!

FIGURE 19–6. Recruitment Ad

RECRUITMENT INSIGHTS

Last but not least, we have Recruitment Insights. How many times did you think your recruiting campaigns were on target but you just weren't attracting the right candidates? Sometimes we're so busy that we get tunnel vision and miss obvious opportunities to improve our recruiting campaigns.

Recruitment Insights is a survey service from LinkedIn that will gather critical data from your target candidates. The survey data will provide you with insights from your target candidates throughout the entire LinkedIn network. Recruitment Insights provides you with valuable data about your potential candidates from a different perspective than you're seeing them. This third-party perspective provides you with many new opportunities to find your ideal candidates.

The survey lets you know which elements of your employment brand matter the most to your target audience. This lets you tailor your messaging so you will attract the very best talent for your company. You can also benchmark your company against your competitors, helping you know where you stand when you are competing for talent.

Recruitment Insights tells you how your recruitment branding campaigns affect your target audience's perception of your company. It also lets you test your campaign effectiveness and measure your ROI, so you maximize your recruiting efforts. Benchmarking your recruiting efforts by yourself is very difficult because you are too close to your own processes. You really need an independent, unbiased assessment of your recruiting efforts to give you the information you need to know what you are doing right and what needs improvement.

The Recruitment Insights survey process is as follows:

1. Define the attributes of your perfect hire. We've seen this many times before. LinkedIn's unique targeting capabilities let you survey your ideal candidate. You can target your candidates by title, seniority, industry, company, region, job function, and more. LinkedIn then surveys a random sample of your ideal target audience.

2. LinkedIn works with you to create a survey that benchmarks your recruiting efforts against your competitors'. The survey also gathers data from your potential candidates so you know exactly what they think of your company and your recruiting efforts.

3. LinkedIn provides a custom report with the detailed insights about your target candidates. This report will tell you in detail how effective your recruiting campaigns are and how you can improve them.

CONCLUSION

Wow, that was a lot of information! As you see, LinkedIn gives recruiters a lot of tools to make recruiting new employees easier and more effective. No matter how big or small your organization, LinkedIn offers a premium recruiting solution to meet your needs. Of course, you could choose to search for new employees using the free search tools, but the automated solutions from LinkedIn will streamline your recruiting efforts so you can stay ahead of your competition.

In the next chapter, we'll explore LinkedIn for Sales and Marketing Professionals, a premium LinkedIn service designed to help sales professionals generate leads for their companies.

LinkedIn for Sales and Marketing Professionals

I f you're in sales, you have to be licking your chops at the opportunities available to you on LinkedIn. With more than 150 million members and growing at a rate of two new members per second, it's a golden opportunity for all sales professionals. Whether your product has a long or short sales cycle, LinkedIn provides the perfect networking platform that enables you to build lasting relationships with clients and prospects alike. Building and nurturing relationships keeps your sales pipeline full.

Assuming you're a seasoned sales professional, we're not going to get into Sales 101 in this chapter. If you're just getting started in sales or are starting your own business, read everything you can about sales, social networking, and social selling. The internet and social media allow sales professionals to cast a wide net to find new prospects for their products and services, if they know how to use these tools properly. The process of selling hasn't changed, but the tools used to find prospects are evolving rapidly, allowing you to reach more prospects with less effort. If you use the internet and social media to attract new leads but don't do it in a strategic manner, you'll attract lots of leads—but not the right ones that lead to relationships and closed deals.

You are probably already well aware of the importance of building a strong professional network and contact database. In the old days, sales professionals used the Rolodex as their contact "database." I use the term database loosely because the Rolodex was just a device that held specially shaped index cards that stored information about your business contacts in alphabetical order. Each contact had his or her own index card where you wrote their contact information and scribbled reminder notes. If you lost that index card, you lost your contact's information. The Rolodex was bulky and sat on your desk next to your telephone, so when you traveled to visit your prospects and customers, you didn't have access to your contact database.

Obviously times have changed and today we carry our entire contact database on our telephones. Our contact database also resides in our customer relationship system (CRM), which is accessible from any internet connection. With the evolution of LinkedIn we can now create our Rolodex on LinkedIn, which makes it accessible from anywhere. The LinkedIn Mobile app lets us add new contacts and search existing contacts right from our smartphones. Today it's easier than ever to build a large electronic database of prospects and customers. Your challenge is to build a targeted database of prospects because it's easy to fall into the trap of focusing on quantity, rather than quality.

BUILDING YOUR LINKEDIN NETWORK

In Chapter 11, "Connecting with Others," I went into great detail about building your network. Now is a good time to review the different networking strategies, so you can decide which approach is best for you—the sales professional. There is no right or wrong answer when it comes to building your professional network, as there are a lot of variables to consider. Let's review a few LinkedIn networking strategies, discuss the pros and cons of each, and help you decide which one is best for you.

We talked about the different ways to build your professional network. The first option was being an Open Networker, where you connect with everyone who sends you a connection request. This enables you to create a very broad network so you have access to literally millions of connections in your first-, second-, and third-degree connections. Being an Open Networker lets you cast the widest net possible on LinkedIn with access to millions of LinkedIn members through your LinkedIn network. Open Networking is a great option for recruiters, real estate salespeople, and some other sales professionals because you have indirect access to so many LinkedIn members. You are never more than two hops away from literally millions of LinkedIn members. The downside is that your network is unfocused, so you have to spend more time digging through your connections to find specific contacts or skill sets within your network. I'll discuss more of the pros and cons of Open Networking in a little bit.

Your other option is to cast a smaller net, which will bring you fewer opportunities, but a more focused network. The audience will be highly targeted, so it's easier to connect with the right people. Building a small, focused network requires you to carefully review every connection request and vet every person who wants to join your exclusive professional network. This means you may opt to exclude some of your friends if they don't meet your stringent standards.

How big should your network be? As previously stated, studies conclude that it's impossible for a human to effectively manage a network of friends or colleagues if it gets too large. It's possible to effectively communicate with 100 to 150 people on a regular basis and maintain a strong relationship. As your network increases in size, your ability to maintain a strong relationship with your network decreases significantly. If you build a network of 2,000 members on LinkedIn, you will not be able to maintain a strong relationship with everyone because you just don't have enough time.

Does this mean you should stop building your network at 150 members? Maybe. It depends what you are selling and how many people are in your target market. If you are selling a specialty product that is only used by senior bioinformatics scientists that reside in the United States, your target market is very small. It wouldn't make sense to connect with 1,500 other people just for the sake of connecting. Bigger is not always better.

The third option—and the most popular one—is to build a network somewhere in between the niche networker of 100 to 150 contacts and the Open Networker who may have more than 10,000 contacts. While most LinkedIn members have fewer than 500 connections, I see many LinkedIn members with somewhere between 500 and 1,000 connections. The longer you've been in the workforce, the more connections you have. I have more than 600 connections, most of which are current and former colleagues. I don't aggressively try to build my network right now because I'm employed at a company full time and I'm not trying to grow my personal business. If I were in sales, I would constantly be looking for quality connections to expand my LinkedIn network in order to generate more leads.

The Pros and Cons of Different Sized LinkedIn Networks

Should you build a professional network that is small, large, or somewhere in between? It depends on what you are selling, whom you sell to, and how much time you want to spend on LinkedIn managing your network. Being an Open Networker gives you a lot of opportunities to connect with others, but you will have to dedicate at least an hour or two a day accepting connection requests and answering emails from your network. Open Networkers tend to be aggressive networkers, so they are constantly reaching out to their network, beating the bush for new leads.

If you are a recruiter who fills jobs nationally or internationally, you need to build a huge network to keep your pipeline full. You have to be willing to dedicate up to half of your working hours working your LinkedIn network for leads to fill open positions and to find new jobs to post. There is nothing wrong with spending 20 hours a week networking on LinkedIn, if it's your primary source to find job listings and quality candidates.

If you are selling niche products, it probably doesn't make sense for you to spend more than an hour or two a day on LinkedIn, if your target audience is small. You probably have a few key contacts on LinkedIn who can connect you with the right people, and you know which Groups to participate in.

Most sales professionals choose the middle-of-the-road approach. They have their professional network of 500 to 1,000 members, which gives them tremendous access to millions of second- and third-degree connections. They also have their core members of their network, with whom they communicate on a regular basis. It's the old 80/20 rule: 20 percent of their network is most active, providing the majority of their leads and sales, while they occasionally benefit from some leads and sales from the other 80 percent.

Figure 20–1 on page 187 contains a table that describes some of the pros and cons of each style of LinkedIn networking. The optimal size of your LinkedIn network depends on a lot of factors that only you can determine. Every situation is different, so weigh the pros and cons of each networking style and determine which is best for the product or service you sell.

Of course you can change your mind if you choose a style that's not working for you. If you start out as a niche networker, you can easily switch to be an Open Networker or a medium-sized network. The difficult transition is if you begin as an Open Networker and connections with 20,000 other professionals, it's hard to easily reduce the size of your network. It's a long, tedious process removing the connections that are not highly targeted. Some people even close their existing LinkedIn account and start over with a brand-new account and rebuild their network from scratch.

If you think building a smaller, more focused network is the way to go, you'll have to be more selective when connecting with others. There is a fine balance between keeping your network small and focused and also having access to those valuable second- and third-degree connections. Of course, you want to have as much access to second- and third-degree connections, but you don't have time to maintain a huge network of first-degree connections.

Take a look at Figure 20–2 on page 188, which is from my profile. I only have a network of 642 first-degree connections, which is manageable. Next look at what happens at the second and third degree. The amount of potential connections I have access to grows exponentially. Imagine what these numbers would look like if I were an Open Networker. Looking at my numbers, it's easy to see why so many sales professionals are choosing this professional networking strategy.

	Pros	**Cons**
Small Niche Network	1. Targeted audience 2. Less noise/emails from connections 3. Fewer connection requests from people you don't know 4. New connection requests are usually more targeted because you are a niche networker	1. Limited ability to reach 2nd- and 3rd-degree connections 2. You may miss some sales opportunities because you don't have as many 1st-degree connections referring you to new connections
Medium-Sized Network	1. You benefit from having a targeted audience and an extended 2nd- and 3rd-degree audience 2. More opportunities to connect with prospects when you need introductions 3. More opportunities to receive referrals from your network	1. You may be limited when you try to reach out to 3rd-degree connections 2. You may receive a lot of connection requests from strangers or people that don't fit your professional network profile 3. You may receive a lot of unsolicited emails from connections
Open Networking	1. You have a very wide audience to sell to and to help refer you to prospects 2. You have access to millions of 2nd- and 3rd-degree connections 3. You are never more than two hops from millions of prospects	1. Your network is very unfocused so you have to work hard to find targeted prospects 2. You will receive a lot of unsolicited emails from your connections 3. You will have no personal relationship with over 90% of your network so you won't be able to refer them 4. You will receive a lot of requests to Recommend people in your network who you don't know very well

FIGURE 20–1. Pros and Cons of LinkedIn Networking Styles

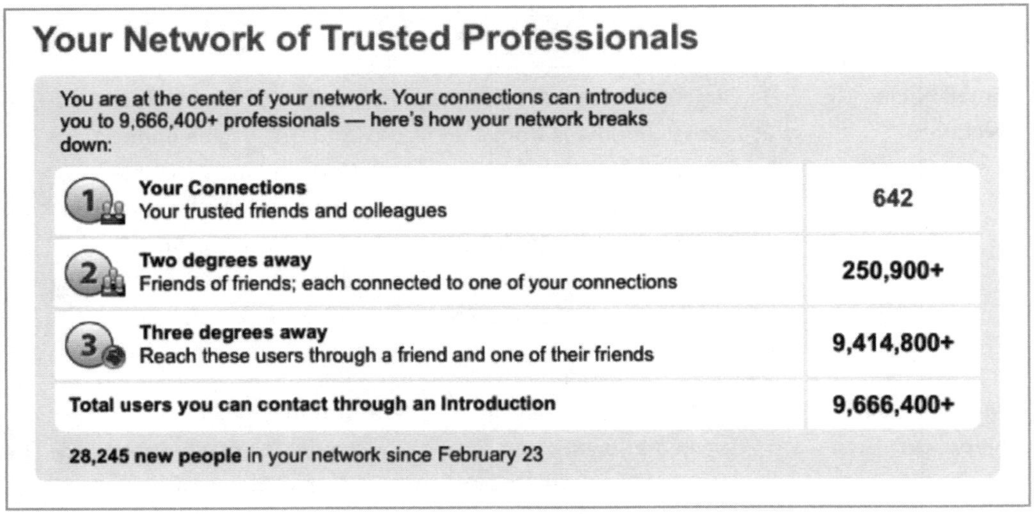

Your Network of Trusted Professionals

You are at the center of your network. Your connections can introduce you to 9,666,400+ professionals — here's how your network breaks down:

1 **Your Connections** Your trusted friends and colleagues		642
2 **Two degrees away** Friends of friends; each connected to one of your connections		250,900+
3 **Three degrees away** Reach these users through a friend and one of their friends		9,414,800+
Total users you can contact through an Introduction		9,666,400+

28,245 new people in your network since February 23

FIGURE 20–2. My Network of Trusted Professionals

As LinkedIn adds two new members every second, I don't have to add anyone to my first-degree connections to expand the potential reach of my second- and third-degree networks. As more of my second- and third-degree connections connect with others, my network is growing exponentially without my lifting a finger. When I started writing this book just two months ago, my third-degree network had around 6 million members. It has grown more than 50 percent in two months and I've only added a handful of first-degree connections.

Also take a look at the statistic at the bottom of Figure 20-2. It says 28,245 new people have joined my network since February 23. I'm writing this chapter on February 24, which means that my network is growing by more than 23,000 new members every day. The growth rate of LinkedIn shows no signs of slowing down, so by the time this book hits the bookstores, my third-degree network could be well over 20 million people. Why would I want to take the time to grow my first-degree network when my second- and third-degree networks are growing like crazy automatically? If and when I need to reach out for new connections, I can easily tap into my second- and third-degree networks to connect with highly targeted connections.

SHOULD YOU GO ANONYMOUS?

I've seen blog posts and articles from LinkedIn experts recommending a technique where you go stealth by creating an anonymous profile and spy on your competitors. I leave it up to you to answer the ethical question. The technique will let you view others' profiles, monitor your competitor's company page and groups, and essentially be an anonymous LinkedIn member. You do this by creating a second LinkedIn account with a fictitious name and lock down your profile, so viewers will only see that Anonymous viewed their profiles. You probably won't be able to join your competitor's groups if they have to approve group memberships, but you can still learn a lot about them. Another technique is where people use fake names, company names, profile information, and even general stock photos as their profile pictures in their stealth accounts to make everything look real.

Again, I'll leave it up to you if you want to use this approach—but personally it's not for me.

LEVERAGING YOUR COMPANY PAGE

Every B2B company should have a LinkedIn company page for many reasons. The obvious reason is that you are a member of the largest and most exclusive business networking site in the world. With more than 150 million members and growing by the second, you have a golden opportunity to get your brand in front of your target audience—for free! In Chapter 7, "LinkedIn for Companies," you learned how to set up and manage your LinkedIn company page. If you didn't set up your company page yet, go back and set one up right now.

Okay, let's assume you now have a LinkedIn company page or you have the right person working on it, so let's get back to the benefits of having a company page and how you can use it to increase your sales. As I mentioned in Chapter 7, your company is accessible to others on the internet even if they aren't a LinkedIn member. Take a look at www.linkedin.com/company/microsoft to see a sample company page. This page is accessible to both LinkedIn members when they are logged into LinkedIn and people who are not LinkedIn members. Your company page also shows up in Google search results, giving your company additional exposure on the internet.

LinkedIn company pages give you the ability to share new product announcements and company news in the Overview section of your company page. You can also recruit the best talent by posting your open positions in the Careers section. The best part of the company page for sales professionals is the Products section. You can feature your top products on this page, which will also show up for both LinkedIn members and non-members. Your customers can write recommendations of your products, building social proof for your company that you can share with your LinkedIn network. If you were selling the Microsoft Dynamics CRM software, you could post links to the product and to the recommendations on your LinkedIn status in your LinkedIn profile and LinkedIn Groups. Here's the link to the Microsoft Dynamics CRM product page so you can see what it looks like: http://www.linkedin.com/company/microsoft/microsoft-dynamics-crm-online-1443/product.

LinkedIn company pages are like mini-websites for your company and your products that you can share with your LinkedIn network. When people see your products and recommendations, they can reach out to you on LinkedIn or visit your website to learn more about your products.

LEVERAGING YOUR COMPANY GROUP

LinkedIn Groups let you build an online community for your company within the larger LinkedIn community. Since most of your customers and prospects are already on LinkedIn, it makes perfect sense to give them access to your Company Group, where they can ask questions, find resources, and get to know your company better. The discussions on your Company Groups can give you insight into what your customers are struggling with and what they want more of. They'll also tell you what they like about your products and they'll even help your other customers by answering their questions.

Sales professionals should always monitor their company's online communities to keep their finger on the pulse of their customers. If customers are complaining about the performance of your product on the discussion board, you can reach out and help them or get the right resources involved to help them out. Being proactive and helping unsatisfied customers is a great way to build strong customer relationships and show prospective customers that your company provides excellent customer service.

PROSPECTING ON LINKEDIN

Imagine having a Rolodex with more than 150 million names of the top business professionals in the world at your fingertips. In addition to the names of every business professional, you have a list of the employees of every major business in the world segmented by the company they work for. You have access to the top employees of companies such as Google, Facebook, IBM, Costco, Target, and every other Fortune 5000 company. If you don't sell to large companies, you have access to thousands of small and medium-sized businesses instead. You even have access to consultants, coaches, and other solo-preneurs who are members of LinkedIn.

Never before has prospecting been so easy for a sales professional. In the past, you would have to purchase lists from list brokers and cold call hundreds and thousands of people. Most of the time you reached the gatekeeper, who would play games with you and maneuver around until you finally got to the decision maker. You spent countless hours on the phone trying to get five minutes of the decision maker's time so you could convince him to meet with you for 15 minutes.

If you weren't purchasing lists, you were scouring the phone book or business directories looking for contact numbers of your target businesses. Prospecting was a lot of hard work and not for the faint of heart. You were essentially a telemarketer being rejected 99 percent of the time when you reached out to prospects.

Today, LinkedIn makes prospecting a lot easier. Using the Advanced Search features, you can find your target audience in seconds. Advanced Search is a fantastic LinkedIn tool, but there are even more ways to find new prospects on LinkedIn. By learning how to use other LinkedIn tools like Answers and Groups, you'll know your prospects' frustrations and hot buttons so you'll know exactly how to approach them and get their attention immediately. People love to use the LinkedIn tools like Answers and Groups to get advice and guidance from their peers.

The key to successfully prospecting on LinkedIn is exactly the same way you network in person. Listen before you talk. You want to get to know a person who is struggling or frustrated and could benefit from your product or service. You'll know how to approach them with your solution when the time is right. The key to success is to hover in the background and observe before reaching out.

Prospecting in LinkedIn Answers

We discussed LinkedIn Answers in great detail in Chapter 14, which means you understand the fundamentals of LinkedIn Answers and how you can use it to demonstrate your expertise. When you answer a lot of questions for people, you can achieve Expert Status in a specific LinkedIn category; once you achieve this you will be regarded as a subject-matter expert by your peers and colleagues.

When you are using LinkedIn Answers for prospecting, you can use the same approach. Be helpful and answer questions so you'll be regarded as an expert on that topic. Remember not to sell your products and services at this point because people will see right through you and think you are just trying to make a sale. You have to be subtle and genuinely interested in helping the person out with no expectation. Once you establish yourself as an expert in your field, it's okay to refer people to your company website for more information—but do it without being sales-y. You can refer people to independent articles that will provide more information or a solution to their problem, or you can suggest they check out an article on your website. Try to phrase it in a way that you are just helping them and don't be too aggressive.

Zig Ziglar—one of the most popular motivational speakers and sales experts of all time—always says, "If you help enough people become successful, you will eventually become successful, too." You should always help others, and, most of the time, they will feel obligated to help you in return. Most don't reciprocate immediately, but some day, when you least expect it, they will reciprocate. Of course, there are a select few who never reciprocate because they are completely self-centered, and you'll notice they eventually fail at what they are doing. I've seen it happen time and time again where people who help others with no expectation eventually come out on top.

If you see a lot of people asking similar questions about the limitations of a product or asking for more features in a product, it's a great opportunity for you to reach out to your product development team to fill that gap. Monitoring LinkedIn Answers lets you identify gaps in your product line or products available in your industry. Look for patterns of similar questions and frustrations and jump on the opportunities to fill those gaps.

Use this same approach of helping others without expectation in LinkedIn Answers, and I guarantee you will sell more than you ever have in the past. People who are self-promoting their products and services and aren't genuinely interested in helping others may make a few sales and pick up a few new clients, but in the long run, the sales professionals who genuinely help others are the ones who rise to the top.

Prospecting in LinkedIn Groups

You can use LinkedIn Groups to find prospects because the Groups have discussion boards where people reach out for support. The discussion boards in Groups are very similar to LinkedIn Answers, but the discussions are more focused. Since LinkedIn Groups are often focused on companies or specific products produced by a company, the questions and discussions go much deeper than they do on Answers.

For example, someone might ask a basic question about Photoshop on LinkedIn Answers. The questions tend to be more general in nature—like at the 10,000 level—and the answers and follow-up comments are very general. A typical question about Photoshop in LinkedIn Answers may be: "How do I crop a photo in Photoshop?" If you join the Photoshop Group, the questions will be about the more advanced features of Photoshop and the answers will be very detailed. You may get three or four great answers that show you how to accomplish the same task using different techniques. A typical question in the Photoshop Group may be something like "JPG and RAW, of course we all know the advantages of RAW. Is there anyone out there who will still use JPG format for professional work?" This question received 251 comments in one month from graphic artists, and the discussion shows no signs of slowing down. A very lively discussion results with many varying opinions and the debate continues. Obviously, this question struck a nerve with many graphic artists who seem to feel strongly one way or the other about which format to use for professional work. You see active questions like this frequently on the LinkedIn Groups focused on specialties and specific products. I highly recommend joining the Groups related to your product, industry, and the vertical markets that use your product or service.

You can also learn about industry trends and your competitors' new advancements in LinkedIn Groups. Companies often use LinkedIn Groups to announce new products and services. They also use the Groups to gather feedback from customers about their products and services by conducting LinkedIn Polls.

The same prospecting rules apply here as we discussed in LinkedIn Answers. Be genuinely interested in helping others and spend most of your time listening to their issues before you reach out. You can also monitor the Groups to find top professionals in your industry. If you notice a certain person reaching out consistently and they're providing excellent advice, you can contact that person to see if he wants to connect on LinkedIn. If he is located in your area, you could invite him to meet for coffee or lunch to talk about industry trends or see if he wants to join a local networking group you belong to. Building relationships with other experts helps extend your professional network, which will help you gain more sales. Of course, you don't want to reach out to others if they are competitors or are connected to your competitors in any way—that could put you in an awkward position with your boss!

LINKEDIN COMPANY GROUPS

In addition to Groups related to specific topics and products, you can join LinkedIn Groups for specific companies. Most companies have Groups in addition to their Company page, so join both if you can. You can learn a lot about your competitors, your industry, and vertical markets where your product or service is used. People always ask me if it's appropriate to join your competitor's Group. Most of the time, the groups are moderated, so they will deny your membership request if they are carefully moderating the Group. Occasionally, you can slip through the cracks and they will grant you access. If that happens to you, I recommend being a silent participant in that Group and just observe, so you can learn as much as possible about the issues your competitors are having with their products or services. You can use this information when selling against your competitors, which gives you a huge advantage. If you join the Group and start participating in discussions, they will become aware that you are a competitor and will remove you from the group.

You should be able to join industry-related groups and vertical market groups without resistance. If you aren't monitoring the other groups in your industry or vertical market companies, you are missing out on a lot of relevant discussions that will help you discover potential sales opportunities. Remember, LinkedIn is one of the largest business intelligence databases available to you, so use it to your advantage to gather competitive information that will give you the upper hand in sales presentations against your competitors.

LinkedIn Company Pages

LinkedIn lets you "Follow" companies similar to the way you can "Like" a company page on Facebook. Once you "Follow" a company on LinkedIn, anything it posts on its company page will be visible on your LinkedIn homepage. This is an easy way for you to monitor prospect companies (and even your competitors) to learn about new product announcements and company news. If you see one of your potential prospect companies just hired a new CIO, it may be a perfect opportunity to get your foot in the door at the company because often that means a clean slate, open to new vendors.

You can also monitor your prospect company pages to see what job openings they have. If you see a lot of new job openings or promotions in a certain department, it may be a great time to test the waters as the company and the new hires might be looking for new products or services.

You can infer a ton of great information from LinkedIn company pages, if you take the time to dig into the job postings, news items, and new product announcements.

LinkedIn Jobs

I touched on this in the previous section. You can learn a lot about a company's strategic direction by monitoring their job postings page. You know your target companies and perhaps even the key decision makers. Spend a few hours a week (or have your assistant do this) and monitor your target companies' job postings. Use the Advanced Job Search features to hone in on the current job openings in the departments you sell to. When you see new job postings for key positions or a lot of listings for similar new positions, it's a sign that you may have an opportunity. If you see they are suddenly hiring 50 new C++ programmers, there must be a huge new product being developed that could mean a huge opportunity for you. With LinkedIn Premium accounts, you can save search criteria in Saved Searches so you can easily replicate your best searches on a regular basis.

LinkedIn Today

LinkedIn Today is a free service displayed on your LinkedIn homepage where you can subscribe to popular news sources, such *The New York Times*, *The Wall Street Journal*, and industry-specific news. I never used to log into LinkedIn on a daily basis until they added features like LinkedIn Today. Now I can log into one website and learn the latest industry news and financial news, and keep up with my professional network from my LinkedIn homepage. Use LinkedIn Today to learn about the latest trends in your industry and the world news in general. I always visit LinkedIn Today when I'm looking for ideas for my next blog post or article. I also use it to find great articles to Tweet.

CardMunch

When you meet new prospects, you can quickly scan their business cards using your mobile phone and add them to your LinkedIn contact database. CardMunch makes it easy to start the connection process because you just take a picture of their business card, and it's uploaded right to your LinkedIn account. Of course, you will still want to connect with them on LinkedIn immediately so you can learn more about them and they can discover more about you and your company. While the CardMunch app isn't perfect, LinkedIn is improving it rapidly because they see it as a very valuable networking tool.

LinkedIn Mobile

The LinkedIn Mobile app has improved dramatically since it was initially released. The app lets you easily access your LinkedIn account from your mobile phone. Before you meet with a prospect in person, you can quickly review her LinkedIn profile, see the latest company news from her company page, and learn about the latest industry news just before the meeting. You will be well prepared and make a good impression on your prospects.

Using LinkedIn Ads

You will learn everything you need to know about LinkedIn Advertising in Chapter 21, so I won't get into great detail here. I do want you to know that you can run very targeted ads to promote your business brand, and advertise white papers, webinars, videos, and workshops for lead generation. The advanced targeting ability of LinkedIn advertising makes it one of the most efficient advertising platforms available online today. Your ads will only be displayed to the appropriate target company, industry, job title, specific keywords, and many other advanced targeting options available in LinkedIn Advertising.

Premium Sales Package

Of course, LinkedIn provides premium packages designed for sales representatives. These are designed to help sales professionals generate leads and manage their LinkedIn network. Figure 20–3 on page 196 shows you the features of the Sales Navigator and the Sales Navigator Plus packages.

Features	Your Current Account **Business**	Recommended **Sales Navigator** Annual: US$39.95/month* Monthly: US$49.95/month [Upgrade]	**Sales Navigator Plus** Annual: US$74.95/month* Monthly: US$99.95/month [Upgrade]
Contact anyone directly with InMail – Response Guaranteed!	3 per month (US$30.00 value)	10 per month (US$100.00 value)	25 per month (US$250.00 value)
Build your pipeline with Lead Builder		Yes	Yes
Pinpoint the right leads with Premium search filters	Premium Filters	Premium Filters	Premium + Talent Filters
Who's Viewed Your Profile: Get the full list	Yes	Yes	Yes
Save important profiles and notes using Profile Organizer	5 folders	25 folders	50 folders
See more profiles when you search	300	500	700
Automate your search with Saved Search Alerts	5 per week	7 per week	10 per day
See names of your 3rd-degree and group connections	First Name	First Name	Full Name Visibility
Get introduced to the companies you're targeting	15 outstanding	25 outstanding	35 outstanding
Let anyone message you for free with OpenLink	Yes	Yes	Yes
Get Priority Customer Service	Yes	Yes	Yes

FIGURE 20–3. Premium Packages for Sales Professionals

InMail

I've talked about the pros and cons of InMail throughout this book, so I won't get into the details of how you can use InMail to your advantage. In Chapter 12, "Using LinkedIn InMail to Reach Out," you can learn how to use InMail to effectively reach out to second- and third-degree connections. With the Premium Business account or the Sales Navigator account, you can receive up to 25 InMails every month, depending on which package you choose. There are many ways to connect with others without using InMail, but sometimes it's much easier and faster to just contact them directly via a personalized InMail message.

Lead Builder

Lead Builder allows you to create and save lists of prospects. You can organize these prospects into folders with your Profile Organizer, which comes with your premium account. As you search for prospects on LinkedIn using the Advanced Search features, you can save your searches in Saved Searches and also create lists of prospects in Lead Builder.

account offers you significantly more search results than a free
when you perform Advanced Searches. This can be good news as
because you can be overwhelmed with search results that you have to
to find what you are looking for. The good news is that you also
h Filters with your upgraded LinkedIn accounts. Figure 20–4
Search Filters you receive with the Sales Navigator and the Sales
s.

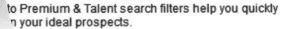

to Premium & Talent search filters help you quickly
n your ideal prospects.

(4 filters)
- rity
- pany Size
- nterests
- Fortune 1000

Premium + Talent (8 filters)
- Seniority
- Company Size
- Function
- Interests
- Years of Experience
- Fortune 1000
- Your Groups
- New to LinkedIn

FIGURE 20–4. Premium Search Filters for Sales Navigator and
Sales Navigator Plus

As you can see, it's worth upgrading to Sales Navigator Plus just for the additional search filters. Being able to filter your searches using the Premium + Talent search filters will save you time and provide more targeted searches.

Who's Viewed Your Profile

This is a vital feature of LinkedIn that lets you see who's been viewing your profile. As a sales professional, knowing who's viewed your profile can tip you off to customers who may be interested in your products or services. As you participate in LinkedIn Groups and Answers and establish yourself as a subject-matter expert, people will click on your profile link to learn more about you. The simple act of a potential customer clicking on your profile link is better than if he opted in on your website to

download a white paper. You'll find out a lot more about a client from his LinkedIn profile than you would just from the name and email address provided to you when he downloaded the white paper.

Profile Organizer

This is another handy feature of LinkedIn Premium accounts. The Profile Organizer lets you save your top contacts in a dedicated workspace within your LinkedIn account. You can organize your leads and top contacts into dedicated folders. You can also add notes and detailed contact information about your conversations, which will help you streamline your sales prospecting.

See More Profiles When You Search

I touched on this feature of LinkedIn Premium accounts a bit earlier. You can see up to 700 profiles when you perform an Advanced People Search, which helps you find more leads in less time. The combination of seeing up to 700 targeted profiles with the Premium Search Filters will help you find more prospects in a fraction of the time you spend today.

Saved Search Alerts

You already know about using the Save Search feature in LinkedIn Premium accounts. As you identify the optimal search criteria to find your ideal prospects, you save them in the Save Search section of the Advanced People Search page. The Saved Search Alerts takes the Save Search feature to the next level by automating your searches. LinkedIn will automatically run up to ten of your saved searches every day and alert you when a prospect is found for you. This is another reason for you to upgrade to the Sales Navigator Plus account—you can receive all ten automated searches every day. With LinkedIn adding at least two new members every second, a new prospect could be signing up right now!

See Names of Your Third-Degree and Group Connections

Normally you will only see the first name and last initial of a contact when you perform a keyword search. If you are doing an Advanced Search for people with the keywords "content management system" in their profiles, by default you will see only their first names and last initials, so it's harder to learn more about them. If you upgrade to Sales Navigator Plus, you will see the full last name on all of your LinkedIn searches. This is yet another reason to upgrade to Sales Navigator Plus.

Get Introduced to the Companies You Are Targeting

Occasionally you try your hardest but, for one reason or another, you just can't make that connection with a key decision-maker in one of your target companies. LinkedIn Introductions will help you make that connection. As you know, you receive five LinkedIn Introductions with your free LinkedIn account. With the Sales Navigator Plus account, you receive up to 35 outstanding Introductions. You can learn more about Introductions in Chapter 11, "Connecting with Others."

Let Anyone Message You For Free with OpenLink

The reason you are on LinkedIn is to connect with as many prospects and customers as possible. Some people lock down their LinkedIn profiles so it's almost impossible to connect with them; this completely defeats the purpose of being on a business networking website. As you know, I'm all about opening up my LinkedIn profile so it's easy for people to get to know me, see that I'm an expert in my field, and connect with me. When you subscribe to any of the LinkedIn Premium accounts, you can enable OpenLink, which allows anyone on LinkedIn to send you a message without seeing your contact details. If you enable OpenLink and receive too many unsolicited messages from people you don't want to connect with, you can disable it at any time. I use OpenLink and I only receive a few messages a month, and most are relevant opportunities. Remember, LinkedIn is a higher-quality network than most online networking websites, so you don't have to worry about being bombarded with spam messages.

CONCLUSION

As you see, LinkedIn provides many free and paid subscription levels. If you are in sales and serious about surpassing your number every month, you need to invest in Sales Navigator Plus to get the most out of LinkedIn. As LinkedIn continues to grow at staggering rates, you will need as many automated tools as possible to help you track down the right leads. The LinkedIn Premium subscriptions are worth the nominal fee you pay and your return on investment will be exponential.

In the next chapter, we'll explore LinkedIn Advertising, one of the fastest growing and most targeted ad networks today. You'll learn how to target your prospects with customized ads that will convert better than the industry average.

LinkedIn Advertising

I remember back in the late 1990s many internet experts were saying, "Banner ads are dead" and "Nobody clicks on internet ads." Based on Google's success—earning more than $30 billion in advertising revenue in 2011—I have to say things have changed. Internet advertising revenue is increasing about 16 percent every year and is showing no sign of slowing down, as the internet continues to become an even bigger part of our lives.

LinkedIn is capitalizing on the popularity of internet advertising by offering a variety of alternatives. LinkedIn provides an affordable way to get your message out to a very targeted audience using many easy-to-use options. Nowhere else on the internet can you create such laser-focused advertising at such an affordable price.

The beauty of LinkedIn advertising is the incredible targeting ability for your ads. You can display one set of ads on keyword-specific content, display another set of ads to specific LinkedIn Groups, and create targeted ads on the LinkedIn Answers page in designated categories, by job title, by company, and a host of other targeting options covered in detail in this chapter. Since LinkedIn is already a targeted, business-oriented community, the ability to use targeted advertising makes your advertising dollar go a lot further and can provide extraordinary results.

LinkedIn members include highly educated, affluent, executive-level, and influential decision-makers in companies. According to The Nielsen Company, @Plan, almost 27 percent of LinkedIn members are business decision makers and more than 34 percent earn over $100,000/year. @Plan is the leading target-marketing platform for internet media planning, buying, and selling. @Plan uses more than 5,000 profile points and 19 profile categories to provide wide-ranging details about the U.S. adult online population.

@Plan also says three out of four LinkedIn members use LinkedIn to keep up with business news and industry trends because they trust the information they read. Over 64 percent of these executives believe LinkedIn helps develop business relationships and grow their businesses.

LinkedIn members are the perfect group to market to because they are receptive to relevant advertising and have the authority to take action when they see products and services that will solve their problems.

ADVERTISING OPTIONS

Your LinkedIn advertising program options include:

- Self-service advertising
- Answers sponsorships
- Content ads
- InMails
- Polls
- Social ads

Each advertising option allows you the flexibility and affordability to reach your target audience, whether you are generating leads, growing your LinkedIn network, recruiting new employees, or growing your LinkedIn company page membership.

Let's learn about the different advertising options available to you on LinkedIn, and then, in Chapter 22, I'll show you how to create powerful, laser-targeted ads that will convert like crazy.

LEAD COLLECTION IN LINKEDIN ADS

Before you start running your ads on LinkedIn, you have to decide if you want to collect the leads yourself, or if you want LinkedIn to collect them and send them to you.

If you are collecting the leads yourself, in your ad you simply add a URL that redirects the LinkedIn member to a landing page on your website. They fill out the web form and they will be able to download your white paper or attend the event you are promoting in your ad.

The other option is to use Lead Collection, which is a feature in LinkedIn Ads. This lets advertisers collect leads directly through LinkedIn ad campaigns. When this feature is enabled, members who click on your ad will be redirected to one of your LinkedIn pages, such as your Company page. Lead Collection adds a button to the top of your company page, or the page you choose, so members can request you to contact them.

The nice feature of Lead Collection is that LinkedIn members don't have to fill out a web form. You have to be logged into LinkedIn to see the ad buttons. Once you are logged in, you don't have to fill out the web form to download your white paper but you can share your email address if you want to be contacted by the vendor. When members click on the button, LinkedIn will automatically send you the member's name, headline, and a link to their LinkedIn Profile. Members have the option of sharing their email address when submitting the request for contact, too.

You'll be able to send a free follow-up message to them on LinkedIn once they've submitted the request for you to contact them.

The disadvantage of Lead Collection is that you are unable to export the lead list and email the contacts later using your email autoresponder program. This is a big drawback because you can't use Lead Collection to build an email list of prospects. The leads do stay in your LinkedIn account so you can email them through LinkedIn, but it's not as convenient as building your own prospect email list.

SELF-SERVICE ADVERTISING

LinkedIn Ads is a self-service advertising solution that allows you to create and place ads on prominent pages and page locations on the LinkedIn.com website.

You specify which LinkedIn members view your ads by selecting a target audience: by job title, job function, industry, geography, age, gender, company name, company size, or LinkedIn Group.

The Components of Your Self-Service Ads

- Headline (up to 25 characters of text)
- Description (up to 75 characters of text)
- From: (your name or any company)
- Image: (50 x 50 pixel image)
- URL (website people visit once they click on your ad)

Locations of Your Self-Service Ads

Your Self-Service ads, as seen in Figure 21–1 on page 204, will be displayed prominently at the top of the LinkedIn page as a text ad, and your full ad with an image will appear in the right sidebar.

FIGURE 21–1. Self-Service Ads

ENHANCED MARKETING SOLUTIONS

The rest of the LinkedIn advertising options are considered *enhanced marketing solutions* and you need to contact the LinkedIn sales team for more information. The starting price for enhanced marketing solutions campaigns is $25,000, but it may be possible to negotiate and start campaigns at lower price points.

Below are the specifications for LinkedIn-approved formats when you run Enhanced Marketing Solutions campaigns:

- LinkedIn accepts IFRAME/Java script tags
- LinkedIn accepts in-banner surveys—no floating layers or pop-ups
- Third-party tags must be allowed so LinkedIn's ad server can track clicks via a click URL macro or redirect.
- All ad content must function uniformly on both MAC and PC formats as well as multiple browser versions of Firefox, Internet Explorer, Safari, and Chrome.
- LinkedIn does not allow the setting of "Flash cookies" (also known as Local Shared Objects, or LSO).

These are very standard ad specifications for those who are familiar with online banner advertising. LinkedIn also accepts the standard ad sizes of (in pixels) 160 x 600, 300 x 250, 728 x 90, and text links.

ANSWERS SPONSORSHIPS

You can place a variety of targeted ads in the LinkedIn Answers section that will appear in different sections of the Answers page. I like to place these ads to promote white paper giveaways because I can offer a white paper that is directly related to the Categories of the questions and answers that are being displayed on the page.

Here's how you can use Answer sponsorship ads. If you are a search marketing consultant and are generating leads by giving away an ebook about search marketing, you can place an Answers sponsorship ad, which will be displayed only in the search marketing category of the Answers section or next to search marketing-related questions and answers. Talk about targeted advertising! As people read questions and answers about search marketing, they see an ad for your ebook out of the corner of their eye, giving you targeted ad placement. Conversion rates for Answers sponsorships are usually very high if you match your ads with the appropriate category.

Below you'll find a variety of Answers sponsorships ads and where your ads will appear on the Answers page:

Answers 245 x 245 Cube

This is a 245 x 245 pixel banner that appears next to the list of the top experts in a category. You choose which categories you want your ads to appear in. This is an image-only placement as you see in Figure 21–2.

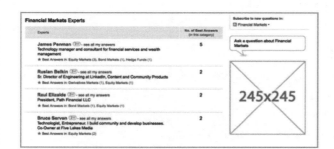

FIGURE 21–2. Image Placement

Answers 245 x 80 Featured Category

This is a 245 x 80 banner that appears on the Answers homepage in a Featured Category section at the top of the sidebar. This is an image-only placement as shown in Figure 21–3 on page 206.

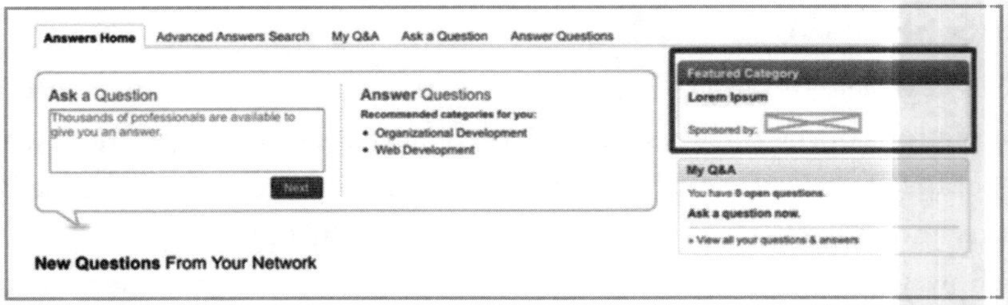

FIGURE 21–3. Answer Banner

Answers 728 x 90

This 728 x 90 banner appears at the bottom of the Answers section just above the footer. This ad can be an image banner, a flash SWF file, or a rich media file, which is a rollover ad. All Answers 728 x 90 ads in this section can contain sound. Figure 21–4 shows you where your banner will appear on the page.

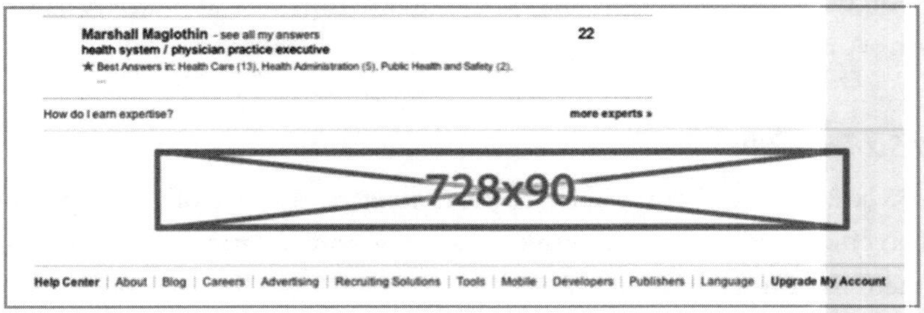

FIGURE 21–4. Bottom Banner

Answers 775 x 25

This 775 x 25 banner appears just above the Open Questions tab. This is an image-only placement. Figure 21–5 shows where your banner will appear.

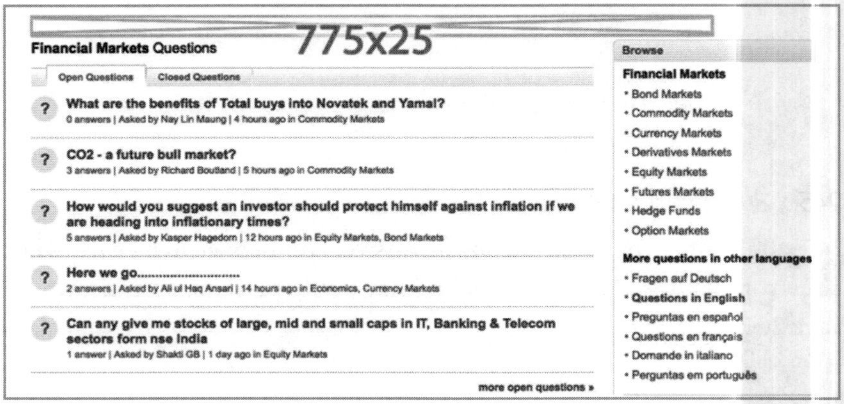

FIGURE 21–5. Open Questions Tab

Answers Co-brand 300 x 250

This is a co-branded image ad that appears in the right sidebar of your LinkedIn homepage. The widget says "LinkedIn Members are Asking" and there is a sample question. Below the question, it says "Sponsored by" and your company name is listed as you see in Figure 21–6.

FIGURE 21–6. Sponsored By Ad

As you see, LinkedIn Answers sponsorship ads give you many options for ad placement. The ad placements are content or category-name driven, so your ads are very relevant to the page content, which increases your conversion rate dramatically. You will be very pleased with the results of your Answers sponsorship because of these highly targeted ad placements.

CONTENT ADS

Content ads are essentially mini-websites that let you display multiple advertising messages in one sidebar widget. You have the chance to display up to four advertising messages in different media formats, so you have more than one chance to catch the reader's eye. Content ads are similar to those rotating billboards you see on freeways where you see three different billboard advertisements as the panels rotate.

Content ads come in just two sizes, 160 x 600 and 300 x 250, but you can add up to four tabs to your ad to create a multimedia experience. You can display your live Twitter feed in one tab, YouTube videos in another, and custom content in the last one. You can mix and match content to make highly interactive ads by offering white papers, podcasts, flash or image banners, or custom videos.

Content ads are a great way to reach many different audiences with just one ad. I like to use them to promote webinars or live events. On the first tab I promote the event with an image ad; on the second I show the live Twitter feed; on the third, I place YouTube videos of the event; and, on the last tab, I post PowerPoint slides from the event. I get to promote four elements of the event in just one ad, which is very effective.

Figure 21–7 shows two sample Content ads with four tabs. As you see, each tab provides the opportunity to display a separate offer or ad campaign.

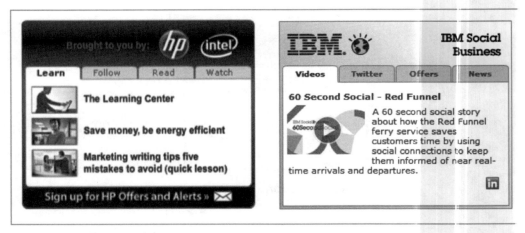

FIGURE 21–7. Content Ads

INMAIL PARTNER MESSAGES

LinkedIn Partner Messages let you use InMail to deliver highly relevant messages to targeted audience segments. Partner Messages are different than the standard InMail message because they're designed to deliver a personalized marketing message to the recipient. When you send an InMail message to someone you don't want to include a marketing message. The sole purpose of an InMail message is to establish contact with the person.

Partner Messages are hand-delivered, personalized messages with space for extensive marketing copy on a co-branded landing page, one ad unit, and a call-to-action. Partner messages are always delivered to the top of the member's LinkedIn inbox, increasing visibility and improving the open rate. LinkedIn members can only receive one partner message every 60 days, so they aren't overwhelmed with unsolicited emails.

When you send a Partner Message, you have the ability to create personalized messages to very specific audiences because you can target any facet of the member profile. For this reason, Partner Messages have an average open rate of 20 percent and a 20 percent click-through rate on the call to action. These are phenomenal open and click-through rates, which are well above the industry standard. Figure 21–8 on page 209 shows you a sample Partner Message.

FIGURE 21–8. Partner Message

POLLS SPONSORSHIP

The LinkedIn polls application is a powerful market research tool. You can collect valuable marketing data from the professional audience on LinkedIn by running polls. The polls are very easy to set up and you receive instant, interactive results. Your poll will be prominently featured on popular LinkedIn pages, which increases the number of responses you receive.

Using the results from your poll, you can create ads that match your poll responses, which will increase the number of comments about your poll and encourages social sharing. Your polls can be targeted to specific segments of LinkedIn members using LinkedIn's enhanced targeting capabilities. This gives you an easy way to start and facilitate conversations around topics relevant to your brand. Like I've mentioned before, it's like having the answers before the teacher hands out the test.

In addition to running LinkedIn Polls for yourself, you can sponsor polls. This gets your brand in front of a very targeted audience, letting you engage with new prospects and gain valuable insights into what they're looking for in a product or service.

LinkedIn Sponsored Polls come in only one size, 300 x 250, as you see in Figure 21–9 on page 210. Your brand image or ad will appear only in the bottom right corner of the 300 x 250 poll widget.

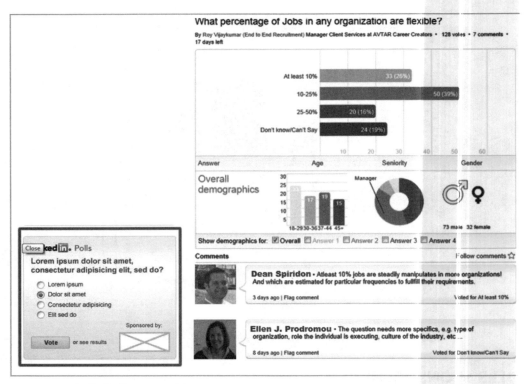

FIGURE 21–9. Polls Sponsorship

When someone clicks on *see results,* they will see detailed poll results as shown on the right in Figure 21–9, including a breakdown of each question and the demographics of the poll responders. Your ad will also be displayed in the right sidebar of the poll results, giving your brand additional exposure to the poll participants.

SOCIAL OR RECOMMENDATION ADS

In 2011, LinkedIn implemented a new type of ad called Social Ads, which come in two ad formats. Figure 21–10 on page 211 shows a sample Social Ad. The first ad format is called a Recruitment ad, which obviously targets job seekers. Recruitment ads are designed to help someone find a job by showing them people in their own personal network who could refer them directly.

These ads are very effective because they show your image in the ad under the headline, "Picture yourself with this New Job" and your new job title under your name. This lets you visualize yourself in this position working at a company you want to work for.

Now that you've seen yourself in your new position you wonder: "How can I get my resume to the hiring manager?" The lower half of the ad shows you exactly who can

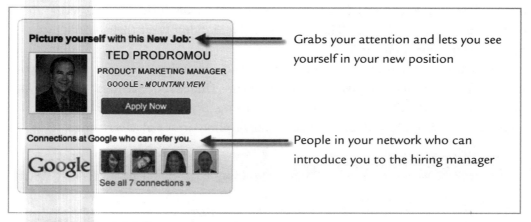

FIGURE 21–10. Social Ad

introduce you to the hiring manager. The ad displays people in your network who are directly connected to the hiring manager, so you now have a direct inside connection to this job opportunity. What could be easier than that?

The second Social Ad is called Ads by LinkedIn Members, as seen in Figure 21–11. At the bottom of the ad you see how many people follow that company on LinkedIn and how many people in your network recommend the product or service. These ads provide instant social proof for your product or service, increasing your conversion rate significantly.

Social ads, which were first introduced by Facebook, were a big hit when they were released—but quickly became controversial. The gist of the method is that users are targeted with relevant ads based on their actions in the social circle. LinkedIn adopted

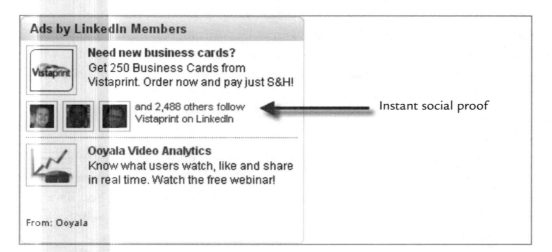

FIGURE 21–11. Ads by LinkedIn Members

this ad format in Social Ads, but users quickly revolted when they started seeing their own pictures in LinkedIn ads. They felt violated and didn't want their profile pictures being used in advertisements.

LinkedIn quickly responded and added privacy controls so you can decide if you want your profile data being used in advertisements. Under your Settings, Account, you now see an option called Manage Social Advertising. If you uncheck the box shown in Figure 21–12, LinkedIn will not use your name or photo in social advertising.

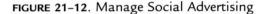

Manage Social Advertising   ✕

LinkedIn may sometimes pair an advertiser's message with social content from LinkedIn's network in order to make the ad more relevant. When LinkedIn members recommend people and services, follow companies, or take other actions, their name/photo may show up in related ads shown to you. Conversely, when you take these actions on LinkedIn, your name/photo may show up in related ads shown to LinkedIn members. By providing social context, we make it easy for our members to learn about products and services that the LinkedIn network is interacting with.

☐ LinkedIn may use my name, photo in social advertising.

Save or Cancel

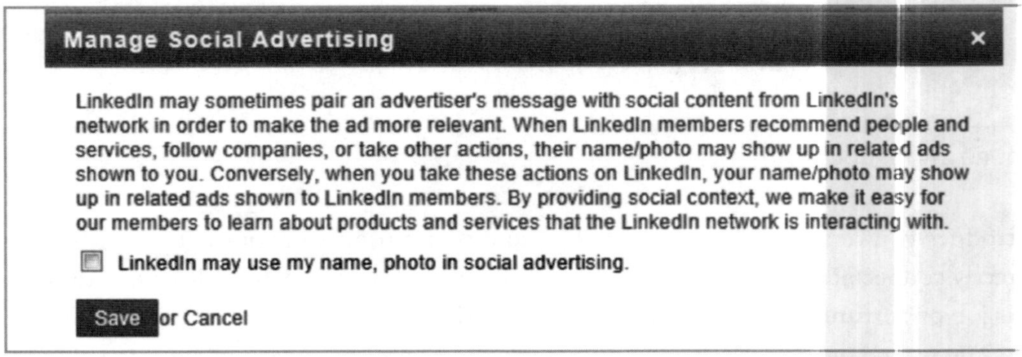

FIGURE 21–12. Manage Social Advertising

I highly recommend unchecking this box, unless you don't mind having your name and photo appearing in ads across the internet. If you choose to let LinkedIn use your name and photo in their advertising, beware that you don't have any control of where the ads will appear or in what context. The ads won't appear on any illegal or immoral websites, but they can appear on websites next to content that conflicts with your personal beliefs or company's policies. I've seen some of my co-workers pop up in ads next to some articles and white papers written by our competition. The problem was that this particular competitor has been known to stretch the truth in some of its white papers, so having our employees show up next to the not-completely-true white paper could have a negative impact.

CONCLUSION

As you see, LinkedIn provides a variety of advertising solutions to help you generate leads, promote your company, and recruit new employees. LinkedIn ads are very targeted and very effective since you have access to so much demographic data. You have the ability to highly target your advertising so your conversion rates are often well above the industry average.

In the next chapter, I'll show you how to write LinkedIn ads that convert like crazy.

Creating LinkedIn Ads That Convert Like Crazy

W
hat makes one ad bring in sales better than another? We've all seen ads that grab our attention and we can't wait to learn more. We've also seen ads that leave us speechless, wondering what the heck the advertiser was trying to accomplish.

Go back and read that last paragraph again. What is the difference between an ad that makes us want to learn more and an ad that leaves us confused? It's simple. Ads that grab our attention aren't visibly trying to sell us anything. Nothing turns us off more than someone giving us the hard sell like a used-car salesman. We like ads that grab our attention and teach us something or entertain us. Those ads turn off our noise filter so the advertiser can build a trusting relationship with us.

Apple is one of the very best at grabbing our attention. Watching an Apple commercial with the catchy background music is an experience that makes us feel cool and hip. Notice that Apple never tries to sell in their ads. Instead, they create an experience where average people just like you and I are enjoying a perfect life without a care in the world. They just happen to be using an iPad to surf the internet or talking to Siri on their iPhone while they're enjoying that carefree life. This makes us associate Apple products with enjoying a life without worry. As a result, we want to run out and buy an iPhone or iPad so we can be just like the people in the commercial. Who doesn't want to feel like that? Owning Apple products is a status symbol like driving a Mercedes or BMW.

On the other hand, have you ever watched a commercial or seen a banner ad that left you feeling angry or annoyed? Or maybe the ad was so offbeat that you had no idea what company produced it and what product they were promoting.

Ads with annoying jingles can turn us off. Annoying characters, such as Flo from Progressive Insurance—the woman with an irritating voice, wearing the white apron, selling insurance like it's a commodity product in a box—is always voted among the most annoying commercials.

Flashing banner ads with too much rapid movement are also ineffective. They may have a great message, but the fast, flashy movements turn us off.

Ads that confuse us often try to sell us something before we even know what the product is. Sometimes the ad does a horrible job explaining how the product can help us, so we get confused and tune out. It may be a product that we really need, but they lost us when they tried to close the sale before we were ready.

So how do we create text and banner ads on LinkedIn that seduce like the Apple TV ads do?

SELLING ON LINKEDIN

Did I say "Selling on LinkedIn"? Sorry about that!

When creating online ads for LinkedIn, you don't want to sell. You want to make a connection with the reader and build a long-term relationship. If you are selling business-to-consumer (B2C) products like you see on sites such as Amazon or Target, it's okay to sell in your advertising because you can entice people to make impulse purchases. The price point for B2C products is much lower and the buying cycle can be seconds or minutes. LinkedIn isn't a great place to advertise B2C products, so you won't see ads for consumer products.

Business-to-Business (B2B) products and services have a much higher price point and a longer buying cycle—sometimes up to a year—so you have to build a long-term relationship with the buyer.

On LinkedIn, you may be running ads for many reasons including:

- Lead generation so your sales reps can follow up with the prospects
- Inviting people to follow your company or join your group on LinkedIn
- Recruitment of new employees for your company
- B2B products or services promotions
- Client case studies or success stories promotions
- LinkedIn polls promotions to gather business intelligence

■ Brand promotions so people will become familiar with your company

LinkedIn advertising can be a very powerful tool if used correctly. As with any advertising campaign, whether it's on LinkedIn or not, you need to create a plan and an objective for your ad campaign. A well-executed advertising campaign will return huge dividends for your company.

CREATE LASER-FOCUSED CAMPAIGNS

If you are creating an ad campaign to generate leads, focus on generating leads. If you are running a branding campaign to publicize your company name, focus on the branding campaign. Do not try to kill two birds with one stone by combining a lead-gen campaign with a branding campaign. You will send a mixed message that will yield horrible results.

When you see an online ad, you should be able to tell if the campaign is designed to promote a brand, advertise a product, generate leads, gather information, recruit new employees, or build relationships. If the intent of the ad isn't obvious to you, the ad is probably a failure because it isn't conveying a crystal-clear message. Remember, people decide in a split second if an ad is relevant and move on if it's not.

Everyone sees thousands of advertisements every day, so it's hard to break through the clutter and grab someone's attention. You need to interrupt a viewer's thought pattern without being annoying. If you grab her attention and pique her interest, she'll click on your ad to learn more. If you don't grab her attention in a second or two, she moves on and can subconsciously block them in the future. This is why you need to carefully plan your advertising campaigns to get the most from your advertising dollar.

LinkedIn advertising has some of the most advanced targeting capabilities of any online advertising platform. You can display specific ads to specific job titles, companies, or LinkedIn Groups. A well-planned LinkedIn advertising campaign includes tracking your results so you know which ads and targeting demographics work best for your products and services.

If you are a web content management software company, you can create ad campaigns to target web developers, IT managers, marketing executives, project managers, and CEOs. You can display technical ads to the developers and IT managers; marketing-focused campaigns to the marketing executives; project-management-related ads to the project managers; and financial-related ads to the CFO and CEO.

Many advertisers don't take advantage of the targeting capabilities and they display all ads to all job titles. The web developers will see ads designed for the CEO and the CEO may see technical ads, which will result in a lower conversion rate. Creating relevant ads and displaying those ads to the appropriate target audience will improve your conversion rate significantly while reducing your advertising costs.

WRITING EFFECTIVE ADS

Remember when you were learning to ride a bike for the first time? You were probably nervous—maybe even scared—because you didn't know what to expect. You were afraid you would fall and get hurt. You thought people would laugh at you.

At first, you were unstable and fell a few times. Maybe you even fell a lot before you got the hang of it.

Eventually, you got the hang of it and before you knew it, you were bombing down the street on your bike. The more you rode, the better you got and your fear completely disappeared.

Copywriting, like bike riding, is a skill you need to practice on a regular basis to get better. We're not born expert copywriters. We get better at it by practicing and making mistakes. It doesn't hurt when you make a mistake when writing copy or ads. It just may cost you a few bucks because your ad didn't convert as well as you expected. Like learning to ride your bike, start slow and hone your skills. If you practice consistently and learn from your mistakes, you will get better.

There are many great books that will teach you the basics of copywriting and ad writing. Any book by Dan Kennedy will make you an expert in direct marketing and copywriting. I highly recommend his book *The Ultimate Sales Letter*, which teaches you how to write powerful, high-converting sales letters. You need to learn how to write these because a great ad does you no good if the landing page (the high-tech version of the traditional sales letter) doesn't convert.

Perry Marshall has co-authored two fantastic books, *The Ultimate Guide to Google Adwords* and *The Ultimate Guide to Facebook Advertising*, that will teach you how to write great online ads. Perry and Bryan Todd study Google Adwords advertising religiously and know the ins and outs better than anyone I've ever met. Their greatest asset is they can take incredibly detailed, complex information, and teach regular people like us in plain English. They are masters at simplifying the complex.

Perry and Thomas Meloche teamed up to write *The Ultimate Guide to Facebook Advertising*, which teaches you how to effectively reach your target audience on Facebook. Creating effective ads on Facebook requires a very different approach than reaching your audience on Google. Perry and Thomas teach you how to write ads that connect with the Facebook community.

The most important thing you will learn from the above books is how to write sales letters and ads from the customers' perspective. The biggest mistake beginners make when writing copy and online ads is that they write from their own perspective. They talk about the features and benefits of their products or services and tell you how wonderful your life will be when you purchase their products.

The key to writing successful online ads is to put yourself in the shoes of the person who is reading your ad. Imagine how they are feeling. Feel their pain points.

Understand why they are frustrated. Once you get into their heads, you can write ads that will grab their attention instantly and make them feel comfortable with you and your products.

LINKEDIN SELF-SERVICE ADS

Okay, now you know the basics of writing good ads and you have some great resources that will make you an expert copywriter and ad writer. Let's explore LinkedIn self-service ads and dig deeper into what it takes to write high-converting ads.

LinkedIn ads consist of the following components:

- Headline (up to 25 characters of text)
- Description (up to 75 characters of text)
- From: (your name or any company)
- Image: (50 x 50 pixel image)
- URL (website people visit once they click on your ad)

The headline and the image are the most important factors in your online ad. Most online advertising experts agree and say the headline can be 80 to 90 percent of your conversion rate. If you don't grab users' attention with a compelling headline or an eye-catching image, they'll never read the rest of your ad, let alone click on the link in your ad.

You could say the headline and image in your online ad is very similar to the title and cover of a book. Research has shown that the title of a book is one of the most important reasons people purchase a book. In 1924, F. Scott Fitzgerald wrote a book titled *Trimalchio in West Egg,* which was later re-titled *The Great Gatsby.* Do you think the original title would have been dubbed a literary classic?

CREATING ATTENTION-GRABBING HEADLINES

Think back to one of your favorite commercials or advertisements. Great ads are more than just words. Great ads tell a story or create an unforgettable experience. The ad headline is the title of the story that makes you want to read more. In fact, great headlines make you *have* to read more, not just *want* to read more.

Well-converting headlines trigger emotions and pique your interest. How many times have you been standing in line at the grocery store and peeked at the cover of *Star* magazine or *Cosmopolitan,* hoping nobody you know would see you? These magazines are masters at creating attention-getting headlines that *make* you pick up the magazine to read the full story behind the headline.

Some sample ads from a recent issue of *Cosmopolitan* include:

- Would you date a dude who looked like this?
- How to turn an office crush into something more
- It drives him wild when I . . .
- Blow his mind every single time
- Five dates that will drive him wild
- The five new ways to lose weight

All these headlines trigger an emotion or grab your attention. Many single men and women have office crushes and they don't know how to take the relationship to the next level, so they're going to read the article.

What guy isn't going to read the articles (in a secret location) about how a woman is going to blow his mind and the five dates that will drive him wild? He wants to know the tricks women are going to play on him!

If you are struggling with your weight and you've tried every diet imaginable, there is no way you are not going to read that article about weight loss.

Of course, it's unlikely your advertising on LinkedIn will trigger these same emotions, but you want to create the same effect when people see your ads. When they read your headline they'll *have* to read the rest of your ad and click to learn more.

FACTORS THAT GENERATE CLICKS

Here are five factors that can make your ads more clickable. Obviously there are other factors, but these work well in online advertising. Not all of these factors will result in clicks on ads for your product or service, so you have to test to see which ones convert best.

- Curiosity
- Benefit
- Emotion
- Credibility
- Expectation

These factors seem pretty obvious, but let's explore them so you're clear on how you can use them in your headlines.

Curiosity

We are curious by nature and want to learn more about subjects that interest us. If you start your headline with phrases like "How I . . ." or "How do I . . ." the reader will be curious and want to read the entire headline. You can also use contradiction in your headline to confuse the reader so you'll grab their attention. Here are some sample headlines that use curiosity to grab your attention:

- "How I turned my business around in the worst economy ever . . ."
- "How do I get top search rankings in Google for my business without spending a fortune?"
- "Social Media is NOT your only way to get web traffic"

Benefit

By providing a clear benefit in your headline, people will click on your ad to find out how they can benefit from what you are offering. You are implying that they will learn something new that may give them a competitive advantage. Some examples of benefit-driven headlines include:

- "3 Easy Ways to Increase Your Click-Through-Rate by at least 40%"
- "How to Convert More Web Visitors into Raving Customers"
- "How to Work Less and Earn More"

Emotion

People respond to certain words, especially when they trigger an emotion. The right words will make people click on your ads and take actions. If you watch one of those Saturday morning infomercials, you will hear and see a steady stream of emotion-triggering words like *amazing, incredible, superb, excellent, free,* and on and on. You may hear them say something like "This amazing formula will help you feel superb, look incredible and make you completely irresistible." Who wouldn't buy that product? Here are some examples of emotional headlines:

- "8 Incredibly Simple Ways to Increase Sales by at Least 25%"
- "Ten Free Social Media Tips that Will Generate More Incredible Comments on Your Blogs"
- "Easily Learn a New Language in Just 20 Minutes a Day!"

Credibility

Most people like concrete or tangible ideas because they are familiar and make sense to them. When you hear "1 + 1 = 2," that is tangible to you because you know it's true. When you hear "How large is space?" you don't feel comfortable because there is no definitive answer. Including familiar experts is an easy way to make your headline tangible and credible. Some examples of tangible headlines include:

- "Warren Buffett Shows You How to Invest Your Money Wisely"
- "Donald Trump Shares His Deepest Real Estate Investing Secrets"
- "How to Start a Social Network by Mark Zuckerberg"

Expectation

It's important to set reasonable expectations in your ad and not over-promise. You can't promise someone that you can get them top rankings in Google for all of their target keywords or guarantee they will lose at least 20 pounds with your home exercise program, unless you can really give them those results. It just not realistic to promise results that you know everyone won't achieve and it's illegal to make promises that you can't guarantee. You need to provide exactly what you are promising in the headline. If you promise a white paper showing seven steps, then you have to provide all seven steps in the white paper—not just one step and then coax the reader into purchasing the next six.

Here are some reasonable expectation-based ads:

- "Voted Best Restaurant in San Francisco 5 Years in a Row by Sunset Magazine"
- "7 Steps to Setting up Your WordPress Blog"
- "Learn How to Recruit the Best Employees on LinkedIn"

You might like to create a spreadsheet to track which factors work best with each product. Figure 22–1 on page 221 demonstrates how you can track your ads. The best converting ad is placed in the box that corresponds with the factor and appropriate product.

So how do you create attention-grabbing headlines that convert like crazy? Here are a few techniques to help you get started.

BRAINSTORMING HEADLINES

Top copywriters like Dan Kennedy, Bill Glazer, and John Carlton teach you to sit down with a blank pad of paper and start writing headlines until you run out of ideas. Just put your pen on the paper and write every word that comes to mind. Don't stop until you've written at least 30 headlines. Most of them will be horrible, but by doing a complete brain dump, you will come up with a few good ones to test.

THE OLD MAGAZINE RACK TRICK

Another great way to get ideas for headlines is to go to your nearest bookstore or grocery store and check out the magazines like I did for the *Cosmopolitan* magazine headlines

Factor	Product A	Product B	Product C	Product D
Curiosity				How I Turned My Business Around in the Worst Economy Ever . . .
Benefit		How to Convert More Web Visitors into Raving Customers		
Emotion	Easily Learn a New Language in Just 20 Minutes a Day!			
Credibility	Warren Buffett Shows You How to Invest Your Money Wisely			
Expectation			Learn How to Recruit the Best Employees on LinkedIn	

FIGURE 22–1. Tracking Factors of Successful Ad Conversion

above. Your local bookstore will have huge magazine racks filled with hundreds of magazines in every niche—or, you can search online.

Write down the headlines and article summaries that grab your attention and use similar wording to create compelling headlines for your LinkedIn ads.

Let's say you sell computer security software and want to advertise on LinkedIn. You could create a targeted advertising campaign that is displayed only to IT professionals. You need some ideas for headlines and ad content, so you check out *PC Magazine* for some ideas. In one issue of the magazine you see the following articles related to computer security as shown in Figure 22-2. You hit the jackpot!

FIGURE 22–2. Article Titles

These are article titles and descriptions that could easily be modified to be powerful ads on LinkedIn to promote your products or white papers that describe your products. What if the first article was a LinkedIn ad? Would you click on this ad if you were in the market for a new antivirus program?

Best Antivirus Software
Still not running antivirus protection?
We'll help you choose the best solution

The headline "Best Antivirus Software" should catch their eye if they see this ad in the LinkedIn Answers section near a question about antivirus software. The simple question "Still not running antivirus protection?" will trigger an emotion if they aren't running an antivirus program or they're using an inadequate or free version that isn't protecting their computers. They're probably thinking, "I'm so stupid for not protecting my business data" or something to that effect. The last line of the ad, "We'll help you choose the best solution," triggers another emotion like "I'm not in this alone. This expert is going to save my business data."

Or, you could promote a white paper that you created to help people decide which solution is best.

Best Antivirus Software?
We reviewed the 21 best solutions
Free white paper helps you decide

This ad works the same as the first ad by grabbing attention and triggering emotions. The person who responds to this ad probably tried to figure out which antivirus program is best, but they were overwhelmed by too many choices or they got lost in technical jargon. They feel great relief when they read this ad and see light at the end of the tunnel because this white paper will guide them to the best solution.

See how easy it is to create ads that resonate with people who are looking for what you are selling?

CREATE A SWIPE FILE

All copywriters create what is known as a *swipe file* where they save articles, magazine headlines, newspaper headlines, and junk mail. Yes, I said junk mail. Those ads you receive in the mail every day are great sources for headlines and ad copy.

Create a file folder where you can save headlines and articles that caught your attention. If you run ads for many different niches or topics, create a separate swipe file for each topic. When you're ready to write new ads, pull out the swipe file for your niche and read through the clippings you've collected. After you read through all the clippings, do the brainstorming exercise I showed you earlier. Your brain is full of ideas from reviewing your clippings, so you should be able to crank out 30 to 50 headlines in a few minutes.

When I was a personal coach, I purchased a lot of personal development programs from Nightingale Conant at www.nightingale.com. They are the premier provider of personal development programs and masters of direct marketing. They send daily motivational quotes via email that happen to have a promotion for a related personal development program. The emails have catchy subject lines, which act as the headline for the motivational tip and personal development program. I copy the emails and subject lines into a huge Word document as an online swipe file. They are also masters at direct mail promotion, so I receive at least two promotional postcards or sales letters in the mail every week. The envelope has a compelling headline that makes you rip it open to read the sales letter promoting the latest method for improving your life. I save every envelope and sales letter in my personal swipe file, so I have content to give me ideas when I'm ready to write ads or web copy.

WRITING YOUR AD COPY

Now that you have a headline, it's time to write your ad copy. Remember how I described the Apple ads that triggered the strong emotions? That catchy jingle, the cool tricks you can do with the iPhone, and the happy people in the ad make you feel happy and hip. When Apple shows you the cool iPhone tricks, they are visually describing the benefits of the product. Some Apple ads don't even show people. They just show an iPhone being held in one hand and a finger sliding across the screen, doing tricks like a magician. The simple, sleight-of-hand imagery is so powerful and makes the iPhone seem so easy to use, like all Apple products. What a huge benefit for a technology product when most people are overwhelmed by the complexity of technology!

Your ad copy should flow like a story that triggers an emotion in the reader's mind so you catch their attention and they take your desired action. If your objective is to get them to download a white paper, they won't hesitate to fill out your web form because they know you are going to provide a solution to their problem.

The headline is the title of the story, the opening line of the ad should describe a benefit of your product or service, and the last line is your call to action or your offer.

Your ad should look like this:

Headline
Describe a benefit of your product or service (paint a picture in the reader's mind)
Offer a solution to a problem in the call to action or offer

THE POWER OF IMAGES

Images in advertising are almost as powerful as your headline and ad copy. Often, the image can be the most important aspect of your ad, depending on what you are promoting. The images you use in your ads are like a book cover. An attractive cover design for a book can increase sales exponentially, just like a compelling book title.

Advertisers have long realized the importance of images in advertising to create mental images in the buyer's mind. Claude Hopkins—one of the great innovators in advertising—was one of the first copywriters to discover that the combination of powerful benefit-driven copy and relevant images increased response rates significantly ("You'll wonder where the yellow went when you brush your teeth with Pepsodent").

This combination of copy and imagery also created a consistency in the response rates of advertising that never before existed. Creating advertising for products was always a hit-or-miss proposition until Hopkins revolutionized the advertising industry.

Selecting the right image for your ad can be up to 70 percent of the reason that someone clicks on it. Your image will make your ad stand out on the LinkedIn page and interrupt the viewer's attention. The image you choose must be relevant to your ad and to your offer. Deception may get the viewer's attention and get them to click on your ad, but they will quickly become disappointed if your offer doesn't match the image.

Images of a real person—from the neck up—convert best on LinkedIn. The image size on the ad is only 50 pixels by 50 pixels, so you don't have much real estate to work with. A simple headshot of a professional man or woman facing the camera works best. You don't want to use casual pictures of a guy in his baseball hat or a woman with a visor. You are targeting professional people on a business-oriented website, so you must choose appropriate photos.

I've done a lot of testing of images on ads in which I gave away white papers, and the results are not surprising. I've run the same ad headline and content and just changed the image in the ad. One ad had a picture of an average-looking professional woman. The second ad had an image of an average-looking professional man—the analyst who had written the white paper—and a third featured an image of the logo from the white paper. The ad with the woman received four times more clicks than those of the man or the logo. She had nothing to do with the ad or the white paper, but she had received more clicks.

The above result may sound sexist but it's true that most of the time people will click on an ad with an image of a woman—even if she wasn't the author of the white paper. Recently, I ran the same three ads but changed the targeting from executives and managers to just a few LinkedIn Groups. The results changed dramatically. The ad with the picture of the analyst outperformed the other ads two to one. I'm assuming the people in the LinkedIn Groups were familiar with the analyst himself and for that reason clicked on his ad instead of the other ads.

FOLLOW EDITORIAL GUIDELINES

Be sure to adhere to LinkedIn's editorial guidelines because they approve every ad before it goes live. Here's a quick list of high-level guidelines for ads:

- Don't deceive or lie.
- Don't use non-standard spelling, grammar, capitalization, punctuation, or repetition.
- Don't use inappropriate or unacceptable language.

- Don't deceive, confuse, or otherwise degrade the experience of members who click.
- Don't use trademarks that you aren't permitted to use.
- Don't use the LinkedIn name or logo.
- Don't use an ad to facilitate collection of a member's data.

A/B SPLIT TESTING

I just showed you why it's important to always test your ads and measure the results according to the group you are targeting. You can never be 100 percent certain which headline, ad copy, or image will perform best. There are many factors that determine this, so you have to constantly test your ads and adjust accordingly.

Testing your ad combinations is commonly called *A/B split testing*. You are testing ad A against ad B to determine which one performs best. You always want to split-test different combinations of headlines, ad copy, and images until you find out the highest converting combination. Once you know this result, use that ad as your control ad and test new combinations of headlines, ad copy, and images until you beat your control ad (or not, as the case may be).

You never know what subtleties will make one ad perform better than another that is similar. Sometimes capitalizing every word works and other times changing one word in the headline does the trick. Some things you can test in your ads are:

1. Create multiple ads for each campaign.
   - Use at least three variations of ads
   - Try capitalizing every word in the headline and ad copy
   - Try different calls to action

2. You can create up to 15 ads per campaign and set different budgets and settings for each ad.

3. Ads that do best will start to be shown more often or you can have all ads displayed equally.

Make sure you track your ads accurately so you know which ones are performing best. Your goal is to achieve the highest click-through rate (CTR) and conversion rate possible. The other important statistic to monitor is the number of impressions, which is the number of times your ads are displayed. You want your ads to be displayed as many times as possible, but they should be displayed to the appropriate audience so your CTR is highest, which reduces your cost per click (CPC).

TARGETING YOUR ADS

One of the most powerful features of LinkedIn advertising is your ability to target the audience where your ads will be displayed. You can create very specific ads for very specific demographics, so your response rate increases dramatically.

You can target your LinkedIn ads based on the following criteria:

- *Geography*. You can target specific regions, countries, states, and cities.
- *Companies*. You can target specific company names or categories of companies, including company size or by industry.
- *Job Title*. You can target specific job titles or categories of job titles, including job categories such as function or seniority.
- *Group*. You can display your ads only to specific LinkedIn Groups.
- *Gender*. You can display your ads to just men or women, as appropriate.
- *Age*. Display your ads to specific age groups.
- *LinkedIn Audience Network*. The LinkedIn Audience Network is a collection of partner websites that display LinkedIn Ads on their pages.

You are probably wondering how to determine where to find the demographic information about your target audience. LinkedIn provides that information for free in LinkedIn Groups. Join a group that is related to your industry or niche. In the right column of your group page you will see a widget as shown in Figure 22–3.

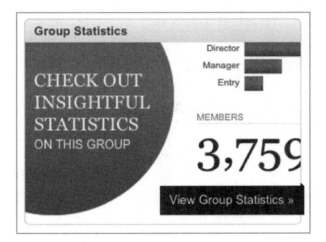

FIGURE 22–3. Group Statistics

Group Statistics is a gold mine of information if you want to run targeted ads. First of all, you can run one set of ads that targets your group, since they are all in your industry or niche. If you want to see the demographics of your group, View Group Statistics shows its seniority, function, location, and industry. This demographic information will let you create custom ad campaigns that should convert very well for you.

BIDDING

For each campaign, you set a payment method of cost per click (CPC) or cost per impression (CPM). You also set a bid (cost per click) for the maximum you're willing to pay for a click or for 1,000 impressions.

For CPC ads, you can enter a bid that's within the Suggested Bid Range. The Suggested Bid Range is an estimate of the current competing bids by other advertisers. The higher you bid within the range, the more likely it is for your ad to be shown and receive clicks. Once you become more familiar with how the bidding works, you can adjust your bids accordingly.

For CPM bidding, you enter the maximum you are willing to pay for 1,000 impressions of your ad. CPM bidding is different because you are paying for ad impressions, not clicks, while with CPC bidding you are paying for each click—not the number of impressions.

You should test CPC versus CPM bidding for your campaigns because sometimes you pay less for CPM bidding and get better results. This varies from campaign to campaign so you have to test it. If you are running a branding campaign to give your brand more exposure via maximum impressions and you don't care about the number of clicks, you should try CPM.

HOW TO MEASURE SUCCESS AND IMPROVE YOUR PERFORMANCE

It's important to define your advertising goals before creating your ad campaign. Clearly defined goals will help you create the right ads, target the right audience, and choose the best landing page.

- *If your goal is to generate traffic* to your website landing page at a certain cost per click (CPC), you can use the My Ad Campaigns section and Reporting section in LinkedIn Ads to track your performance. You can track the number of clicks you've received, which is the number of visitors to your website, and your total budget spent.

- *If your goal is to generate leads,* you need to track users' actions on your website using a web analytics tool like Google Analytics. Using web analytics, you can track the number of web visits from LinkedIn, the number of conversions, and the conversion rate.

You can use a chart like the one in Figure 22–4 to manually track your ads and see which perform best. The chart shows you everything you need to know about your campaigns, including the number of conversions and your return on investment.

Ad Name	Impressions	Clicks	CTR	Cost	Cost Per Click (CPC)	Conversions	ROI
Ad 1							
Ad 2							
Ad 3							
Ad 4							

FIGURE 22–4. Ad Performance Tracking

CONCLUSION

Online ads that convert best are relevant to the target audience and are written with clear, compelling words.

- Remember to use emotion-triggering words that grab the reader's attention in the headline.
- Make sure the description in your ad clearly describes the benefits of your offer.
- Use an image that readers will notice and is relevant to your offer.
- Always include a clear call to action like "download now" or "try it for 30 days" in your ad.
- Use special offers, trials, or free reports to entice them to click on your ad.

In the next chapter, we'll explore finding a job. You are likely a small-business owner and probably not looking for a job, but it's a good skill to know. If you understand the process of how others use LinkedIn to find a job, you'll be able to spot good talent more easily.

Finding a Job
on LinkedIn

A lthough this book is focused on LinkedIn for business owners and
you probably aren't looking for a full-time job, you should always
be prepared to do what you have to do to survive. The economy has
been an absolute roller coaster over the past 15 years. We hit the highest
of highs with the dotcom explosion and we hit the lowest of lows with the
economic collapse in 2008. Personally, my business collapsed twice in the
past decade and I had to give up my dream of owning my own business
to return to the workforce full time to support my family. I had no choice
because my business was focused on providing web marketing services to
small businesses and my clients either went out of business or stopped
spending money completely when the economy tanked in 2008. I had to
find a full-time job or we would have faced foreclosure and bankruptcy.
Luckily, I landed a great job, and while I miss the freedom and flexibility
of owning my own business, the steady paycheck at this point in my life is
just what the doctor ordered.

So, let's say you're looking for a job. I bet you joined LinkedIn because
everyone says it's the best place to find a job. Almost every time I mention
LinkedIn to someone, the person inevitably responds: "I signed up for
LinkedIn, but I never use it because I'm not looking for a job" or "I signed
up for LinkedIn a year ago to get a job and I still don't have one." It seems

like most people think LinkedIn is exclusively a job opportunity website like Monster. com. Of course I tell everyone that LinkedIn is a great job opportunity website—but it is so much more.

Yes, LinkedIn is a great place to find a job if you know what you are doing and you are willing to make the necessary effort. So many people think they just have to sign up for a LinkedIn account and companies will magically find them and offer them a job. Well, I have some bad news for those folks: Just signing up for LinkedIn will not get them jobs. Like everything else in life, good things don't come to you unless you work for it. You need to put in the effort to find a job, whether it's on LinkedIn, another job website, or in person.

Finding a job is so much more than updating your resume, posting it on job websites, and responding to Craigslist ads. How many times have you applied for a job online that you knew you were perfect for and yet you never heard back from the company? Most of the time, they don't even acknowledge they received your resume because they are so inundated with responses to their ads.

To get a job in today's job market, you need to stand out above the crowd. You are competing against hundreds of applicants every time you apply for a job. You may be more qualified than most of the applicants, but somehow they get noticed by the employer and land the interview while your resume goes unnoticed. What are they doing that you aren't? Is their resume flashier than yours? Are they optimizing their resume, so it will get through the automated scanners that detect certain keywords? Do they know someone in the company who passed their resumes directly to the hiring managers?

The key to getting hired today is to catch the attention of the hiring manager. It's not about having more education or experience than other job applicants. Don't get me wrong. Education and experience are very important when you are looking for a new job. But there is so much more employers consider when they're looking to hire new employees. They are looking at the big picture, like your LinkedIn image where you demonstrate your skills and expertise in a variety of ways. You need to establish a presence on LinkedIn, as well as social media sites like Twitter, SlideShare, blogs, or article websites, and even YouTube.

Employers are looking for well-rounded, flexible people because jobs are so dynamic these days. Most jobs require a diverse skill set and adaptability because the business environment is changing so fast. The skills I use in my job as an online marketing and search engine optimization analyst didn't exist a few years ago. I had to learn these new skills to be qualified for my job and these skills are changing constantly. In a few years, I will have to be an expert at an entirely different skill set because the tasks I do at work today will evolve into something completely different. I have no idea what skills I will be using in five years, but I know that the internet and online marketing will be very different. Google will probably be replaced by another company that doesn't even exist today. Employers are looking for employees who understand this and are willing to adapt quickly to the latest and greatest trends in their industry.

What can you do to rise above your competition for jobs? First of all, do you know who your competition is? What are their qualifications, experience, and skill sets that make them competitors when you're applying for a job? Why might they be more qualified than you for the position you are applying for? Let's go to LinkedIn and do a little research to find out who your competitors are and how you can rise above them.

Let's say you are looking for a position as a social media manager in a midsized business. This position is one of the hottest new jobs and there are a lot of people competing for it. We should learn a lot from this example, since it's a job that didn't exist a few years ago and it's an evolving career.

Let's start by searching for some job openings to see what qualifications these companies are looking for and comparing them with your skill set. This will tell you if you are qualified and what skills you need to learn to be a top candidate for an open position as a social media manager.

Go to the LinkedIn Search box and in the dropdown menu, change People to Jobs. Let's start by searching just for "social media," so we don't limit our search results. You want to carefully review the qualifications and the responsibilities of the jobs you are interested in. Are you qualified? Can you quickly learn new skills you may be lacking? After reading the job responsibilities, is this a job you really want? Sometimes you have the skills for a position but you don't like the responsibilities. Maybe the list of responsibilities is unfocused or includes tasks you don't want to perform. The good news is that there are plenty of jobs out there in high tech, so you can keep searching until you find the right job for you.

Below is a list of qualifications for a position as social media manager for a software company located in Silicon Valley. Competition for this job will be very stiff since the Silicon Valley is full of social media experts, so you want to make sure you meet most, if not all, of the qualifications. Many times some of the qualifications are vague so you want to be sure to ask the hiring manager for clarification if you are lucky enough to get an interview. Let's go through these qualifications for the social media manager position and see if this is a job for you.

Job Qualifications

- *Minimum of 3 to 4 years professional social media work experience, including demonstrated success using social media to grow a consumer or enterprise brand through creative, out-of-the-box thinking that drives measurable results*

- *Strong project management or organizational skills*

- *In-depth knowledge and understanding of social media platforms and their respective participants (Facebook, LinkedIn, YouTube, Twitter, etc.) and how they can be integrated using tools and third-party applications*

- *Knowledge of blogging ecosystem relevant to Informatica's technology*

- *Experience using Radian6 preferred*

- *Team player, with the confidence to take the lead and guide other departments and team members when necessary*

- *Good technical understanding and can pick up new tools quickly*

- *Have a good knowledge of the principles of SEO*

- *Public relations, marketing, and community management experience a plus*

- *Candidates with past experience as a community manager are preferred; additionally, data integration and related industry experience are ideal*

- *A candidate's ability to forge strong connections cross-functionally and across business units will be key for success*

- *Advanced knowledge of how to leverage social networking sites, tools, plug-ins, video and photo-sharing sites, etc., is a plus*

Most of these qualifications are very vague and full of jargon like "out-of-the-box thinking," which you will see in many job descriptions. The good news is this is your first opportunity to rise above your competition! I'm sure you have some examples of times you "thought out of the box" and created a unique and effective social media campaign. Of course you will add that successful "out-of-the-box" campaign to your resume and to your LinkedIn profile, but to stand out, you need to show them the campaign in a creative way. You could create a YouTube video demonstrating how you executed the social media campaign. If the campaign is no longer active, you could create a narrated PowerPoint slideshow that explains the campaign in detail, including why you created the campaign, what you were promoting and, of course, the fabulous results. Maybe your campaign resulted in 1,000 new Facebook Likes, or 5,000 new Twitter followers. You can turn the narrated PowerPoint presentation into a YouTube video and promote the heck out of it on social media sites such as Twitter, Facebook, LinkedIn, blogs, and other social media to help it go viral. You can measure the number of Tweets, reTweets, Facebook Likes, and other social media measurements and share them in your PowerPoint and YouTube video. This demonstrates your ability to measure your social media activity, which is another requirement of the job. What would be more impressive than creating a successful social media campaign demonstrating your skills and creativity as part of your application process for the job?

Demonstrating your expertise in this manner gives you a huge advantage over your competitors. Submitting your resume with your education, qualifications, and experience has a fraction of the impact of creating your own multimedia social media campaign. Essentially, it becomes your video audition for the job, and it has the potential to grab the attention of the hiring manager if you do it correctly. If you can't catch the hiring manager's attention using social media, you need to rethink your desire to be a social media manager because that is the primary skill you need to succeed in the position.

Okay, we know you are qualified for the position and you've made a huge splash with your viral social media campaign—but that still may not be enough to get you an interview. As I mentioned before, competition is fierce for social media managers in Silicon Valley. Not only that, you may be competing against people from other areas, as companies are increasingly hiring remote employees. This means you are competing nationally—or even globally—for jobs, so you have to do everything you can to stand out.

Let's start by looking at the LinkedIn profiles of the top social media experts. They may not be in direct competition with you for this particular job, but if they are appearing at the top of a LinkedIn Search for "social media" you want to know how they got there.

Go back the LinkedIn Search box, change the search type to People, and click on the Advanced link, so we can perform an Advanced People Search. Let's enter just "social media" in the job title and click Search to see who comes up. We'll leave the search filter on Relevance for now so we can see the most relevant search results. Figure 23–1 on page 236 shows our initial search results.

The first thing I notice about the top search results is that every social media expert is a Premium LinkedIn member and an OpenLink member. Remember, OpenLink members are open to receiving messages from any LinkedIn member and they don't have to use InMail to reach out. Being a Premium LinkedIn member and using OpenLink should not affect your search rankings, but it does give people a great first impression of you. They see you are committed to LinkedIn and willing to pay for the enhanced features and networking capabilities. Being open to receiving messages from anyone tells everyone you are using LinkedIn to network with others to grow your professional network.

Notice the following common characteristics of the top search results:

■ All the top search results use "social media" liberally in their Profile Headline. They also use "social media" in their current and most recent past position.

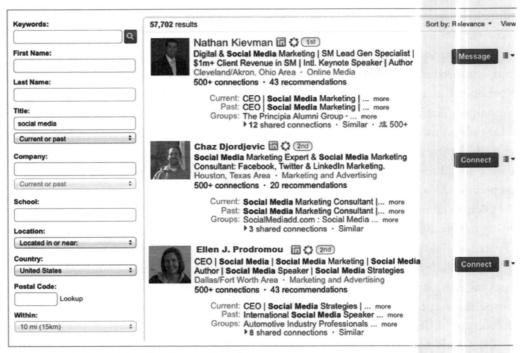

FIGURE 23–1. Social Media Search Results

- All the top search results have 500+ connections; this shouldn't affect their search ranking in a Relevance-related search, but it shows viewers they are active LinkedIn members.
- All the top search results have a lot of Recommendations, which add a tremendous amount of credibility to their LinkedIn profiles. Having a lot of Recommendations helps your search ranking when you sort by Relationship – Recommendations.
- Everyone in the top search results belongs to numerous Groups. Again, belonging to LinkedIn Groups will not affect your search ranking, but it will add to your credibility.

For this example, let's focus on the top search result, Nathan Kievman, and dig into his profile to see if he is more qualified than you. Just because someone outranks you in a LinkedIn Search doesn't mean he is more qualified than you, but you can still learn a lot by reviewing his profile. You want to figure out what keywords, experience, or profile content made that person rise to the top of the search result, which is where you want to be. The best way to catch the attention of a hiring manager is to be one of the top search results for a job title.

FIGURE 23–2. Nathan Kievman Profile Snapshot

My first impression of Nathan's profile summary is very impressive. The first thing I notice is a lot of credibility-building information in his Profile Headline. See his effective Profile Headline in Figure 23–2.

Nathan makes it very clear that he does digital and social media marketing and he's a social media lead-generation specialist. The second line of his Profile Headline clearly separates him from his competition with some impressive facts.

$1m+ Client Revenue in SM | Intl. Keynote Speaker | Author

Nathan lets everyone know that he's helped clients generate more than $1 million in revenue for clients using social media. That's a significant accomplishment and one he should share as often as possible. If you have significant accomplishments like Nathan's, you need to let people know in a number of prominent places. Add it to the professional summary section of your resume, so people notice it immediately. Also, add your accomplishments to your LinkedIn Profile Headline in an abbreviated form like Nathan did. In the Accomplishments section of your LinkedIn profile, provide more details and let people know what you accomplished. Be proud of your significant accomplishments! If you are afraid to toot your own horn, get over it. Everyone else is doing it, so you need to let others know how good you are.

If I were Nathan, I would create a formal case study that documents step-by-step how I generated more than $1 million in revenue for my clients. You don't have to mention the customer's name if they aren't comfortable with you sharing the details of your campaign, but you can still create a powerful case study. Get in the habit of documenting all your projects in great detail so when you do hit a home run, you have the step-by-step process to use over and over again. You can post those case studies in your LinkedIn profile in the Box.net application. In your resume you can refer people directly to the appropriate case studies that are relevant to the position you are applying for.

What else can we learn from Nathan's Profile Headline? A lot. We'll get to the rest of his profile in a minute, but take note how much information we've learned from just 92 characters in his Profile Headline. Besides being a digital and social media marketing consultant, he's a social media lead generation expert, he generates a ton of money for his clients, and he's an international keynote speaker and an author. That's a lot of very relevant information in a Profile Headline.

Take some time now to revise your Profile Headline so viewers know exactly what you do and how you can help them. Add key accomplishments such as being an author or a speaker at your industry events. See how much you can pack into 100 characters, and don't be afraid to use industry abbreviations or acronyms and the | symbol (shift plus the backslash key) to separate your accomplishments as shown in Figure 23–2 on page 237.

Let's move on and examine Nathan's profile in more detail. You want to review the profiles of your competitors to see how they convey their messages and strengths to prospective customers. Every LinkedIn profile is different, and you can learn a lot about your competitors by reviewing their profiles. See what they're doing well and aren't doing so well in their profiles. Some LinkedIn profiles are just awful, while others convey a clear, succinct message to prospects. When you come across a profile that resonates with you, use the same approach when you write your profile. Use the "best of the best" from many profiles so your profile will stand above your competitors.

Take a look at Nathan's LinkedIn Summary:

Nathan Kievman is a highly sought after Digital Strategist, Speaker & Social Media Consultant & Trainer with a heavy focus on LinkedIn and B2B social media initiatives. He uniquely bridges Business Strategy, Targeted Objectives and ROI with Social Media, Digital Media and Traditional Marketing Initiatives.

Mr. Kievman is also the Executive Editor of LI & Business, now with more than 14.5 million subscribers, SocialMediaMags.com. Considered one of the leading authorities on Social Media and LinkedIn with a robust following as the owner of the number one LinkedIn Strategies Group on LinkedIn while having taught more than 35,000 people how to master the platform. He has authored three books on the topic, including the currently available LinkedIn Mastery: An All-Inclusive Guide to Mastering LinkedIn and presented as the keynote speaker on Social Media Strategy for the National Speakers Association winter meetings in 2011.

Companies hire Nathan for one of the following three reasons:

1. *To Launch a Digital or Social Media Company Initiative*

2. *To Generate Leads through LinkedIn, Social & Digital Channels*

3. *For Training on LinkedIn*

He has consulted with Fortune 500 companies, INC 500 companies, well-known business leaders, and many small to mid-sized businesses.

Mr. Kievman holds two masters degrees in Business and in Sports Administration from the highly acclaimed sports program at Ohio University. He is married to his beautiful wife Leah and has three vibrant children. He currently resides in Cleveland/Akron area of Ohio.

Specialties

- *Social Media Marketing*
- *Social Marketing Fulfillment*
- *Understanding Social Media ROI*
- *Social Media Lead Generation*
- *Social Media & Strategic Alliances*
- *Social Networks & Joint Ventures*
- *Sports Social Media*
- *Event Marketing & Promotion*
- *Online/Offline Marketing*
- *LinkedIn Strategies*
- *Internet Marketing*
- *Building Teams through Social Media*
- *Automated Lead Generation & Online Marketing*
- *Internet Marketing*

Note how Nathan starts out by telling you that he's a highly sought after digital strategist. Then he lets you know that he's a thought leader in his field as the executive editor of a very popular social media publication, a published author, speaker, and group leader. After establishing himself as an industry thought leader, he tells you exactly why companies hire him and what type of companies hire him as a consultant. Next he tells you a little bit about his personal life to help you get to know him, and closes with a list of his specialties.

Nathan does a brilliant job establishing himself as an industry leader and expert in his field, telling you how he can help you, showing whom he's helped in the past, and letting you get to know him personally in just a few paragraphs. This is one of the best professional summaries I've seen on LinkedIn. If you are a social media consultant, you need to create a summary as good or better than this in order stand out as an expert in your field.

If standing out as an expert is your goal, you need to demonstrate how you are a leader in your industry. Here are a few things that help: Join industry associations; become a board member in your associations; start a Meetup group, if you want to attract small business owners; write a book; or become a public speaker to get your message out there.

Continue reviewing every section of your competitor's profile and see how you can improve yours and stand out. Don't make things up or exaggerate facts in your LinkedIn profile to look better than your competitors. Be honest and leverage your accomplishments. Set long-term goals and make a plan to increase your visibility in your industry so you will eventually be considered a leader in your field. Using the combination of LinkedIn and social media, you can quickly become known as a thought leader.

You get the idea. You know your top competitors, so do some surveillance work and check up on their online activity. Document what your competitors are doing well to promote their businesses online and also note what they aren't doing so well. Take advantage of their weaknesses so you can stand out where they aren't. With a clear plan of action and some hard work, you will eventually become a leader in your industry and your business will never be the same. Employers or clients will be pursuing you instead of the other way around.

Action Steps

We've covered a lot of material in this chapter, so in this section we will help you create your plan of action. The internet and social media make it relatively easy for anyone to get noticed and stand out above their competition. The key to success is to consistently post content online on LinkedIn, your blog, your website, Twitter, or Facebook. You can also be a guest blogger, write articles, and participate in LinkedIn Answers and Groups. Sharing your expertise on a daily basis will help you rise in the LinkedIn and Google search results, which will make you appear as an expert in your field. Once you have reached that level, you will never have to look for a job again. Great opportunities will come your way on a regular basis and you will have your choice of jobs.

Here is the process I use to identify my ideal job, the company I want to work for, and how I'm going to update my LinkedIn profile to attract attention from my target employers:

1. Identify your ideal job in great detail.

    a. What is your job title?

    b. What are your job responsibilities?

    c. Do you manage others?

    d. What is your boss like?

    e. What are your co-workers like?

    f. What is the company culture?

    g. Can you work from home or do you have to commute?

    h. Describe any other characteristics that make this your ideal job.

2. Identify the top five companies you want to work for.

3. Complete your LinkedIn profile! Fill out every detail of your profile, including the skills and accomplishments that are relevant to the jobs are you are pursuing. Go back and read Chapter 4, "Supercharging Your LinkedIn Profile," to make sure your profile is optimized so you will appear when people search for your expertise.

4. In your Profile Headline, add a statement that you are currently seeking a position in (fill in the job title you are looking for). Say something like, "Currently pursuing a senior management position in the biotech industry." The more detailed you can make it, the better.

5. Get at least three excellent references for each position you've held in the past ten years. The more excellent, relevant references you can get, the better. Coach the people you reach out to for the references and let them know what skills and accomplishments you want them to highlight. We covered Recommendations in great detail in Chapter 10, "Giving and Receiving LinkedIn Recommendations," so feel free to go back and read Chapter 10 again to refresh your memory. Excellent references will open a lot of doors for you.

6. Add your LinkedIn badge on your website and blog to let people know you are an active LinkedIn member

7. Add your Twitter account to your LinkedIn profile so your Tweets will appear in your LinkedIn Status

8. Add your blog to your LinkedIn profile using the WordPress or BlogLink apps. Blog at least three times a week about current events in your industry to show hiring managers that you know what's happening in your industry. Don't just write a summary about current events. Give your opinion about the current events and make predictions about industry trends so you establish yourself as a thought leader in your industry. Read the blogs of thought leaders such as Seth Godin or Chris Brogan to see how they convey their message. Create your unique style so you can differentiate yourself from other thought leaders in your field. Always Tweet a link to your blog post to drive traffic to your blog.

9. Add the Reading List app to your LinkedIn profile and share what you are reading with others. Read at least two books per month that are related to your industry or about business in general. Don't just post the books you are reading or want to read. Make comments on the books you list and tell people why you are reading the books. Don't forget to let people know what you thought of the book after you finish it!

10. Add the SlideShare app to your LinkedIn profile and share your best presentations. Create new presentations about relevant topics in your industry.

11. Upgrade your LinkedIn account to the Job Seeker or Job Seeker Plus level. This lets people know you are looking for a job andgives you numerous tools to help you with your job search. I'll describe the Job Seeker and Job Seeker Plus packages in detail at the end of this chapter.

Now that your profile is in order, it's time to start looking for your ideal job. I've covered LinkedIn Search and Advanced Search techniques numerous times in this book so you should be very familiar with them by now. If you are not familiar with them, what are you waiting for? Becoming an expert at LinkedIn Search is your key to leveraging LinkedIn to find a job, finding hot leads, reconnecting with colleagues, and building your professional network that will carry you to success. Start practicing your LinkedIn Searches now!

Create a detailed strategy for growing your professional network to help you achieve your career goals. Search for thought leaders and key decision-makers in your industry and connect with them. Don't be afraid to reach out to them or ask one of your connections for an introduction. You would be surprised how approachable many industry leaders are if you simply ask. Being associated with the leaders of your industry gives people a better impression of you. Remember, quality over quantity is best in my opinion when you are growing your professional network. Don't connect with people, unless you have a specific reason to add them to your network. LinkedIn is not a popularity contest where the person with the most connections wins. You want to connect with the right people, not with people who can't help you achieve your career goals.

Sometimes you aren't sure if you should connect with someone who is not in your industry or you may not see immediate value in connecting with them. See whom they are connected to and see if they are actively networking on LinkedIn. For example, it's okay to connect with someone who isn't in your industry or not a key executive, if they are connected with a key individual in your industry whom you want to meet through an introduction.

LET'S FIND A JOB!

I'm assuming your LinkedIn profile is 100 percent complete, including your excellent recommendations that make you sound like the best thing since sliced bread. If your profile is not 100 percent complete, stop reading right now and get to work on it, now! I know I keep harping on this fact, but it's so important to present a great first impression when a prospective hiring manager looks at your profile. If they see an incomplete or unprofessional profile, they're going to click right by you and move onto the next candidate.

In case you didn't know, many hiring managers search LinkedIn and monitor their industry-related Groups and LinkedIn Answers for exceptional people. It's not hard to spot the A-list players in your industry when they answer questions in the Answers section or in Groups. There are many wannabes that think answering 1,000 questions a week makes them more qualified for a job, but you will notice their answers are shallow and lack expertise. These people don't have time to answer in depth because they're answering a question every two minutes to meet their 150 questions per day quota.

When a hiring manager sees an exceptional person on LinkedIn, they will proactively reach out to this person and court them. Many times, a hiring manager will hire an exceptional person whether he has a job opening or not. Great companies proactively hire the best talent when they are available. If you haven't read the book *Good to Great* by Jim Collins, then make it your next read (after you finish this one, of course). In his benchmark book, Collins describes great companies as hiring the right people first, then putting them in their positions. He says, "Get the right people on the bus first, then decide where the bus is going." Most successful companies believe hiring the best people is the key to success. Microsoft overpaid for software engineers in the 1980s to get the very best. Today Google, Facebook, and other internet companies are paying premium wages and huge stock options to attract the very best talent.

Now do you understand why I keep harping on you to finish your LinkedIn profile? Hiring managers may be looking at your profile this very minute, so you want to impress the hell out of them on first glance; it may be your only one, so it had better be good.

Remember, you can see who has viewed your profile by looking at the Who's Viewed Your Profile widget in your sidebar. You see either limited information about who viewed your profile with your free LinkedIn account, or the full list of people if you are a LinkedIn Premium member. The full list is included with your paid Business account as well as the Job Seeker and Job Seeker Plus accounts. This is yet another reason for you to upgrade! If you are serious about wanting to get the most out of LinkedIn—whether you are looking for a job or building your professional network—you need to invest in a Premium account. It's a relatively small investment of a few hundred dollars a year and it lets people know you are a serious networker.

When you are searching for a job and you find the perfect one, you will want to learn something about the hiring manager to determine if he or she is someone you want to work for. Once you click on the hiring manager's profile, it will register in their Who's

Viewed Your Profile widget and they will most likely click on your profile link to check you out. Once they see your outstanding LinkedIn profile that knocks their socks off, they're going to reach out to you. That's why it's important for you to let them see your full profile summary when they click on your link. Figure 23–3 shows you what they will see after clicking on your link.

FIGURE 23–3. The Three Configuration Options for the What Others See When You've Viewed Their Profile

It's hard to understand why anyone would want to remain completely anonymous or just show the company name in this situation. You are trying to find a job, so you want to be as accessible as possible so hiring managers can find you. If you remain anonymous, they'll never know you are a top performer in your industry and you are looking for a new opportunity.

You know what position you are looking for and the top five companies you want to work for, so let's start searching. First, let's see if any of those companies you want to work for have any job openings for you. Let's stay with the social media manager position we discussed earlier and assume the top five companies you want to work for are:

1. Google
2. Facebook
3. Salesforce
4. Cisco
5. Intuit

These are all great companies to work for and you wouldn't mind being part of any of them. Your decision will mainly come down to your supervisor, the team you will be working with, the salary, the benefits, and perhaps other factors, such as the commute. For now, let's assume the other factors won't be an issue—you can work virtually or relocate, if necessary—and you want to do some research on these five dream employers. Go to LinkedIn Advanced Search (you know how to get there by now!), enter "social media manager" in the job title field, select Google as the company, and click on Search.

As you see in Figure 23–4, there aren't any jobs open for social media manager at Google right now.

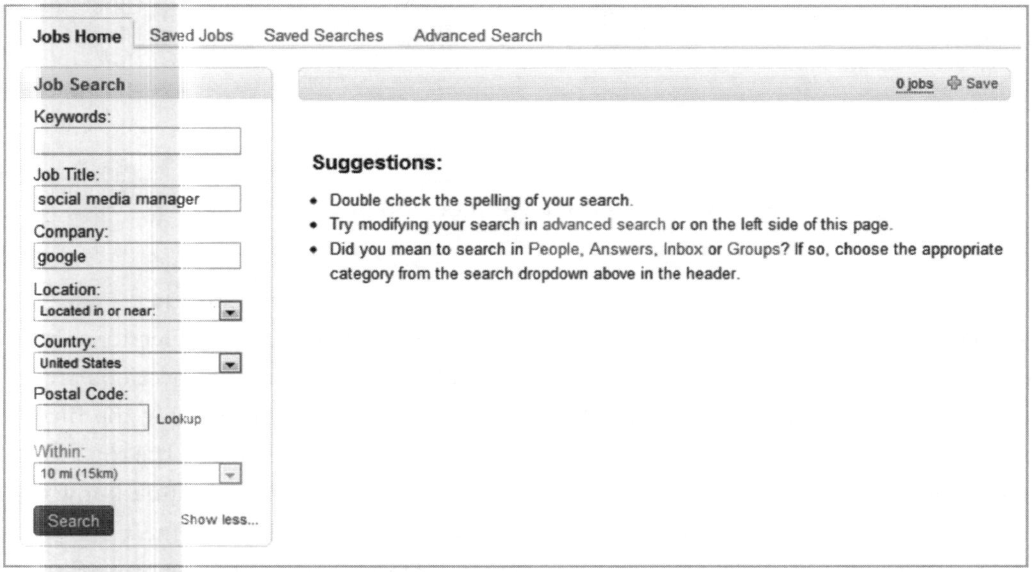

FIGURE 23–4. Search Results for a Social Media Manager Job at Google

LinkedIn has partnered with Simply Hired, a job search network, to expand the LinkedIn Jobs Network. LinkedIn first searches the LinkedIn Jobs Network and, if it doesn't find a match, it searches the Simply Hired partner job site. In this case, no open positions were found at Google, so let's search the other companies. You can also modify the job title to just "social media" to expand the search, since there may be a similar job title. You can also leave the title field blank and enter "social media" in the keywords. Try different combinations of searches because companies use different terminology in their job descriptions and titles. Sometimes you need to get creative, as job titles and job descriptions vary from company to company.

It looks like the only open social media manager position today is at Cisco. Notice the job title is "Social Media Marketing Manager," not just "Social Media Manager." This is why you need to experiment with your search terms so you capture all open positions. Figure 23–5 shows the open position and suggests there are additional positions on Simply Hired.

FIGURE 23–5. Social Media Marketing Manager Position at Cisco

The cool thing about searching for jobs on LinkedIn is the way they help you connect with the hiring manager. In this case, two of my first-degree connections work at Cisco and 653 other people who are my second- or third-degree connections are at Cisco. I can reach out to my first-degree connections to see if they know the hiring manager. I can get feedback on the hiring manager and get my resume to the top of the pile if my connection knows him or her. If my first-degree connections don't know the hiring manager, they may know some of my second- and third-level connections who can connect me with the hiring manager. This is professional networking at its finest! This is so much easier than randomly submitting your resume to Craigslist ads and job sites and praying they'll see your resume.

Let's take a look at the job posting for Cisco's social media marketing manager position to see if it's a fit.

R915797 Social Media Marketing Manager

Cisco Systems—San Francisco Bay Area

Job Description

Cisco is seeking an experienced Social Media Marketing Manager to drive online marketing activities and increase engagement via social channels. In this role, you will manage the social media strategy for Cisco's Collaboration solutions, including social awareness for Cisco Collaboration launches and events.

The ideal candidate is extremely flexible, has strong project management skills, is an excellent communicator, and is comfortable working with multiple contributors on a variety of projects.

Key Responsibilities include:

- Develop the social media strategy for Cisco Collaboration campaigns, launches, and events—coordinating with stakeholders across the company to ensure its effectiveness.
- Manage Cisco's presence in social networking sites including Facebook, Twitter, YouTube, and other community sites.
- Manage day-to-day social media activities and interface with corporate social media team to leverage broader awareness campaigns and activities.
- Become an advocate of the company in social media spaces, engaging in dialogues and answering questions where appropriate.
- Measure the impact of social media programs. Analyze, review, and report on effectiveness of campaigns in an effort to maximize results.
- Manage social media monitoring activities, reporting, and trend analysis.
- Interact with other Cisco social media leads across different regions to develop global campaigns and promotions.
- Facilitate monthly TweetChats between Cisco followers and subject matter experts.
- Drive innovation and incorporate new social techniques/tools into social media marketing plans.

The successful candidate will possess the following skills:

- Proven experience managing social media channels (i.e., Facebook, Twitter, YouTube, Foursquare, Flickr, blogs, wikis, RSS, social bookmarking, discussion forums, and community software). Previous experience managing or working with online communities.
- Experience with online monitoring and measurement platforms including, but not limited to, Facebook Insights, YouTube Insights, Google Analytics, Radian6, and Sprinklr.
- Ability to innovate and define new tools and practices.
- Experience creating and identifying quality social media content related to Collaboration technology is preferred.

- Strong written, oral, and presentation skills with the ability to clearly and simply articulate concepts, messages, and strategies.

- Excellent interpersonal skills with the ability to thrive in a team-oriented culture.

- Data, analytics, and metrics oriented.

- Ability to manage simultaneous projects in a fast-paced, cross-functional environment.

- Able to communicate with and influence a geographically dispersed, international team.

- BS/BA degree in marketing, communications, or public relations, and 4-6 years of experience in social media marketing.

This looks like a pretty standard job description for a social media manager. You need to be well-versed in using social media platforms, such as Twitter, YouTube, and all the other popular social media channels. You need to be able to measure your social media activity using popular tools like Radian6 and Google Analytics. They're looking for creativity, initiative, and the ability to manage the day-to-day activities of the social media team. I don't see any big red flags in this job description, so I think it's time to move to the next step, contacting the hiring manager.

Reaching Out to the Hiring Manager

It's not always easy to find out the name of the hiring manger, but I'll show you some tricks that may help. For this job posting on LinkedIn, you can see who posted the job in the right column of the page. See Figure 23–6 to see the Posted By widget that shows who posted this job.

FIGURE 23–6. The Posted By Widget

In this case, Jane Smith is a third-degree connection to us. The most obvious option is to send Jane an InMail to learn more about the position, and maybe she will be willing to provide you with the name of the hiring manager. Some companies are very open and will tell you who right away, while other companies only share that information with people who make it past the initial screening process. Every company is different and there is no rule of thumb how they will respond.

Before we send Jane an InMail, let's do some exploring to see if we can find this information on our own. By the way, if you don't care about the name of the hiring manager, you can go right to the Apply on Company Website button and apply right now. Most of the time you won't know the hiring manager in a huge company like Cisco, so it doesn't matter. If you have friends who work at Cisco, they may know the hiring manager and they'll warn you if it's a person you won't want to work for. If they do know the hiring manager and have positive things to say about him or her, they may be able to pass your resume on to them and put in a good word.

Let's take a look at Jane's profile to see if we're connected to anyone who can connect us with her in order to find out more about this job opening and the hiring manager. Figure 23–7 shows us how we are connected to Jane or if any of our first- or

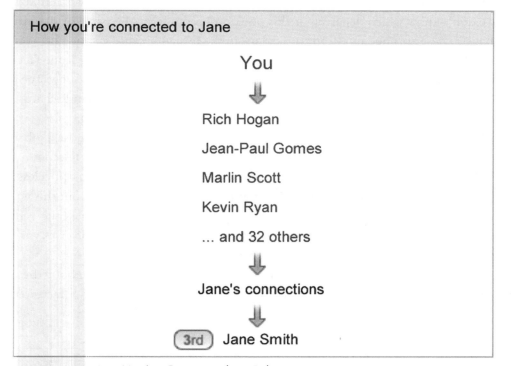

FIGURE 23–7. How You're Connected to Others

second-degree connections are connected with her. It looks like we have no connections who can connect us directly to Jane.

At this point you have two options. You can send Jane an InMail to introduce yourself and learn more about the job, or you can click on the Apply on Company Website button and apply for it. I recommend the former for three reasons: First, when you send an InMail to someone, there is a very high chance you will receive a response from a recruiter, which increases your InMail rating and benefits you when you send future InMails; second, the recipient of the InMail knows it cost you money to send that InMail, so they know you are serious about the position; last, but not least, getting to know the recruiter before you apply for the position almost guarantees he or she will take a longer look at your application. Applying blindly, without reaching out to the recruiter or hiring manager first, is almost the same as blindly applying to jobs from Craigslist ads.

Before you send that InMail to Jane, let's check one more thing. I know you think I'm teasing you, but this is an important step. Let's click on the Apply on Company Website button and take a look at the job posting on the Cisco website to see if we can learn more about the position before reaching out to Jane.

The job posting on the Cisco website is exactly the same as the posting on LinkedIn, so we don't know which department this position resides in or the name of the hiring manager. These are good questions to ask Jane in the InMail because it shows her you've researched the job and have some very relevant questions. However, there is one fact on the Cisco website that we didn't see on the LinkedIn website. Figure 23–8 shows the job is located in San Jose, California, but there is an alternate work location in Richardson, Texas.

The fact there are two potential work locations suggests that this may be a job you can work from any town or city and telecommute. Many Cisco employees telecommute, which is a huge benefit. Not having to commute to and from work is priceless to someone with infants or school-age children at home. You can ask Jane about this when you reach out to her via InMail. The more relevant questions you can ask, the better. It shows you are doing your homework before you apply for the job. This gives you an advantage over the candidates who did not reach out in advance.

It looks like you aren't going to learn any additional information about the job online, so it's time to write your InMail to Jane. Sending an InMail to a recruiter is

Job Title	Area of Interest	Primary Work Location	Alternate Work Locations ▲
Social Media Marketing Manager	Marketing	UNITED STATES.CALIFORNIA.SAN JOSE	"Richardson Texas"

FIGURE 23–8. The Primary and Alternate Work Locations

relatively easy because you should have a 100 percent open rate. Recruiters are always looking for talent to place in jobs so they're going to open every InMail sent to them, unless it has a horrible or offensive subject line. Here are some tips to help you write an InMail to a recruiter:

- Introduce yourself immediately and let the recruiter know which job you are inquiring about. Include the job number or requisition number with the exact job title listed in the job posting.

- Keep your correspondence short and to the point. You don't want to waste the recruiter's time with idle chatter.

- Be curious and ask important questions about the position or job responsibilities that aren't included in the job posting. Don't ask too many detailed questions in the first correspondence because your intent should be to start a dialogue with the recruiter. Ask no more than one or two important questions in your initial InMail. Be careful not to ask very obvious questions that are answered in the job posting because it shows the recruiter you did not carefully read the entire job description. Remember, you want to start a dialogue with the recruiter so she can get to know you and remember you.

- Refer the recruiter to your LinkedIn profile so she can learn more about you. Since your LinkedIn profile is 100 percent complete and ready to knock her socks off, she should be sufficiently impressed.

- Follow up with the recruiter in a timely manner after she responds to you. Get back to her as soon as possible—definitely within 24 hours to show her that you are a responsible person.

- If you are interested in the position, let the recruiter know you are interested and will be applying for the job online. Send them your resume and any other information they may request from you.

- Make sure you follow up with the recruiter a day or two after you apply for the position to let her know your application has been submitted. Also thank her for her time.

Reaching Out to Your Connections

I'm assuming you reached out to your first-degree connections at the company you're thinking of applying to see how they feel about the company and what they like about their job. It's always good to get feedback from the company's current employees to make sure the company culture is right for you. If you haven't reached out to your first-degree connections, this is a good time to contact them. Let them know you are thinking of applying for the position and see if they know anyone in that department who can put in a good word for you. Since you've reached out to the recruiter and applied for the job, you know more about the position and which department the job reports to. Get as much information as you can about the department, other people who work on the social media team, and any other relevant information that may help you during the interview process. The more you know, the better prepared you will be for the interview process. Also, by learning about the department members and who's on the team, you can reach out to them in advance and familiarize them with your name and background, which will give you a leg up during the hiring process.

If your first-degree connections refer you to others in the company and help you get your foot in the door, don't forget to thank them for their effort. Even if you don't get the job, show your gratitude and offer to help them in the future.

Keep Going!

That seems like a lot of work to apply for one job, but that's how it works these days. You have to be proactive and aggressively go after the jobs you want. Being aggressive doesn't mean being annoying and bothering recruiters and hiring managers. Show them you are interested and keep in touch with them, but don't overdo it or you will ruin any relationship you have established.

Now that you applied for one job, go back to LinkedIn Job Search and keep looking. Try different keywords and job titles and follow the same process you just completed. Keep track of your activity in a spreadsheet so you know when you reached out to a recruiter, when you applied for the job, every time you followed up with her, and when you interviewed for the job. Also include any appropriate notes from your correspondence with the company, so you look and sound organized.

Keep following this process, and you will have the job of your dreams in no time. Don't get discouraged if you have to apply and interview over and over. Stay positive and keep networking. Persistence is the key to success.

JOB SEEKER PREMIUM

LinkedIn offers two premium packages called Job Seeker and Job Seeker Plus. It can't be overstated: If you are serious about finding a job, you need to invest in yourself. The Job Seeker and Job Seeker Plus give you additional tools that will accelerate your job search. I know most of you hesitate when it comes to paying extra when you get so many fantastic tools for free. The Job Seeker Plus subscription is $49.95 a month or $39.95 for the entire year at once. If you are looking for a $100,000+ salaried job, don't you think it's worth investing $100 for a couple of months of the Job Seeker

Plus subscription to get you a great job faster? That's an investment of one-tenth of 1 percent of your annual salary.

What You Get with Job Seeker and Job Seeker Plus

Here's a summary of what you get with your Premium Job Seeker packages. Figure 23–9 shows the benefits of each package. Currently, I am a business member and I receive some features that help with searching for jobs. Let me describe the benefits in detail so you can decide which package is best for you. Personally I'm not sure why you would invest in an Annual package because it shouldn't take you an entire year to find a job—even in today's economy—if you follow my approach.

Features	Your Current Account **Business**	Recommended **Job Seeker** ● Monthly: **US$29.95**/month ○ Annual: **US$24.95**/month* [Upgrade]	**Job Seeker Plus** ○ Monthly: **US$49.95**/month ○ Annual: **US$39.95**/month* [Upgrade]
Contact anyone directly with InMail -- Response Guaranteed!	**3 per month** (US$30.00 value)	**5 per month** (US$50.00 value)	**10 per month** (US$100.00 value)
Who's Viewed Your Profile: Get the full list	Yes	Yes	Yes
Zero in on $100K plus jobs with detailed salary information²		included	included
Move to the top of the list as a Featured Applicant		included	included
Exclusive access to our job seeker community		included	included
Get noticed by recruiters and hiring managers with a Job Seeker Badge¹		📷 on your profile	📷 on your profile
Join Lindsey Pollak's webinar: "Job Seeking on LinkedIn"		Yes	Yes
Get introduced to the companies you're targeting	**15 outstanding**	15 outstanding	25 outstanding
Let recruiters message you for free with OpenLink	Yes	Yes	Yes
Get Priority Customer Service	Yes	Yes	Yes

FIGURE 23–9. Job Seeker and Job Seeker Plus Comparison

There are many great features included in your free LinkedIn account when you are searching for a job. Each premium level gives you additional features, helping you find your dream job. Below is a list of the features included with the premium Job Seeker accounts.

■ *InMails.* This is a great tool for reaching out to others, but you can usually connect with someone you don't know through a first- or second-degree connection or by joining Groups. I rarely have to use InMails to connect with others.

- *Who's viewed your profile.* Viewing the full list is included in every package, including your business account.
- *Detailed salary information.* This is very useful information if you are looking for a job that pays more than $100,000 a year. Usually you can estimate what salaries will be based on the job title and responsibilities, though not always.
- *Move to the top of the list as a Featured Applicant.* This is worth the $49.95 investment alone. Hundreds of people apply for some positions, so being able to move to the top of the list is invaluable.
- *Exclusive access to the job seeker community.* This is a nice benefit because the community can give you the additional support you may need to get a job. The community will help review your resume and your LinkedIn Profile; they will also give you interviewing tips and help cheer you up when you get discouraged.
- *Join Lindsay Pollack's webinar, Job Seeking on LinkedIn.* You get great tips about using LinkedIn tools to find your perfect job.
- *Get introduced to the companies you are targeting.* If you don't have first- or second-degree connections who can introduce you—or you're not having any luck connecting with the right person in Groups—this feature will help you get connected with the right people in your target companies.
- *Let recruiters message you for free.* Recruiters are your friends when you are looking for a job. Let them help you as much as they want to.
- *Get priority customer service.* I've never needed any help on LinkedIn, but it's always nice to know it's there if and when you need it.

CONCLUSION

As you see, there are some nice features and benefits in upgrading to the Job Seeker Premium packages. I'll let you decide which one is best for you. I may sound like I'm a salesman for LinkedIn, but I'm not. The Job Seeker Premium package is only $49.95 per month and one you should strongly consider, if your financial situation allows it. Most people are able to find a job in a couple of months to the $100 investment is well worth it.

In the next chapter, we reach the end of this book but the beginning of a new phase of your career. If you implement just a portion of what you've learned in this book, your business will never be the same.

Commencement

Many authors call the last chapter of their books "Conclusion," "Wrapping it Up," or something to the effect that you've successfully reached the end of the book. I prefer to call it "Commencement," because this is a new beginning for you—not the end. I want to be the first to congratulate you for reaching this chapter because you now know more about LinkedIn than 95 percent of all LinkedIn members.

As I mentioned many times throughout the book, most LinkedIn members never reach the milestone of seeing that magical message saying their profile is 100 percent complete. I hope your profile now says 100 percent complete, and if it doesn't, you need to commit to yourself that you will reach that milestone in the next day or so. You've seen the benefits of completing your profile completely, and it will make a world of difference to your business and career.

A lot of people still think LinkedIn is only a website for finding a job. After reading this book, you now know that LinkedIn is so much more than a job website. You learned how to use LinkedIn to give you a huge competitive advantage over your peers, co-workers, companies you are selling against, people you are competing against for jobs, or other consultants who are looking for new consulting engagements. It's time to put into practice what you just learned about LinkedIn and blow away your competition.

Throughout the book, I demonstrated the power of LinkedIn and how you can use it to rise above your competition. Here are a few of the highlights:

- Determine your reason for being on LinkedIn—whether it's to find a job, recruit new employees, prospect for new clients, connect with former colleagues, build your professional network, promote your company, or to become an industry thought leader.
- Use LinkedIn as a business intelligence search engine to find the best employees, find a new job, connect with key decision makers, monitor trends in your industry, keep an eye on your competitors, or increase your sales.
- Optimize your LinkedIn profile so you and your company can easily be found on LinkedIn and Google.
- Build your professional network with the right people, whether you decide to become a LinkedIn LION with a massive network, build a small, niche network, or somewhere in between.
- Use LinkedIn Tools so you can easily keep up with industry trends, connect with others, and automate many LinkedIn functions.
- Use LinkedIn Apps so you can easily access LinkedIn from your computer or mobile device to keep your LinkedIn profile up-to-date, read the latest industry news, connect with others, and find new prospects.
- Use LinkedIn Answers to get advice from other industry experts by asking questions or demonstrating your expertise by answering questions posted by others.
- Use LinkedIn Groups to build strong relationships with others, learn from other group members, and demonstrate your expertise.
- Establish a presence for your company on LinkedIn so others will learn about your products your company employees, and culture; to recruit new employees; and to generate leads.
- Effectively use LinkedIn Advertising to promote your brand, generate leads, recruit new employees, and promote events.
- Use LinkedIn Premium services like Job Seeker, Business, Talent Finder, or Sales Navigator to help you get the most out of LinkedIn.
- And so much more! LinkedIn is constantly evolving, growing, and adding more great stuff, so stay tuned for developments as they occur.

Now that you qualify as an expert LinkedIn user, you have to use that knowledge on a regular basis to maintain the competitive advantage you just gained. I could create a generic 30-day LinkedIn plan for you, but since everyone uses LinkedIn for different reasons, I recommend you create your own that fits your needs. Keep your plan very simple and ease into LinkedIn gradually. In no time you'll be logging into LinkedIn every day.

Some suggestions to get you started include:

1. Change the start page in your browser to LinkedIn.com so you automatically log in every time you open your browser.
2. Get in the habit of logging into LinkedIn every day, and check out LinkedIn Today to read your industry news.
3. Check out the People You May Know widget on your LinkedIn homepage and connect with a few people every week.
4. Recommend one person every week.
5. Ask for recommendations from your current co-workers or past co-workers and bosses.
6. Read some of the new questions posted in the Answers section.
7. Join a Group and read some of the popular discussions.
8. Check out the profiles of people with the same job title as you and update your profile so it's more focused than theirs.
9. Follow some companies that are leaders in your industry.
10. Check out the Jobs section and see what new opportunities are out there—even if you aren't looking for a job.
11. As you become more comfortable with the way Group and Answers discussions work, try posting some provocative questions. When you're even more comfortable, start answering other people's questions. Remember, don't self-promote! Just answer the questions in an unbiased way.
12. Help at least one person every day on LinkedIn by answering their question or by giving them a recommendation.
13. Install one LinkedIn App every week so your profile becomes more robust.
14. Learn one LinkedIn Tool every week so you can become more efficient with LinkedIn.
15. Install the LinkedIn Outlook Toolbar if you use LinkedIn.
16. Set a goal of connecting with at least one key third-degree connection every week.
17. Practice using InMail by sending one to someone you know but aren't connected to. This will increase your chances of them opening it and replying, which helps your InMail score and lets you practice writing interesting InMails. Ask them for feedback and see if they would have opened the InMail if you were a stranger. Practice with them and review their InMail messages in return for helping you.

18. Upgrade to at least the Business account after you become comfortable with the basic LinkedIn functions.

19. Do a Google search on your name and see if your LinkedIn profile comes up. If it does come up, does your Profile Headline let people know exactly what you do and how you can help them?

20. When you are comfortable with your LinkedIn profile, start promoting it by adding a link in your email signature, and add the LinkedIn badge to your blog and website.

Well, that was easy! There are 20 ideas to help you get started on LinkedIn. Do one item each day for the next 20 days and you'll be hooked on LinkedIn.

The key to success in business is consistency. If you consistently use LinkedIn every day to grow your professional network, help others and demonstrate your expertise by answering questions, participate in Group discussions, and display your blog posts, articles, and SlideShare in your profile, there is a good chance you will be considered a thought leader in your field. I've seen it time and time again on the internet—when someone consistently posts fresh, relevant content and helps others, they are soon considered a leading expert in their field. What's stopping you from becoming a leading expert in your field?

I really enjoyed sharing my LinkedIn experience with you and I hope you use the information wisely. If you use just a fraction of the information I taught you, I guarantee your career will never be the same. Will you do me one more favor? When your career takes off because of what you learned in this book, please share your success story with me at ted@tedprodromou.com.

To your LinkedIn success!

LinkedIn Glossary

First-Degree Connections: LinkedIn members who you've agreed to connect with. Your First-Degree Connections are usually friends, co-workers, or colleagues. If you are a LinkedIn LION, your First-Degree Connections are anyone who sent you a Connection request since you want to connect with everyone. You can send messages to them directly without using InMail.

Second-Degree Connections: A "friend of a friend," or the LinkedIn connections of your 1st Degree Connections. You must request an introduction from a first connection if you want to connect with your Second-Degree Connections. You can only contact your Second-Degree Connections via an Introduction or InMail unless you are members of the same Group.

Third-Degree Connections: The connections of your second-degree connections. You must request an introduction or use InMail to contact your Third-Degree Connections unless you are members of the same Group.

Activity Broadcasts: Your Status Updates are sent to the Activity Feed and visible to others. You can edit your Status Updates.

Activity Feed: Displays your network activity such as joining/starting groups, comments, profile changes, and application downloads. You can control which activities appear in your Activity Feed in your LinkedIn Settings.

Anonymous Viewers: You can choose to keep personal identification information private. Recruiters often choose to remain anonymous to remain discreet.

Answers: This is where you can demonstrate your expertise by answering questions posted by other LinkedIn members. You can also ask questions and receive answers from subject matter experts. Answers are found under the "More" tab of your LinkedIn homepage.

Applications: Applications can enhance your LinkedIn experience, by integrating other social media networks such as Twitter, Facebook, and WordPress, and by enhancing your professional profile with a reading list or portfolio app. Applications can be found under the "More" tab of your LinkedIn homepage.

Basic Account: A free LinkedIn account that most members use. The features of the Basic account are limited but meet the needs of most LinkedIn members.

Business Account: A Premium LinkedIn account which offers more features for business users. Business accounts include three InMails per month, enhanced profile search results, expanded profiles, and storage space.

Business Plus Account: A Premium LinkedIn account which offers more features for business users. Business Plus accounts include 10 InMails per month, enhanced profile search results, expanded profiles, company introductions, and storage space.

Connection: LinkedIn members who have accepted an invitation to connect to become your First-Degree Connection.

Events: LinkedIn Events is an application that allows you to see what events your LinkedIn network is attending and allows you to find events recommended to you based on your industry and job function. With LinkedIn Events, you can:

- Create an event
- Search for events
- Share an event
- See attendees and read comments about events

Executive Account: A LinkedIn Premium account that features 25 InMails per month, premium search results, maximum storage, third-degree connection info, and enhanced search filters.

Groups: LinkedIn Groups provide a place for professionals in the same industry or with similar interests to share content, find answers, post and view jobs, make business contacts, and establish themselves as industry experts.

You can find groups to join in the Groups Directory or view suggestions of groups you may like. You can also create a new group focused on a particular topic or industry.

IDK response: When you receive a connection request, one of your options is to choose "I don't know this person" or IDK. If someone receives more than three IDK responses, their account may be suspended to prevent LinkedIn spamming. Always personalize your invitations with a greeting to let the person know why you want to connect with them and how you know them.

InMail: InMails are messages you can send directly to another LinkedIn member you're not connected to. Any member can purchase an InMail, or you can get them with a premium account.

Intermediary: The process whereby a first-degree connection must request an introduction from the secondary connection in order to connect to the 3rd.

Invitations: Invitations are how you make connections on LinkedIn. When one LinkedIn user sends an invitation to another person who then accepts the invitation, they become 1st-degree connections. If the person receiving the invitation isn't a LinkedIn member, they'll be prompted to join LinkedIn in order to accept the invitation. Each new connection can increase your access to thousands of professionals in your network.

Job Seekers Account: A LinkedIn Premium account for people looking for a job. You can choose Job Seeker Basic, Standard, or Plus to enhance your job search. Job Seeker accounts let you get introduced to the companies you want to work for, you can be contacted by anyone using OpenLink, and you can post a Job Seekers Badge on your LinkedIn profile.

LION: An acronym of "LinkedIn Open Networker," which is usually posted on people's profile as an "open networker" or "LION." When you are a LION, you agree to connect with anyone, regardless of industry or connection, to increase your network size.

Local Connection: Connections that are in your local area listed on your account.

Network: Your LinkedIn professional network, which consists of a group of users that can contact you through connections up to three degrees away.

Network Statistics: The Network Statistics feature offers a variety of information about your network, including estimated size and regional and industry access. To learn more about the professionals in your network, move your cursor over Contacts at the top of your home page and click Network Statistics.

News: The News tab, located on your LinkedIn Toolbar, can be configured to be your newsreader displaying content from popular websites like *The Wall Street Journal*, *The New York Times*, and other popular websites and blogs. You can easily add any website or blog that contains an RSS feed.

Open Link Network: A network that Premium members can join, which allows any LinkedIn member to send them an InMail free of charge, regardless of relationship.

Polls: You can create up to 10 free polls at a time on LinkedIn to survey other members. A poll can help facilitate a business or market research decision.

After you add the application and create your poll, you'll be able to see the results in a graph. Each poll can have one question and up to five multiple-choice answers.

Profile: Creating a LinkedIn profile is an excellent way to establish and own your professional identity online. LinkedIn profiles typically appear among the top search results when people search by name.

Profile Organizer: Profile Organizer is a feature that comes with any LinkedIn Premium account. From a single location, you can save and organize profiles, add notes, and track your messages to clients, experts, and candidates. When you upgrade from a Basic to a Premium account, you'll find Profile Organizer under the Profile menu at the top of your homepage.

Recommendations: A recommendation is a comment written by a LinkedIn member to endorse a colleague, business partner, student, or service provider. People interested in hiring or doing business with someone often consider recommendations in making their decisions.

Skills: The Skills page is found under the More menu at the top of your homepage. LinkedIn Skills helps you discover the expertise that other professionals have and see how the demand for these skills is changing over time. The skills information shown is based on data LinkedIn members enter on their profiles.

Index

A

A/B split testing, 226
accounts, creating, 9–13
action plan for job seeking, 240–242
ads. *See* advertising
Ads by LinkedIn Members, 211
Advanced Search
    for finding job candidates, 164–167
    importance of, 53–54
    for job seeking, 242, 245
    premium accounts and, 35, 60
    for prospecting, 191
    for sales professionals, 54–60
advertising, 201–229
    annoying ads, 214
    Answers sponsorships, 205–207
    attention-grabbing ads, 213, 217–218

A/B split testing in, 226
bidding in, 228
content ads, 207–208
conversion rates and. *See* conversion
editorial guidelines for, 225–226
enhanced marketing solutions for, 204
focused campaigns for, 215
generating clicks with, 218–220, 221
headlines in, 217–223
images in, 224–225
in InMail, 208–209
lead collection with, 202–203
options for, 202
Partner Messages, 208–209
performance tracking in, 228–229
Recruitment Ads, 179–180, 210–211

for relationship building, 214–215
Self-Service Ads, 203–204, 217
Social Ads, 210–212
Sponsored Polls, 209–210
swipe files in, 223–224
targeted ads, 201–202, 227–228
writing effective ads, 216, 224, 229
analytics, 42, 229
anonymous profiles, 188–189, 244
Answer button, 126–127
answering questions, 30, 122–127, 243
Answers, 117–130
about, 117–119
advertising in, 205–207
answering questions, 30, 122–127, 243
asking questions, 119–122
Expert Status in, 130, 191, 243
prospecting using, 54–57, 191–192
self-promotion in, 129
Suggest Expert option, 127
writing effective answers, 128–129
apps (applications), 135–146
Blog Link, 141
Box.net, 146
CardMunch, 148–149, 195
Creative Portfolio Display, 139
E-Bookshelf, 139
Events, 142, 160
experimental apps, 69, 149–151
GitHub, 143
Google Presentation, 138
Lawyer Ratings, 144–146
LinkedIn Mobile, 147–148
MOCHA (Military Occupational Clas-
sification Hack for Advancement),
150
MyTravel, 143
for polling, 143–144, 154, 193, 209–210

Projects and Teamspaces, 141
Reading List by Amazon, 142–143
Real Estate Pro, 144–145
Signal, 150–151
SlideShare Presentations, 137–138
SpeechIn, 150
Swarm, 69, 150
Tweets, 135–137
Veterans, 150
Wordpress, 139–140
asking questions, 119–122
automated connections tools, 9–10
automated profiles, 93–96

B

basic accounts, 103
Behance Network, 139
bidding, 228
black-hat SEO techniques, 61–64, 72–73
Blog Link, 141
blogs, 139–141
Box.net, 146
broad matches, 71
bulletin board systems (BBSs), 117. *See
also* Answers; groups
business accounts, 99–100, 196, 243
business card scanning app, 148–149, 195
business networking sites, 7–8

C

CardMunch, 148–149, 195
Career Pages, 41–42, 175, 176–178
closed groups, 109–110, 155–157
coding community app, 143
company groups, 190, 193–194
company homepages, 41
Company Page Setup Wizard, 44–45
company pages

administrators for, 45
Analytics tab, 42
benefits of, 189–190
components of, 40–44
creating, 44–46
employee profiles on, 43–44
following companies using, 194
job postings on, 41–42
leveraging, 189–190
monitoring, 45
negative remarks on, 45–46
premium accounts and, 169
searching for, 39–40
setup wizard, 44–45
status updates on, 44
competition
   company groups of, 193–194
   in job seeking, 231–240
   maintaining competitive edge, 255–258
   monitoring, 193–194
   profiles of, 238–240
competitive analysis, 49, 67–69
competitive edge, 255–258
configuration settings, 20, 29–31, 33–37,
   154–157, 244
connection tools, 9–10
connections. See also networking;
   networks
   defined, 260
   first-degree, 96–97, 167, 246, 251–252,
     259
   with hiring managers, 210–211, 243–
     244, 246, 248–251
   job seeking with, 251–252
   monitoring, 131–134
   removing, 97
   requesting, 96
   screening invitations for, 94–96

   second-degree, 92–93, 167, 186, 188,
     253, 259
   tagging, 134
   third-degree, 186, 188, 198, 259
   tools for, 9–10
contacts, importing, 9–10
content ads, 207–208
conversion. See also advertising
   ad performance and, 228–229
   A/B split testing and, 226
   bidding and, 228
   copywriting for, 217, 224
   factors contributing to, 218–220, 221
   headlines and, 217–218, 220–223
   images and, 224–225
   improving rates, 215
   targeted ads for, 227–228
copywriting. See writing
creating accounts, 9–13
Creative Portfolio Display, 139
credibility in headlines, 219–220, 221
curiosity triggers, 218–219, 221
customer relationships, 190, 214–215
customer service, 45–46, 190

D

deleting connections, 97
description, company, 43
discussion boards. See groups

E

E-Bookshelf, 139
educational background, 12
email, 34, 114–115
emotional triggers, 219, 221
employee profiles, 43–44
employee referral engine, 172
etiquette in groups, 162

Events, 142, 260

exact matches, 71–72

expectation-based headlines, 220, 221

experience questions, 121

experimental apps, 69, 149–151

expert status, 130, 191, 240, 243

F

Facebook, 3–5, 77

fake profiles, 93–94

Feedback Scores, 103–104

file sharing app, 146

finding jobs. *See* job seeking

first-degree connections, 96, 167, 246, 251–252, 259. *See also* connections

following companies, 194

forums. *See* groups

Friendster, 7

G

generating leads, 4, 196, 202–203. *See also* prospecting

getting found. *See* search engine optimization (SEO)

getting started, 3–8

GitHub, 143

Google Docs presentations, 137–138

Google Keyword Tool, 70–72

Google Presentation, 138

Google search, 65

group connections, 198

Group Discussions, 119–125

Group Rules, 160–161

groups

closed, 109–110, 155–157

company, 190, 193–194

configuration settings, 154–157

defined, 109, 260

descriptions of, 153–154

discussions in, 109–110, 112, 114–116, 156

effective use of, 115–116

email notifications, 114–115

etiquette in, 162

evaluating, 111–114

finding, 110–111

joining, 110, 114–115

managing, 160–162

membership in, 155–158

moderating, 161

open, 109, 155–157

optimal number of, 110

permissions in, 155

polls in, 154, 193

promoting, 158–159

prospecting using, 192–194

restrictions in, 155

rules for, XPOST Group Rules

self-promotion in, 162

starting, 153–154

top contributors in, 161

H

Hackdays, 149

headlines in ads

attention-grabbing, 217–218

benefit expressed in, 219, 221

credibility in, 219–220, 221

curiosity triggers in, 218–219, 221

developing, 220–223

emotional triggers in, 219, 221

expectation-based, 220, 221

swipe files for, 223–224

headlines in profiles, 16–18, 237–238

hiring managers, connecting with, 210–211, 243–244, 246, 248–251 homepages, 33–37, 41

I

IDK (I don't know this person), 261
image
    groups and, 162
    profile as reflection of, 16, 18–19
    recommendations and, 80
images
    in advertising, 224–225
    in profiles, 18–19
importing contacts, 9–10
InMail, 99–108
    advertising in, 208–209
    benefits of, 101–102
    defined, 99–100, 261
    delivery rules for, 104–105
    Feedback Scores, 103–104
    introductions vs., 99–100
    Partner Messages in, 208–209
    premium accounts and, 100–103
    purchasing InMail credits, 100, 102–103
    sending, 102–103
    writing tips for, 105–108
introductions, 99–100, 199, 242
invitations, 9–10, 94–96, 159, 261

J

job listings, 41–42
Job Seeker accounts, 242, 252–254
job seeking, 231–254. *See also* recruiting
    accounts for, 242, 252–254
    action plan for, 240–242
    answering questions and, 243
    competition in, researching, 235–240
    competition in, rising above, 231–234
    connecting with hiring managers, 210–211, 243–244, 246, 248–251

hiring managers needs and, 242–243
    job listings, 41–42, 175–178
    Jobs Network for, 173–176
    network building for, 242
    premium packages for, 252–254
    qualifications for job openings, 233
    reaching out to connections, 251–252
    recruitment ads in, 179–180, 210–211
    Simply Hired network for, 245–246
    social proof and, 77–78
Jobs for You Web Ads, 175–176
Jobs Network, 173–176

K

key statistics, 42
keywords
    LinkedIn search and, 48–50
    researching, 67–72, 150
    search result sort by, 50–52
    selecting, 65–67
    target keywords, 17–18, 51, 65–66
knowledge questions, 121

L

Lawyer Ratings, 144–146
Lead Builder, 196
Lead Collection, 202–203
lead generation, 4, 196, 202–203. *See also* prospecting
Like buttons, 77
LinkedIn
    advertising on. *See* advertising
    answers on. *See* Answers
    applications for. *See* apps (applications)
    as business-oriented search engine, 1–2
    for companies. *See* company pages
    connecting on. *See* connections; networking

creating accounts in, 9–13

e-books on, 139

Facebook vs., 3–5

finding jobs on. *See* job seeking

functions of, 6–7

getting found on. *See* search engine
optimization (SEO)

getting started, 3--8

groups on. *See* groups

homepages on, 33–37, 41

InMail on. *See* InMail

maintaining competitive edge with,
255–258

monitoring networks on, 131–134

objectives of, 5–6

opportunities in, 3–5

privacy settings on, 29–31, 244. *See also*
configuration settings

profiles on. *See* profiles

recommendations on. *See* recommendations

recruiting on. *See* recruiting

for sales and marketing professionals.
See LinkedIn for sales professionals

search on. *See* search

selling on, 214–215

tools on. *See* apps (applications)

value to recruiters, 163

versions of, 10–11

LinkedIn Ads, 195

LinkedIn Advanced Search, 164–167

LinkedIn Answers. *See* Answers

LinkedIn apps. *See* apps (applications)

LinkedIn for sales professionals, 183–199

advanced search, 54–60

anonymous profiles, 188–189, 244

building your network, 184–188

CardMunch, 195

company groups, 189–190

company groups of competition,
193–194

company pages, 189–190, 194

contact databases, 183–184

job posting pages of competitors, 194

LinkedIn Today, 194

monitoring your competition, 193–194

prospecting, 54–60, 190–199

LinkedIn Groups. *See* groups

LinkedIn Introductions, 99–100, 199

LinkedIn Jobs, 194

LinkedIn Labs apps, 69, 149–151. *See also*
apps (applications)

LinkedIn Mobile, 147–148, 195

LinkedIn Network, 35

LinkedIn Open Networkers (LIONs), 93

LinkedIn Recruiting Options, 169–181

Career Pages, 175, 176–178

Jobs Network, 173–176

Recruiter Corporate Edition, 169–170

Recruiter Professional Services, 170–172

Recruitment Ads, 179–180

Recruitment Insights, 180–181

Referral Engine, 172

Talent Direct, 172–173

Work With Us, 178–179

LinkedIn Skills, 12, 262

LinkedIn Sponsored Polls, 209–210

LinkedIn Today, 150, 194–195

LinkedIn Tools. *See* LinkedIn Apps

LIONs (LinkedIn Open Networkers), 93

M

marketing professionals. *See* LinkedIn for
sales professionals

Martindale-Hubbell Client Review
Ratings, 145

Martindale-Hubbell Peer Review Ratings, 145–146
messaging with OpenLink, 199
MOCHA (Military Occupational Classification Hack for Advancement), 150
monitoring connection networks, 131–134
MyTravel, 143

N

negative remarks, 45–46
Network Statistics, 131–134
networking
    automated profiles and, 93–96
    monitoring networks, 131–134
    removing connections, 97
    requesting connections, 96–97
    screening invitations, 94–96
    types of, 91–93
    websites for, 7–8
networks, 35
    building, 183–188, 242
    defined, 261
    extending, 193
    monitoring, 131–134
    size, 184–188
new hires, 43
News, 34, 35, 194–195
niche networks, 185–187

O

open groups, 109, 155–157
open networking, 91, 93, 184–187
OpenLink Network, 167, 199, 235
opinion questions, 121–122

P

Partner Messages, 208–209

pay per click (CPC) bidding, 228
pay per impressions (CPM) bidding, 228
permissions in groups, 155
personal profiles. *See* profiles
phony profiles, 93–94
photographs, 18–19
phrase matches, 71
pictures, 18–19
Polls app, 143–144, 154, 193, 209–210
portfolios, 139
PowerPoint, 137–138
premium accounts
    Advanced Search and, 35, 60
    company pages and, 169
    InMail and, 100–103
    for job seeking, 252–254
    job seeking and, 235, 243
    recruiting and, 167–169
    for sales, 194–197
    search and, 197–198
    Slideshare and, 137
Premium Search Filters, 197
presentation apps, 137–138
privacy settings, 29–31, 244. *See also* configuration settings
products and services, 42
Profile Organizer, 60, 196, 198, 262
Profile Wizard, 9–12
profiles, 11–31
    anonymous, 188–189, 244
    for companies. *See* company pages
    company pages and, 13
    components of, 15–16
    creating, 11–13, 240–242
    educational background in, 12
    experience/employment sections in, 20–23
    fake, 93–94

headlines in, 16–18, 237–238

homepages in, 33–37

links to websites and blogs on, 24–26

logos in, 19

optimizing, 11–12, 66. *See also* keywords

pictures in, 18–19

primary, 29–30

privacy settings for, 29–31, 244. *See also* configuration settings

promoting, 28

prospecting using, 197–198

public, 30–31

purpose of, 15

recommendations on. *See* recommendations

registration wizards, 9–12

researching competitor, 238–240

search and, 15

sidebars in, 12–13

skills in, 12

social media feeds on, 26–27

status updates in, 20

summaries in, 11–12, 238–240

symbols in, 16

viewers of, 30, 35, 197–198, 243–244, 254

project management tool, 141

Projects and Teamspaces, 141

promoting groups, 158–159

promotions, company, 43

prospecting

with Advanced Search, 191

collecting leads, 202–203

with company groups, 193–194

with company pages, 194

generating leads, 4, 196, 202–203

job posting monitoring for, 194

in LinkedIn Answers, 54–57, 191–192

in LinkedIn Groups, 192–193

LinkedIn tools for, 194–199

premium sales packages for, 195–199

using profiles, 197–198

Q

qualifications for jobs, 233

R

ranking, 80. *See also* search

Reading List by Amazon, 142–143

Real Estate Pro, 144–145

reciprocal recommendations, 86–87

recommendation ads, 210–212

recommendations, 75–89

based on skills, 87–89

benefits of, 80–81

defined, 262

education on, 23–24

effective, 82–83

giving, 30, 79, 83–87

optimal number of, 81

purpose of, 78–80

quality of, 81–82

ranking and, 80

reciprocal, 86–87

requesting, 21–23, 87–89

as social proof, 75–78

Recruiter Corporate Edition, 169–170

Recruiter Professional Services, 170–172

recruiting. *See also* job seeking

careers on company pages, 41–42

paid recruiting options. *See* LinkedIn Recruiting Options

premium accounts and, 167–169

recruiting employees, 163–181

finding candidates, 163–167. *See also*
  search engine optimization (SEO)
survey data for, 180–181
tips for, 167–169
Recruitment Ads, 179–180, 210–211
Recruitment Insights, 180–181
Referral Engine, 172
registration wizards, 9–12
relationship + recommendation sort, 50,
  52
relationship building
  in ads, 214–215
  with customers, 190
  with other experts, 193
relationship sort, 50, 52
relevance sort, 49, 52
removing connections, 97
Reply Privately option, 127
requesting connections, 96
Ryze, 7

S
Sales Navigator, 195–197
Sales Navigator Plus, 195–199
sales professionals. *See* LinkedIn for sales
  professionals
Save Search features, 198
screening invitations for connections,
  94–96
search, 47–64
  advanced, 51
  Advanced Answers Search, 61
  Advanced Job Search, 60–61
  Advanced People Search, 58–60
  black-hat SEO techniques in, 61–64,
    72–73
  company pages and, 39–40
  functions of, 47–48

importance of advanced search, 53–54
keywords in. *See* keywords
premium accounts and, 197–198
recommendations and, 80
Reference Search, 60
results of, 71–72
saving searches, 60
search options in, 48
SEO and. *See* search engine optimization (SEO)
sorting options in, 49–52
using Answers to, 54–58
search engine optimization (SEO)
  black-hat techniques in, 61–64, 72–73
  competitive analysis and, 67–69
  Google Keyword Tool for, 70–72
  keywords in. *See* keywords
search results, 71–72
second-degree connections, 92–93, 167,
  186, 188, 253, 259. *See also* connections
self-promotion, 129, 162, 192
Self-Service Ads, 203–204, 217
selling on LinkedIn, 214–215
Send Invitations Wizard, 159
services and products, 42
Share This option, 127
sidebar widgets, 35
sidebars, 12–13
Signal, 150–151
Simply Hired network, 245–246
skills, 12, 231–235, 262
SlideShare Presentations, 137–138
Social Ads, 210–212
social media feeds, 26–27
social proof, 75–78
sorting options, 49–52
spam, 93
SpeechIn, 150

Sponsored Polls, 209–210

sponsorship advertising, 205–207

statistics, 42

status updates, 44

status updates timeline app, 150–151

strategic networking, 91, 92–93

Suggest Expert option, 127

summaries, 11–12, 238–240

Swarm, 69, 150

swipe files, 223–224

T

Tags, 134

Talent Direct, 172–173

target keywords, 17–18, 51, 65–66

targeted ads, 201–202, 227–228

third-degree connections, 186, 188, 198, 259. *See also* connections

tools. *See* apps (applications)

travel information app, 143

Tweet spam, 93–94

Tweets, 135–137

V

vertical search engines, 65

Veterans, 150

videos, 137–138

Viewers of This Profile Also Viewed, 30

W

web analytics, 229

websites for networking, 7–8

Who's Viewed Your Profile, 35, 197–198

Who's Viewed Your Profile, 197–198, 243

Who's Viewed Your Profile, 243–244, 254

wizards

    Company Page Setup Wizard, 44–45

    Profile Wizard, 9–12

    Send Invitations Wizard, 159

Wordpress, 139–140

Work With Us, 178–179

writing

    editorial guidelines, 225–226

    effective ad headlines, 217–221, 229

    effective ads, 216–217, 224, 229

    effective answers, 128–129

    effective InMail messages, 105–108

X

Xing, 7–8